Praise for *Simple Soulful Sacred*

'*Simple Soulful Sacred* is a heartfelt offering that honours the wisdom and presence within each woman's journey. May this book become a trusted resource for all women.'

Elena Brower,
Author of *Practice You*

'*Simple Soulful Sacred* addresses a pivotal question asked by women everywhere: how can we step into our true power as women, and live an intentional, purposeful, happy life? Megan's wisdom cuts through the noise and gets to the heart centered truth. We can create more simple lives. We can awaken to our true potential. We can redefine womanhood. We can claim our sovereignty. If you've been waiting for a book to help you rise up in all areas of your life and become the woman you want to be, this is it.'

Rebecca Campbell,
Author of *Light is the New Black* and *Rise Sister Rise*

'The future is feminine. And powerfully so. *Simple Soulful Sacred* is the brilliant road map that will help women everywhere rise into their greatest potential. The inspiring truth, wisdom, and love that this book imparts is just what we need to reconnect to our souls and tap into the sacred flow of purpose, power and genius that all women were born to express.'

Kelly Noonan Gores,
Writer/Director/Producer, HEAL Documentary

'*Simple Soulful Sacred* is the bible for women who want less hustle, more flow and to get sacred with what matters. If you want to live your passion and purpose from an authentic place, and learn how to radically take care of yourself on all levels, this book is a must read.'

Lisa Messenger,
Founder and Editor-in-Chief, Collective Hub

'So much heart and wisdom. An absolute gem.'

Bronnie Ware,
Author of *Top Five Regrets of the Dying*

'*Simple Soulful Sacred* gives deeply-rooted guidance to women to awaken to the power that lies within them. Filled with wisdom, stories, questions, sacred practices and soulful inquiry, this book will become a treasured and trusted guide for women everywhere.'

Dr Ezzie Spencer,
Author of *Lunar Abundance*

'*Simple Soulful Sacred* is a gift. A gift for your awakening soul and spiritual journey. Every chapter is a heart opener that will leave you feeling more aligned and in love with your sacred life, and with a deeper clarity about your passion and purpose. Read it from cover to cover in one juicy sitting, or simply open up to a divinely chosen page for daily guidance. A gorgeous gem of a book that deserves to sit permanently on your desk or bedside table.'

Julie Parker,
Founder, Beautiful You Coaching Academy

'*Simple Soulful Sacred* inspires us all to say yes in more powerful ways. Megan's wisdom helps us get clear and declare what we want by trusting our own guidance and bravely taking the action we know we want and need to take.'

Emma Isaacs,
Founder and Global CEO, Business Chicks

'*Simple Soulful Sacred* is an irresistible invitation to lead a more meaningful, purposeful and soul-aligned life. Megan lights the path for women to get clear on what they truly want, own their feminine power and claim what's sacred in their lives. Her wisdom has the power to not only validate women's struggles, but to heal all that is in need of love, comfort and awakening. Importantly, Megan guides women to know and trust themselves. In a world that still tells women who to be and what to think, this is profound guidance. This book is a powerful permission slip for women to live the life of their creation. Read it and share it with everyone woman you know.'

Rebecca Van Leeuwen,
Founder, Soul Sister Circle

Simple
Soulful
Sacred

*A woman's guide to clarity, comfort
and coming home to herself*

MEGAN DALLA-CAMINA

HAY HOUSE, INC.
Carlsbad, California • New York City
London • Sydney • New Delhi

For all the awakening women.

ACKNOWLEDGEMENT OF COUNTRY

I acknowledge the Australian Aboriginal and Torres Strait Islander peoples of this nation. I acknowledge the Traditional Custodians of the land, the Gai-mariagal peoples, on whose land I reside. I pay my respects to ancestors and Elders, past, present and future.

EVERYONE IS WELCOME HERE

While the terminology used throughout this book is biological/gender based (women/woman/she/her/they), please know that everyone is welcome here. No matter your gender, colour, race, age, sexual orientation, religion, persons with and without a disability – you are welcome. This book has been written with love and the intention to serve all those who may need it, and all who might resonate with this work. Everyone is fully welcomed and celebrated in this book.

CONTENTS

Part 2   **LIVELIHOOD**

Part 3   **WELLBEING**

Part 4 **COMFORT**

Part 5   SOULFULNESS

Part 6   CONSCIOUSNESS

Part 7   SACREDNESS

Part 8 **COURAGE**

Part 9 **WOMANHOOD**

Part 10 **SOVEREIGNTY**

INTRODUCTION

Welcome to your simple, soulful, sacred journey. I'm so pleased you're here. I hope this book will become a trusted companion on your journey home to yourself.

How glorious it is to be a woman, in all of our complexity, wisdom and radiance. It's such a gift, our womanhood, to be witnessed, treasured and honoured. But let's be honest: some days it's not easy being a woman. Our lives are complicated, and they can be furiously fast and busy. We can lose ourselves among the juggle of everything on our to-do lists: our work, family, children if we have them, and the busyness of our lives. We can also lose touch with the woman we long to be, and lose sight of the dreams we once held for our life.

Too many of us feel frazzled, rushed, overloaded and burnt out. We may want to live a happy, fulfilled life, but it can seem all too hard. We want to do purposeful work in the world, but it gets lost in the mix of our endless days. We'd love to make a greater contribution, but have our hands full just doing what's in front of us. And we long to be vibrantly well, but even that can feel like an impossible goal.

Perhaps most of all, so many of us want to be living, working, loving and leading in our feminine power, as sovereign women with agency over our own lives. But in a crazy world and with so much to do, where do we even start?

We can start here, together. What I have learnt, from working with thousands of women and doing decades of research, is that what many of us are really seeking is more sacredness in our lives. We want to step out of the noise and chaos and live more simply. We want time and space for what's most important. And we have a deep longing for connection—to ourselves, with each other, with the earth, and with the soulfulness in our lives.

Many of us also want to create work and businesses that we're passionate about, that fulfil our purpose and potential, and make a difference in the world.

My purpose is to share love, wisdom and tools for your rising. To help you tap into the core of what you want most, and help illuminate the pathways for you to live it. To shine a light on just how magical you really are, so that you can finally see it. To further awaken and shift your consciousness, so that you can deeply feel it. And to share all of the possibilities for how you can create it. All of it.

This is the path ahead of us. With this book as your guide, we will explore themes that can help lead us home: Simplicity, Livelihood, Wellbeing, Comfort, Soulfulness, Consciousness, Sacredness, Courage, Womanhood and Sovereignty. As you work your way through the chapters and explore these themes, there are questions for you to ponder, and affirmations to inspire and support your journey. You may like to start a new notebook to capture your discoveries and innermost thoughts as your path unfolds. Or you can download the beautiful free *Simple Soulful Sacred Journal*, which you will find at megandallacamina.com/sssjournal

This is a gentle journey and there is no prescribed path. You can start at the beginning and read through to the end; or you can go to the chapter that's calling to you the most. You might even choose to use the book as an oracle, and simply open a page to see what message lies waiting for you. Let yourself be led by your inner guide and know that however you choose to use this book, you will get what you need.

While the journey is gentle, it is also deep. Because if you're like many of the women I know, you are ready for so much more than the life you are currently living. We're ready for a new definition of womanhood. Ready to throw off the shackles of the patriarchy. Ready to step out of the cloak of masculine traits that keep us driving and striving for a version of success that isn't even our own. Ready to be radiantly well, instead of anxious, stressed and burnt out. Ready to stop hiding, playing small, comparing ourselves to everyone everywhere. Ready for financial abundance and, yes, ready for sovereignty.

We're ready for more from our lives. Ready for more clarity, time, space, money, freedom, simplicity, alignment, abundance, purpose, joy, hope, meaning, creativity, truth, consciousness, love, connection, health, wellbeing, softness, power, radiance, spirituality, soulfulness, sacredness, *magic*.

We're ready to find our voices, speak our truth and own our power. Our feminine power. Because while the feminine may have been disowned and devalued for centuries, *we are so done with that story now*. We know in our bones that the feminine is where our true strength resides. It's time to remember who we are, reclaim her and redefine our womanhood for ourselves.

This is our work. It's the work we need to do for ourselves. And it's the work that the world needs us to do. We are women. Mothers, partners, seekers, teachers, healers, dreamers, creators, leaders. We are breaking the chains and stepping out of the shadows.

It's time for us to heal. It's time for us to create. It's time for us to speak. It's time for us to lead. And believe me when I say this, my sister, and feel it resonate and reverberate deep into your soul: *It's time for us to rise.*

Throughout my life, there have been many books that have guided my path, nurtured my spirit and helped me unfold into my womanhood. My wish is that this book may be one of those books for you. That it may help you to see all that is possible for your beautiful life. And that it may bring clarity, comfort and light on your path, as you journey home to who you truly are.

　　With love, Megan x

PART 1

Simplicity

START WHERE YOU ARE

It's never too late—never too late to start over,
never too late to be happy.

~ JANE FONDA

O ften when we want to embark on a new journey, we don't know where to start. We think that we need to make some grand gesture to the Universe that we are ready. Ready to transform, to show up, to change. But this is often where we get stuck, because it can all feel too big and too hard. And sometimes we don't even get off the starting line.

As you embark on this simple, soulful, sacred journey, I invite you to start from exactly where you are right now. With all of your beautiful flaws and perceived inadequacies. Don't worry, we all have them. And with all of your stories about how hard it is to change, how you aren't really ready, and how much it's going to hurt. You are ready and it won't hurt a bit.

This is a journey of small steps. No big leaps. No scary requests. Just ideas and thoughts for you to ponder, one at a time. Little by little, they will support you in creating a life that is simpler, more soulful and much more sacred.

Wade on in. The water is lovely and warm. And I've got you.

AFFIRMATION
I am safe to start a new journey.

THIS IS YOUR LOVING
WAKE-UP CALL

*Sometimes all it takes is a subtle shift in perspective, an
opening of the mind, an intentional pause and reset, or a
new route to start to see new options and new possibilities.*

~ KRISTIN ARMSTRONG

You are here. You picked up this book, or perhaps it was
given to you for a reason. There are no accidents. Nothing
is random. So let this book be your loving wake-up call. Your
intervention. Your open invitation. To pause, to check in, to evaluate where you really are in your life and whether that's where
you truly want to be.

Nothing may be necessarily wrong. In fact everything may
be going along just beautifully. I hope that is the case for you,
and if it is, this book will guide you on a deeper journey into
yourself. But if all is not well, that's okay too. Perhaps you're in
a rocky period, working out the next move in your career, or
maybe what's next in a relationship. Perhaps you've been feeling
restless, or feeling a yearning for something you can't quite name.

Often a wake-up call comes in the midst of drama. Of
something bad happening. A job loss. Relationship breakdown.
A life-changing diagnosis. The death of a loved one. It's sometimes the only time we stop to reassess where we're truly at, how
we really feel, or what we want most.

But you can also need a wake-up call to the relatively subtle
things that are keeping you from stepping into your best life,
even if that seems a long way off for you.

Because maybe you're living by default instead of by design, on auto pilot and just going through the motions.

Or perhaps you put everyone in your life ahead of yourself—from your boss to your kids, your partner, your friends.

Maybe you're chasing a version of success that you're not sure is even yours, or you don't know what success looks like for you at all.

You could be numbing yourself down, selling yourself short, or doing what we have all done at some point, self-medicating with anything from shopping too much, working too hard, indulging with food or with your drug of choice.

Or maybe, just maybe, you're exhausted; on the verge of a burnout or breakdown, or just up to your eyeballs in stress.

Wherever you are, it's okay. Let this be your call. No matter where you are right now, let this be your sacred space to reflect, dream, hope, assess, vision and create what you actually want for your life.

Waking up is the first step. Answering the call comes next. I know you're ready. And it's all here waiting for you.

AFFIRMATION
I heed the call to wake up to my life.

YOUR LIFE VISION

How we live our days is how we live our lives.

~ ANNIE DILLARD, *Teaching a Stone to Talk*

One of my all-time favourite questions is this: *What is your life vision?* It's a question I have posed hundreds of times to clients, friends, women at events I'm speaking at, and countless times in my writing. It's one of the most important questions we can ask ourselves. And yet it's also one we spend the least amount of time contemplating.

How can that be? After all, this is our one and only life— well, in this lifetime anyway. How is it that we spend so little time envisioning how we want to live it? The easy answer is that we're busy. Caught up in daily demands and our never ending to-do lists. Frantically trying to navigate our way through the days and weeks unscathed and unbroken. Just trying to get through it all.

If that's the easy answer, there is a tougher one as well. And that is that it can be hard. Hard to get quiet with ourselves. Hard to sit with our truth. Hard to admit that the life we are living bears little resemblance to the life we were hoping to live, or would hope to live if we gave ourselves enough space to dream about what it looked like. It can be hard to be with ourselves in the truest essence of our souls and listen to the simple desires that sit in our deepest places.

So we stay busy, filling up our schedules and social lives. Scrolling through endless social media feeds in the hope of distracting ourselves from the sense of disappointment we can feel if we sit with ourselves for too long. But if you could be brave for a moment, and I asked you to jot down in a stream of consciousness what you truly wanted for your life, what would you write? What words and visions would flow onto the page? What would your heart beckon so that it could finally be heard?

I invite you to spend a little time to get clear. What do you want for your life? What would you want most if you gave yourself permission? Think about your family life, friends, work, creativity, spirituality, community, charity, activism, wellbeing, romantic and social life … what would it all look like? Get an art journal with blank pages and some coloured pens or pencils. Write, draw, cut out pictures from magazines, use a Pinterest board, write inspiring quotes, dream larger than the life you are currently living. Vision it all. This is your one and only life. Give yourself the gift of living it.

AFFIRMATION
I hold a clear vision for my life.

SEE WHAT'S POSSIBLE

Without leaps of imagination, or dreaming, we lose the excitement of possibilities. Dreaming, after all, is a form of planning.

~ GLORIA STEINEM

Picture this: A woman sits in front of me. She is amazing, but doesn't fully realise it. We start talking. She has come to see me for coaching because she wants more for her career than she is currently experiencing. Secretly, she actually wants more for her life. She feels stuck. Stifled. And more than a bit over it. We unpack what's going on. Work. Home. Wellbeing. Life.

As our conversation unfolds and the time passes, we go deeper. I ask her, 'If there were no limitations regarding time, money, commitments or expectations, what would you be doing with your life? What work would you be doing? How would you be living?'

She stares at me blankly for a moment. It's a big question. Then a few things happen like clockwork. First, a glimmer of hope flashes across her face. Her eyes light up. A smile starts to twitch the corners of her mouth.

And then ... the cloud comes over her. The frown begins to form. The hope she felt just a moment before seems to be dashed. Her eyes fade.

I know this scene. I've been here before. 'Tell me what happened in the last thirty seconds ... explain it to me,' I ask.

She looks at me shyly, like she has a big secret. 'Well, I thought of something I'd really like to be doing with my life, but well, you know ...' she stumbles, her voice fading just as the glimmer in her eyes had done a moment before.

'What do I know?' I ask.

'Well, you know, that would never, ever happen, so I'm just dreaming and it's not realistic,' she says, shoulders slumping down a little further, seemingly defeated.

Yes, I do know. This is a scene that has played out dozens, if not hundreds, of times with women I have spoken with, particularly the amazing women I coach. When I ask questions around what my clients want for their careers, businesses and lives, it's not that they don't have a dream. It may well be long buried, may not have had a look-in for a decade, but there is always a spark of excitement about something if you dig in the right areas and ask the right questions.

But here is where we get stuck. We give up on ourselves too easily, and it shows in that thirty-second window: I ask the question, she ponders and feels the hope, then she shuts it down just as fast as it comes up.

As we play this story out through a coaching relationship, many magical things happen. Because she has to—having showed up, paid the money and made the commitment—this woman dwells on the possibilities of her life. What could the dream look like, who would be involved, what would she be doing, how would it change her life, what would the ideal day look like and what would the very next small action be? It's just the two of us. There is nowhere to escape and no place to hide.

But she isn't trying to hide from me, only from herself. Because I am just the mirror and the question bearer.

Having created space for the dream to unfold, the vision to build and the plans to be developed, I have witnessed what would before have seemed miraculous: careers reimagined, businesses birthed, books written, relationships changed, lives completely transformed. And invariably this was because a woman was willing to show up, do the work and plan for change with honesty and grace (and, yes, a little grit too).

Experience would tell me that this may sound familiar to you. That you dream of something more for your career, your business or your life. So I ask you to contemplate on these questions:

- *What possibilities have you shut down or closed off in your life?*
- *What would you truly love to be doing if there were no limitations?*
- *What permission do you need to give yourself to unpack those possibilities?*
- *What stories and beliefs are stopping you from taking action?*

If I know one thing from all of the work I have done, it's that you have to start by getting real about where you are at, who you really are and what you truly want. Give yourself the gift of your truth. Make a cup of tea, diffuse some calming oils, put on some relaxing music and get out your journal. Pick up a pencil and write. Answer the above questions. Just let yourself dream about what could be possible for you, if you were brave and open enough to wish for it.

Then decide on the smallest step that you can take this week to inch yourself in the direction you want to head. You don't need any grandiose plans. Not just yet. One small action, followed by another, is enough to get you started. Enough to begin building momentum. The magic is made with the little things. And it all starts by giving yourself permission to see what's possible.

AFFIRMATION
I get out of my own way and dream
about what's possible for my life.

WHAT IF YOU DID KNOW?

Sometimes deeper mental clarity is
preceded by great internal storms.

~ YUNG PUEBLO

I'm sitting on the musty Victorian chaise longue, trying not to look at my coach. She is staring at me with her typically intent, patient gaze, waiting for me to process the game-changing question she's just asked.

Moments before, I was speaking aimlessly, wafting my words into the air the way an old perfume atomiser sprays scent, directionless puffs appearing and disappearing as quickly as they come.

I wasn't saying anything meaningful. Just trying to work through an issue in my life that had me on the endless cycle of an imaginary merry-go-round, when all I wanted was to get clarity and get off the ride. However, I wasn't willing to do the work that would allow me to get off.

'I don't know,' interspersed every fifth sentence I mumbled, uttered as an endless and weak excuse, so I wouldn't have to go any deeper. 'I don't know,' I sighed again.

Then a pause. Awkward silence. Fidgeting in my seat. Sweat forming in my palms.

And then she hit me with it. 'What if you did know?' she asked, her penetrating gaze making me feel like she could see every part of my soul, along with every dark secret.

'Huh?' I avoided.

'What if you did know?' she asked again, ignoring my diversion tactics.

Oh. Hunh. What if I did know?

What if I stopped distracting myself, playing the avoidance game, dancing with my words in the perfumed mist and just sat with the knowing.

What if I did know? What then?

Well, then there I would be—alone, naked, vulnerable. Because in that place there is only truth. And because I knew. Of course I knew. We always know. We only need to get quiet enough, real enough, true enough and brave enough to listen.

AFFIRMATION
I listen for my truth.

LIVE MORE SIMPLY

*Be as simple as you can be. You will be astonished to see
how uncomplicated and happy your life can become.*

~ PARAMAHANSA YOGANANDA

I've been thinking a lot lately about how my grandparents used to live. And their parents, and all those who came before us. In simpler times. When people would rise with the sun and rest when the sun set. When people took the time to lovingly prepare meals cooked with real food and then sit at the table together to eat. When all food was organic because it came from nature. Where there was time and space and connection and community.

I have memories of my Scottish grandparents on Dad's side and what seemed like strict rituals around how they lived, that now seem oddly comforting. How my Grandma would prepare half a grapefruit each night before bed for her and my Granddad, cutting little wedges and drizzling them with honey before placing them in the fridge, always in the same pastel bevelled glass dishes from the 1960s. How that would be the first thing they ate at 6am, followed by homemade muesli sprinkled with lecithin, served with a glass of orange juice then tea—always made on the gas stove, placed in the teapot and covered with a hand crocheted tea-cosy that my Grandma had made.

How they never owned a dishwasher and every dish would be mindfully washed, dried and put away after meals. Every meal was eaten at the dining table, together, at set meal times. We used to joke when we went interstate to visit family that we had to make sure we were at their place by 6pm, no matter what, or we would miss dinner. No exceptions.

The only television they watched was the ABC, and only in the evenings before early bedtime. The large backyard was speckled with grape vines, apricot, lemon and plum trees. Granddad spent plenty of time in his shed carving, fixing and working with his hands, while my Grandma would cook, bake, mend and garden. It was a simple life. A long and happy life. One that I, and perhaps you too, could take some lessons from.

AFFIRMATION

I look for ways to live more simply.

USE WHAT YOU HAVE

Out of clutter, find simplicity.
~ ALBERT EINSTEIN

It's a typical scene. You're out shopping with girlfriends having a great time. In the fun and excitement of it all (or the sheer adrenaline of the hunt), you buy a few beautiful new pieces to add to your already full wardrobe. When you get home, you open your wardrobe to hang up the new tops, only to see two that are almost identical, hanging right there in front of you. You had forgotten they were in there, stuffed together and pushed towards the back to save space.

You have your grandmother's best china in your cupboard. You don't like to get it out in case it breaks or gets chipped, which would break your heart. They were her favourite pieces and you treasure them. So they sit on the shelf, behind closed doors, waiting for a special occasion that is deemed worthy of the risk. But the occasion rarely arises and even when it does, you forget about getting the china out until the moment has passed. Oh well, you think to yourself, next time.

The same can be said for all of our possessions. We forget what we have, buy what we don't need, replace what hasn't been used, discard what isn't broken. And in the process, we accumulate more things, cramming the already stuffed corners of our lives even more.

Go through your closets and give away anything you don't love, so that you can see all that brings you joy. Get out your grandmother's china. She would have wanted you to use it, not hide it away in a musty cupboard. In fact, go through all of your cupboards and take out the pieces that delight you, so that you can see them, hold them, and make use of them in your everyday life.

Stop buying what you don't need. Seek both joy and utility from the beautiful and practical. Use what you have.

AFFIRMATION

I use my possessions with gratitude and joy.

YOUR IDEAL MORNING

I would like to learn, or remember, how to live.

~ ANNIE DILLARD

I wake up early, before 6am. I can hear the peaceful sound of birds chirping outside: kookaburras singing their morning song, lorikeets beckoning to each other, parakeets squawking loudly. I hop out of bed, eager to get into the day. After my morning rituals (oil pulling, saltwater mouth rinsing, teeth brushing, lemon water), I head out for my walk.

I love this time of the morning. Only a few locals are out. The streets are clear. The light is magical, optimistically bright for what the day might bring. I walk through the bush track along the long harbour trail, then eventually make my way down to the beach. I have a swim in the ocean, meditate on the beach, contemplate my Universe and then walk home again. I finish off with a yoga practice to the tunes of Stevie Nicks, before showering, making a green smoothie and settling in for some writing time— dressed in my silk kaftan, essential oils in the diffuser, chai latte in hand. For me, that's as close to a perfect morning as it gets.

Rewind, not even a decade ago, and my morning looked vastly different. The alarm would go off and I'd hit snooze until the last possible moment, before dragging myself out of bed. Dreading what was ahead of me not just for the morning but for the entire day, I'd trudge into the shower, waking my kid up on the way. Then it was a stressed-out hustle to get us both ready, him fed and off to school and then me to the office. Suited up from my head to my heels, I'd grab a coffee and maybe some toast and suffer through a never-ending morning of grind. And more often than not, there were hot frustrated tears along the way.

Your morning sets your mindset for the entire day. Back in those days, I used to have an ideal morning when I was on vacation, but could never quite replicate that in my 'real life'. Then one day coming back from a week at the beach, I just decided that I wanted to bring that energy home with me. It wasn't enough to only have a beautiful morning experience a few times a year; I wanted it daily. And while I was still working my corporate job at that time, I managed to create a version that brought me similar energy and positive emotions, and that set me up to carry that energy throughout my day.

What does your ideal morning look like? No matter how much or how little time you have, work out a ritual that will support you, have you looking forward to the morning like a child on Christmas Day, and infuse positive energy into every cell of your body.

AFFIRMATION
*I cherish my morning routine and take time to
nourish myself, bringing joy into my day.*

YOU CAN STRIVE FOR LESS

I'd rather have roses on my table than diamonds on my neck.

~ EMMA GOLDMAN

What would it feel like to strive for less, instead of more? You may need to sit with this one for a few moments. We are socially programmed to always want more. More money. A better job. A bigger business. A newer car. A larger house. The latest fashion. The biggest, most fabulous next-thing-on-the-list.

It can be motivating. But it can also be emotionally draining, energy sucking and, for many, soul destroying.

But what if more wasn't better? What if we could learn to be happy and content with what we have and where we are at right now, and let that be enough? Contemplate that for a moment.

If you could let go of the expectation that more and more is better, and instead practise gratitude for all that is present, how would you feel? Would it help you relax, safe in the knowledge that your striving, driving persona could take a back seat for a while? Would that mindset help you to actually see all that you have to be grateful for? Would it let you enjoy your life more, perhaps even soothe your soul a little?

When you give up the need to achieve and stop driving yourself so hard, you free up energy for magic to happen. For things to evolve. For space and time to breathe and be and enjoy.

So just for now, stop striving. Be at peace with what is and what you have right now. And let that be enough.

AFFIRMATION
I am content with where I am right now.

CREATING SPACE

I have made my world and it is a much
better world than I ever saw outside.

~ LOUISE NEVELSON

A woman is sitting in front of her therapist. Georgia came to see him, desperately seeking a relationship. After many sessions, the therapist asked her what space she had created for this new relationship to come into her life. 'Have you cleared out part of your wardrobe?' he asked.

'What for?' Georgia questioned.

'For the new man you're calling in. Where will he put his belongings, if there is no space for him?' the therapist enquired.

The question had never occurred to her. Georgia wanted the relationship, but she wasn't creating any space, energetically or physically, to allow it to come in.

This is a simple example of a powerful creation tool. Where are you creating space for what you really want?

If you want more balance but keep taking on more work, you aren't creating space.

If you long for a spiritual practice, but won't set your morning alarm for ten minutes earlier to meditate and reflect, then you aren't creating space.

If you want to deepen your romantic relationship, but you keep cancelling your weekly date night, then you aren't creating space.

Today, think about how you can create space for what you say you want most. Even in the busyness of your life, you have a beautiful opportunity to create space for yourself and what you truly desire.

Find some small moments to allow what you want to flourish in your life. Start with the little things if you need to, then grow from there. Space is created with intention and action. What will you create space for?

AFFIRMATION

I create the space for what I really want.

THE SPACES BETWEEN

There are things known and things unknown
and in between are the doors.

~ JIM MORRISON

There are spaces between the moments. Between successes. Between relationships. Between projects. Between purposes. The time seems endless. You can feel the restlessness.

You want to move, to plan, to do the doing that will get you to the next place, the next phase. To keep up with the endlessness, and prove that you're still good enough to be in the game.

To be there. To be seen. To matter.

But wait, dear heart. You can wait. You can pause, breathe, and take the space that is there in front of you.

You won't miss it. You have time. What is for you will not pass you.

The space in between the moments you think matter is where the moments that matter are.

Learn to soften. To sit in the spaces between where you are going and where you are right now. In that gloriously uncomfortable space between your being and your becoming. And sit in the knowing that what is right here, right now in this space, is enough for today and all of your tomorrows.

AFFIRMATION
I sit with grace in the spaces between.

SIMPLE ACTS

What a wonderful life I've had. I only
wish I'd realized it sooner.

~ COLETTE

I'm standing on the pavement outside my house. Black leggings, yoga top, cashmere wrap. On my feet, there's one blue sock on my left and a pink sock on my right, because I can never find a matching pair. It's almost winter, but the midmorning sun is shining strongly. This footpath is the only place around my house where the sun shines so brightly at this time of day.

I stand there, cars passing by, with my eyes closed and face tilted upwards. Probably for only two or three minutes, but I'm feeling like I'm lost in a timeless vortex, rooted in place. As I feel the warmth on my face and body, and bask in the glory of it, I say a silent prayer to the Universe.

Beings of light, please bring my guides to me today as I write. Let their knowledge and wisdom come through me into this work, and out into the world for all who need it. Thank you.

It's a simple act, standing outside in the sunshine in my odd socks, grateful for the warmth on my skin, praying to my guides. Simplicity in one of its many forms. And it brings me a moment of connection to self, to nature and to the universal energy forces that guide my being and all existence.

AFFIRMATION
I connect to source in simple ways every day.

WHAT DO YOU WANT
MORE THAN THIS?

You can only lose what you cling to.

~ BUDDHA

Anytime you feel stuck or you're not sure about something, ask yourself this simple, powerful question: *What do I want more than this?*

It applies to pretty much any situation, and it helps to shift our focus from what we don't want to what we do. When we want to create a change, the activation energy that's required to get started can be amped up by bringing our attention to the positive images and feelings that can pull us forwards.

Perhaps you'd like to lose some weight. Instead of focusing on how hard it is to shift the kilos, ask yourself what you want more than to be at your current weight. You may want to feel lighter, more energised, fitter, sexier. That's what you want more than the heaviness you are currently sitting with. So focus on that.

You may be yearning for a new job. Instead of focusing on how unhappy you are in your current role, ask yourself what you want more than this. You may want a better environment, to use your creativity more, to have a boss who supports you, or better benefits. By focusing on specific areas that you want more of, you can activate your energy and mindset to go about creating them.

You may be unhappy in your relationship but can't quite put your finger on what the issue is. What do you want more than this? More love, support, romance, soulful sex, or a more intimate friendship? What can you do to communicate that to your partner, so you can work together to create a more connected relationship?

Get in touch with what you really want and focus on moving towards that, instead of sitting in a story about how unhappy or dissatisfied you are with where you're at. It will help you visualise, activate and enable the change you want to create in a positive way that will pull you forwards into your new future.

AFFIRMATION

I focus on what I am moving towards.

HOW SIMPLE CAN YOU MAKE IT?

True life is lived when tiny changes occur.
~ LEO TOLSTOY

Think about your day tomorrow. If you were to take out all of the superfluous activities, from parts of your morning make-up routine to wasted time on your schedule, what would your day look like? How simple could you make it?

For the next week, try this ...

Minimise the number of things you need to do in the morning before you start work.

Reduce the number of things you need to take with you as you leave the house.

Simplify your diet to just a few things like a green smoothie for breakfast, salad for lunch, and soup for dinner.

Limit the number of meetings, phone calls, emails and items on your to-do list to the bare necessities.

Stay off social media for the week, don't watch the news, and check emails only once a day, to reduce the number of inputs coming in and distractions circling your brain.

Eat your meals with loved ones. Just you and them. And blessed food to give thanks for.

Go to sleep early, to arise fresh for the next day.

Repeat.

Life can be as simple as we make it. Try it and see.

AFFIRMATION
I make my life as simple as possible.

RADICAL RELEASE

There is nothing permanent except change.

~ HERACLITUS

My client Paige came home one day and decided to give away practically all of her belongings. She'd been working with me for a while on her next career step. At the same time, she had also been on a deep spiritual path of learning to be a meditation teacher. That's some journeying. You can guarantee that major shifts will happen, especially combining both paths of awakening.

Once Paige decided that she wanted to be free of her things, no-one could talk her out of it, although friends and family tried. She gave it all away. Everything. Her expensive couch that she loved. All of her lounge and dining room furniture. Most of her clothes. A lot of her personal belongings. She felt deep in her soul that this was the right thing to do, that she was being called to do it. And she followed through on that calling.

But it didn't come without regret. In the days after the release came the doubt. What had she done, she thought to herself, as she looked around her empty apartment. All of her friends told her she was crazy. She started to question her very sanity.

As days passed, Paige found that with the release of her belongings came another kind of release. One night after work, she sat on her lounge room floor and cried and cried. For all she'd let go. For all that remained. For all the unanswered questions on her path. For what would come next. More than letting go of her possessions, what Paige had really wanted was emotional release from letting go of her emotional baggage.

Often we hold onto our belongings because we are invested in them. Financially, emotionally, socially. There is a sunk cost, because we paid money for our things, so we hold on for fear of losing more than the item itself—also the time, energy and money spent acquiring it.

But what if you could release all that you no longer needed? You don't have to do what Paige did, which was extreme. Just walk through your home room by room, with a box or bag, collecting items that no longer serve you. It could be a cathartic exercise for you.

What can you release? What can you intentionally let go of, in the hope that it can serve someone else? What would that make space for in your life? Interesting questions to ponder. I wonder what your answers will be.

AFFIRMATION
I am safe to release what I no longer need.

THE GIFT OF SOLITUDE

In solitude we give passionate attention to our lives,
to our memories, to the details around us.

~ VIRGINIA WOOLF

Virginia Woolf wrote about it when she declared that every woman *needed a room of one's own.* Henry David Thoreau described it when he set out for his journey into the woods near Walden Pond, writing: *I went to the woods because I wished to live deliberately, to front only the essential facts of life.*

They were both seeking solitude. Woolf in her room, Thoreau in the woods.

The world is clearly much busier, noisier and more hectic now than it was in those times. It's even more essential today that we step away from the hustle and find our own kind of solitude, for it has much to teach us about life and about ourselves. We can only find that when we are alone.

When we seek out the quiet of solitude, we have the opportunity to calm ourselves, quieten the inner workings of our mind, and get in touch with the whispers of our soul. It's what allows us to focus, to create, to bring our magic into the world. It can be what allows us to stay sane when the world around us seems to be too frantic to deal with.

We need to intentionally create space for our solitude. For many, the ideal time is first thing in the morning, before the kids or partner arise, or the phone starts ringing. It doesn't matter whether it's your meditation practice, or a cup of tea while listening to the birds outside, only that you are alone and have time to just be. For others, it is on the way to work, perhaps a train or bus ride, where solitude can be found even among the bustle of the commute. Or maybe it's an afternoon nature break or a quiet evening that provides the respite. Wherever you find it, schedule it in so that it becomes part of your day.

Solitude can be uncomfortable because when we are truly alone, we have to face ourselves. Without distraction, it is just us. But with practice it becomes a less daunting endeavour. Over time, it will become like a secret refuge, a magical escape from the busyness of your life that will welcome you like a long-lost lover into its warm embrace.

AFFIRMATION
I create time and space for my solitude.

GETTING IN ALIGNMENT

The system is always going to collapse until you're on course.
~ CAROLINE MYSS

You say you value health and fitness, yet you haven't been to the gym in months and your new Nikes still sit in the box in your cupboard. You say you value family, yet time with your kids seems to be the last thing on your to-do list and your partner barely gets a look-in. You say you want to change careers, yet you've done nothing to investigate that new job or speak to the potential mentor who offered to help you. You say you want to save money, but your new car that you didn't really need is contradicting that.

Does your life reflect what you say is important?

When I say 'you', of course I also mean 'me'. I teach wellness, along with leadership, confidence and all aspects of women's development. Yet there was a brief time in my business when I didn't feel at all comfortable speaking of and teaching women about wellbeing. I would stand on stage and speak of green smoothies, no sugar and exercise and yoga. But there was a contradiction between what I said was important and how I was living my life.

You see I was about ten kilos overweight. I felt heavy and uncomfortable in my body. And it was clear to anyone who looked at me, including myself, that there was a gap between what I was saying and what I was actually doing. Yes, I was drinking the green smoothies. But I was also secretly comfort eating, still dealing with the emotional pain of a recent break-up. I would eat clean all week, then often binge on pizza and ice cream on the weekend, stuffing down my food to cover up my feelings. And while I would walk and do yoga, I wasn't actually working too hard, barely breaking into a sweat. And so I stayed stuck. And my values remained out of alignment.

Take a really good look at your life. With all of the self-compassion you can muster, ask yourself these questions: *Does your life reflect what you say is important? Where are the gaps in values?* Be gentle with yourself. You can close these gaps like I did, over time and with some dedicated work. You can get into alignment. Start small—awareness today, one small action tomorrow. And then another and another. Until one morning you can wake up and walk through your life knowing that, yes, your life does reflect what you say is important. And it feels amazing to live in alignment like that.

AFFIRMATION

I live in alignment with my values.

LOOK FOR THE SMALL WINS

You are the one who can stretch your own horizon.

~ EDGAR MAGDIN

When you look for the signs that you are being 'successful' at work or life, look for the small things. The little moments. The tiny wins that, when you notice and acknowledge them, can make you feel like you really are making progress, not just wading through mud while trying not to get stuck.

I was rushing to the airport last week after a long day of work, just making my check-in. Practising the art of small wins, I wrote this in my journal:

> *Small wins = big gratitude. After two days of speaking events including eight hours of workshops today, I rushed to the airport and made the bag drop with about two seconds to spare. Grateful. Had time to change out of my heels and into my sneakers before checking my bag. Grateful. Then found out that on an overbooked flight, I had been magically moved from the very last row to near the front. Grateful. It's in the small moment sometimes. Oh, and having a Netflix episode downloaded on my phone, as my kid has shown me that that's a thing now. Grateful. Feel like I'm winning.*

It's the little things. The small wins. The simplest gratitudes. The event organiser telling me I'd received great feedback from my workshop. The woman who came up to me after the workshop in tears because something had shifted for her. Making the check-in. A seat move. Having a show to watch on my iPhone. The nice woman who sat next to me. The decent in-flight meal. Being picked up at the other end at 11pm, when I was bone-tired.

The text from my mother, checking I got home okay. Sleeping in my bed after travelling. All of it.

What are those small moments for you? It might be rushing home after a long day in the office, in time to have dinner with your partner. Maybe it's kissing your kids as they lie sleeping in their cosy beds, after you come home from working the night shift. It could be your morning coffee, the unexpected 'well done' from your boss as she walks past your desk, or the little moment you had sitting under the tree in the park during your lunch break.

The small moments add up. The days of noticing these tiny wins end up accumulating into a week of feeling pretty good about the events that have passed. It sure beats the alternative: looking out for every small defeat or frustration as another indication that life is terrible, that it's all too hard and so very stressful. I used to live in that place. Trust me when I say that there is no joy there.

Life happens. Sometimes we don't get to choose how we show up; events can overwhelm us and we just have to ride that wave. But most days, we get to choose our mindset, what we notice and what we acknowledge. I don't always get it right; in fact, I often get it wrong. But last week, even among the crazy, I sure felt like I was winning. And this week, I'll try it again and look for the small wins, what I have to be grateful for and staying in the moment of what's working, no matter how tiny that moment is.

AFFIRMATION

I look for and celebrate the small wins.

NAME WHAT YOU WANT

I am where I am because I believe in all possibilities.
~ WHOOPI GOLDBERG

Name it. That thing that you are secretly longing for. Name it right now. Grab a piece of paper, the back of an envelope, your phone or your notebook, then write it down. Quickly, before you lose your nerve.

Name it.

What is it, this thing you really want? Is it on the top of your mind and close to your heart? Or do you need to really do some digging to find it? Have you been avoiding it for years, trying to talk yourself out of it because it seems too unattainable, unacceptable or unachievable?

Pause. Think about it now for a moment.

I believe you know what it is. You may have to sit quietly for a while for it to come into your consciousness, especially if you've been denying yourself the truth for a long time. But you know. It's there, waiting for you like a beloved family dog, impatiently patient while you go about your business of living. But ever waiting. To be acknowledged. To be seen. To be told, 'Yes, I'm ready now'.

You can't claim it until you name it. Tell the truth. It's just you and me. You are safe here. And you deserve to tell yourself all of the truths about who you are, what you want and why you want it. Then you can decide that you really can move towards it, this thing that you want. You can. With just one small step, you can start to bring it into existence. You are safe here. I know it seems scary. But I know you can do this. Shed some light on the darkness.

Take the step. Name it now.

AFFIRMATION

I am safe to name what I truly want.

WHAT WOULD IT LOOK LIKE IF IT WERE EASY?

Live life as if everything is rigged in your favor.
~ RUMI

What would it look like if it were easy? That thing you have been putting off, because you think it's going to be too hard. The work project you don't want to start, because you're terrified it will be a struggle like the last one. The conversation you're dreading with your partner, because it's going to be awkward. All of those things on your to-do list.

Pick just one. What would it look like if it were easy? If there was flow. And grace. And oodles of ease. If everything that could go to plan, went to plan. If you felt great while doing it. What would it look like?

Plan for easy. Plan for ease. Actually work out and write down how the pieces would come together, how the conversation would go, how the work would pan out, if it were easy. Create a visual picture and an internal dialogue that supports that path.

It doesn't have to be so hard, this life you are living. You can manifest and create ease. You can do easy. You can choose it.

AFFIRMATION
Easy is a viable path for me.

PART 2

Livelihood

FOLLOW THE BREADCRUMBS

If you don't know your purpose, then your
immediate goal is to figure that out.

~ OPRAH WINFREY

A decade before I wrote my first book, I was walking around the streets of New York. I was lost in the back streets of SoHo and was meandering along when I came across a big bookstore. In the large window display was a range of books on how to be a non-fiction writer. At this stage I hadn't even dreamt of writing a book. But before I knew it, I was walking back on the street with one of those how-to books tucked in my bag.

That was the first of many crumbs and over the course of the next fifteen years, it would lead to my purpose. That day a seed was planted and more clues would follow. A close girlfriend telling me that I should put 'all that stuff I talk about' on women's journeys and my own journey into a book because 'no-one talks about it and we need to'. Or the crumb of an idea to start a blog, after completing my yoga teacher training and my second Masters degree in Wellness, to share that knowledge with the world.

Following those crumbs led to my first blog and website, when I was still working for a global tech company. And those crumbs would eventually lead to more blogs, businesses and, yes, my first book deal with many more to follow. Contrary to what many people imagine, it wasn't an instant grand awakening, but a purposeful path that unfolded over time. We think that we're going to get struck by our purpose, that the heavens will open and we'll hear a booming voice declaring what work we should do in the world. But researchers tell us that it rarely happens like that. Instead, it happens by following the sparks of curiosity, seeing where they lead, and continually re-triggering this interest until it either dies out or blooms.

If I had squashed the flutter in my stomach when I saw those books in the window in New York; if I'd brushed aside the comment made by my girlfriend about writing a book when I knew there was something in that for me; if I had resisted the creative urge to start a blog by telling myself that I had a day job and didn't have the time (or no-one would read it); and if I hadn't followed through on my idea of writing a book proposal and submitting it to a publisher, even though the idea of being a published author seemed crazy at the time—then who knows, I might still be back in my old job, wondering what my purpose was and how I could walk a different path.

But I did follow the breadcrumbs, even when I didn't know why. Even when it didn't really make sense. Even when it looked like there was no purpose to any of it. I followed them anyway. Because something inside of me was whispering that there was more to be found on my path. Because I believed that things show up on our path for a reason, even if we can't rationalise it. And because I knew that curiosity is one of the greatest teachers we have; that we should follow the trail when it appears in front of us; and we should trust that it knows where it's going, even if we don't.

AFFIRMATION

*I follow the breadcrumbs of my curiosity
and trust my purposeful path.*

IS THIS SUCCESS?

Success is liking yourself, liking what you
do, and liking how you do it.

~ MAYA ANGELOU

How do you define success? At this very moment, considering your work and career, would you call yourself successful? Whether you answered 'yes' or 'no', what were the measurements that you used? What's on your checklist for how successful you deem yourself to be?

Many of us are striving for success and yet we don't really know what that looks like for us. So we look around at our friends, our peers, even strangers on the internet, and as we absorb the cultural narrative into our consciousness, we get to work. Driving, striving, pushing, hustling, always trying to get to the next goal post. Climbing a ladder when we don't even know if it's against the right wall. Running our businesses and careers like crazy women, when we're not even sure if the work is on purpose.

What are you driving and striving for?

Pause for a moment. Grab a sheet of paper. A quarter of the way down the page, draw a horizontal line. Below that line, write a list of all the things that really matter to you, as many as you can think of. Family, friends, money, abundance, health, wellbeing, happiness, creativity, freedom, spirituality, service, spaciousness, activism, culture, art, children, relationships, business, philanthropy, community, legacy.

Now choose the three to five things that are absolutely most important in your work and life. Really feel into it. These are the things that matter more than anything else on the list. Write those selected few things above the line. This is what success looks like for you, these items above the line. These are the things that matter. These are your 'yes' items.

When you find yourself driving and striving for success, check in with yourself: Does this even matter to you? Does it relate to something on your 'above the line' list? If it does, then go for it. If not, stop and reconsider whether what you are doing matters.

We need to be intentional about how we define our success, because it drives our decisions and our actions. Every day we trade our time and energy for something. Make sure you're not trading away your integrity, your dreams or what matters most to you, for a version of success that isn't your own.

AFFIRMATION

I am intentional about my definition of success.

THE PHD I DIDN'T NEED

When you come to the fork in the road, take it.

~ YOGI BERRA

I was in Philadelphia with my PhD professor, about to discuss the fourth version of my dissertation outline. As I tentatively held my breath waiting for her comments, she looked at me with a stern kindness.

'Megan, this is a very good dissertation outline. Your early research is sound. You can absolutely write this paper and it will be very good.'

I felt myself exhale. This was great news. I was on my way to New York for the US release of my first book, with the next few books already lined up to be written. I was buzzing with the excitement about the path that lay ahead.

But then my professor paused. I felt myself holding my breath again, as she drilled into me with her all-knowing eyes. 'But I want to know *why.*'

'Why what?' I asked.

'Why are you doing this PhD? You are well advanced in your career. You're already a global thought leader around women's empowerment and the areas you want to research. You don't want to be an academic. You have a thriving business.'

Another pause.

'You don't actually need this PhD. So why are you spending tens of thousands of dollars and years of your life doing it?'

I stared back at her with a deep sense of panic. My breath caught in my chest. I could feel my heart racing.

Because this is who I am, I thought, my mind exploding. I am following the path. I am becoming an expert. I did not one, but two Masters degrees. I now need this PhD for the final layer of my legitimacy. To be accepted. To be seen.

As these thoughts settled, I looked somewhat blankly at my professor. And a new understanding landed with such a weight that it almost levelled me: *I'm doing it to be validated.*

I wanted to do my PhD because I was waiting for that next level of acknowledgement from the people I had been trying to impress from inside the structures where I had worked my entire adult life. I wanted them to see me, to like me, to value me. I was doing it for them, not for me.

I was struck with such instant insight it was like God, the angels and the Universe had all colluded to shine the brightest light directly into my brain, my heart and my soul simultaneously, so that I couldn't possibly miss it.

I didn't need it. I didn't want to do it. In fact, I was doing it for all the wrong reasons. And truth be told, the rebel in me just wanted to run away from another patriarchal masculine model of 'success' as fast as I possibly could.

'I feel that what you really want to do, Megan, is write books. You're a truly gifted writer. So go and write.'

That conversation was cause for me to take a long look at my motivations, where I really wanted to head in my business, my very identity. I walked away from Philly that day, leaving behind the study that I no longer needed, to step into the life I was truly longing to live. On my own terms. And without anyone's validation except my own.

AFFIRMATION
The validation I seek is mine alone.

EMBRACE YOUR INNER REBEL

Life is either a daring adventure or nothing. To keep
our faces toward change and behave like free spirits
in the presence of fate is strength undefeatable.

~ HELEN KELLER

G ood girls. It's a syndrome you know. We see them every
day. All over the world, you can spot them a mile away.
They're the ones working diligently. Playing the game by the
numbers. Doing as they're told. Not being too loud, too vocal
or opinionated. Being obedient.

Whether working for someone else or even in their own businesses, good girls are doing it like they think it should be done.
Like they've seen it done before. Like they've been told to do.

Constantly worried about what other people will think, how
they will be judged, if they will be liked, how they will be able
to succeed. Always thinking about how to fit in, not stand out,
not be too much, and certainly of how they will measure up.

Good girls. Are you one of them?

I used to be. Followed the patriarchal rules to the letter. Played
nice. Fitted in. Gloria Feldt wrote that to succeed in a man's
world, women need to either be liked by men or be like men.
Good girls are definitely in the former category.

But didn't you hear? We're smashing the patriarchy—the
very systems and masculine modes that have kept the good girl
in us in place, locked down, quiet, controlled. We're breaking
those paradigms down. Busting out of those boxes that have
kept us constrained. Saying no, thank you very much, we are
so done with that.

The time of the good girl is over. It's time for your inner rebel to come to the party. To come and play. To raise your head from below the line and find the voice that is resting inside you.

She is just bursting to come out. She is a rebel with a cause. And the cause is you. Your voice. Your work. Your power. Your everything. She is waiting for you. Let her roar!

AFFIRMATION

I embrace my inner rebel. And she is glorious.

TWO QUESTIONS ON PURPOSE

A calling is the sense that you are on this earth for a reason,
that you have a destiny, no matter how great or small.

~ THOMAS MOORE, *A Life At Work*

I was listening to Chase Jarvis on his podcast recently, while out for my walk. He was talking about creativity and entrepreneurship, but for me he distilled a whole lot of thinking around career, passion, pursuits and purpose into these two questions:

- *What do you care about?*
- *How can you become masterful at that?*

If you stopped stressing about finding your purpose and making money from your calling and instead asked yourself these two questions, what would you discover about yourself and your work in the world?

Take out all the concerns about how you could turn a passion into a vocation. Take any income out of the equation. Take out the worries about when, where, what people will say, and how on earth you can transition. Just start by asking: *What do you care about?*

Is it education, disrupting the system, empowering teenagers, re-homing animals, nursing, making pottery, being a general manager, starting a small business, wellness coaching, making art? Are you passionate about publishing, jewellery, creativity, fashion, interior design, banking, how things are made, books, crystals, teaching, food, travel, photography, coffee, retail, podcasting, child care, recruitment, people, culture, minimalism, diversity, politics, feminism, changing the world, self-help, spirituality or relationships?

What do you care about? Make a list. A big list. Circle the things on that list that really light you up. Things that you would do or have in your life, even if no-one ever noticed, cared or paid you. Then go and do those things, or one in particular, in whatever way you can. Keep doing it. Explore it. Play with it. Ignite and reignite your passion for it. Then work out how you can become masterful at it.

The rest, those elusive purpose and profit questions, will take care of themselves when you show up and do the thing that you are most passionate about with enough curiosity, consistency and mastery.

So work out what that is. Go and do that. And let your journey unfold.

AFFIRMATION
I become masterful at what I care about.

WHAT YOU DO MAKES
A DIFFERENCE

*There are two ways of spreading light; to be
the candle or the mirror that reflects it.*

~ EDITH WHARTON

Every day I come into contact with women who wonder whether anything they do really matters. Whether their voice, their work, their life, really makes a difference to anybody. I often think this too. Do the words I write matter? Does the talk I just gave really impact anyone? Will the coaching help create a tangible breakthrough? Does my parenting reach my child in a profound way?

Then a client will email me to share that they went after that big deal they were too scared to consider before our coaching session, and landed the contract. Or the business owner I've been working with calls to tell me she had that crucial yet hard conversation with her team member and got to the bottom of the issue. Someone sends me a message on Instagram telling me that the blog I wrote made them cry, and then they acted on it. My kid texts me with a decision he made from that random chat we had last week, and he feels good about it.

It matters. Even when you don't think it does. The way you show up. The kindness you share. The time that you take. The words you exchange.

It's a 14-year-old girl from Germany, who sends a message on Instagram to Sarah, a well-known influencer and podcaster. The young girl had been dealing with depression and an eating disorder and wrote that Sarah's posts about loving and accepting yourself the way you are helped her so much. 'You saved me and made me believe in myself and I am forever grateful.' As Sarah commented when she shared the post, 'Your story matters. Don't ever underestimate the power of changing one life with your story and words.'

And it matters in small ways every day. The smile you gift to the elderly woman in the pharmacy. The way you hold the elevator door for the stressed woman racing towards you, with hope beneath the strain in her eyes. When you take the time to say 'thank you' and mean it. When you ask how someone's day is going and really listen for the answer.

The way you put your heart into what you do. Your soul into your work. Your love into your relationships.

What you do makes a difference. Please believe it. And when someone makes a difference for you, make sure you tell them too.

AFFIRMATION
I do what I do because it matters.

THE PORTFOLIO CAREER

*If you powerfully believe in the value of what
you have to offer the world, your love and
passion for it will be an unstoppable force.*

~ YOGARUPA

If you're old enough, you may remember that back in the day everyone had one career, perhaps even one job, and that was it. You were kind of locked into that lane, and moving or changing was a really big deal. It feels so 1980s right now. Things have changed dramatically and our working lives are much less linear than they used to be.

When I share with women I work with that they aren't restricted to their 'nine to five', and that they have the opportunity to create more than one type of work for themselves, many are disbelieving. This is so outside the realm of reality for most women, just as it used to be for me. Even those running their own businesses can still feel 'locked in' and it can take a while for this new paradigm to sink in.

But it's true. It's liberating. And you have permission to do it (just in case you were waiting for it).

Like Tara, who managed her big banking job for twenty years before asking to work four days a week, so she could focus on blogging and start a style consultancy on the side.

Or Louise, who started taking on a small number of energy healing clients on the weekends while she worked her full-time role in government, so she could fulfil her passion and start to build a presence online for her soul work.

Or perhaps you might relate to Stacey, who ran an events company and built an online global community for women while at home with her young family.

Or Mary, who runs her small accounting business while designing jewellery at night, selling it at markets on weekends.

You can create a portfolio career that nurtures many of your passions, in a way that supports you financially, creatively and perhaps also serves a community as well.

Whether you run your own business or work for someone else, take a look at the make-up of your work. Are you feeling fulfilled? Do you have variety in the work you are doing? Could you add a little portfolio spice into your life (with some extra income)?

We are living the future now. Portfolio careers are real and tangible and could make a difference for you in more ways than one—especially if you're in a position where you can't quit your day job but really long to follow your passion. Take a look at how this can apply and add value to your own life. Open yourself up to the possibilities.

AFFIRMATION

I create a portfolio career that lights me up.

NO-ONE IS HERE TO DO
WHAT YOU ARE

There are far more people in need of your gifts
than there are people giving those gifts.

~ GABRIELLE BERNSTEIN

How often do you look around and see people doing what you want to be doing, then shrug your shoulders with a sigh, feel defeated, and tell yourself that it's already been done, it's being done better, so why even bother?

It's a derailing story. But it's just not true. Let me share why: *Nobody else is you.*

That may sound simple enough. And completely obvious. And perhaps even unhelpful in the real world you inhabit with all of your big beautiful dreams. But it's the simple truth. Nobody else is you.

Nobody has what you have. No-one else has your background, experiences, stories, perspectives, relationships, skills, energy, narrative, view on life, mindset, personality, attitude. Nobody else has had the jobs you have had, lived where you lived, met the people you have met, learnt the same knowledge in the same way, or sees life just the way you see it.

Nobody else is you. Nobody else is here to do exactly what you came here for, in exactly the way you came here to do it. It hasn't all been done before, because you haven't done it yet. And no-one else can do it like you will do it. So if you don't do it, guess what? It won't get done.

Next time you think about what you really have your heart set on, but turn around and say, 'Meh, she's doing it better than

I ever could', remember that she isn't you. You are amazing. And the world needs your unique contribution, whatever that may be. So if you are going to believe in any story, believe in that one.

AFFIRMATION
I follow my unique purpose and trust my gifts.

YOU'LL DO IT WHEN YOU'RE READY

Be happy with what you have, while
working for what you want.

~ HELEN KELLER

Rose came to me for coaching a few years ago. She was a burnt out marketing executive, struggling to keep up with the demands of her job. In truth, her passion had completely run out. As we began working together, I could see that beneath the greyness that had become her working life, amid the hustle and grind, there was a vibrant, creative and dynamic woman waiting to be released.

As we worked together, Rose dug into what she truly wanted for her life. We looked at what her most purposeful work would be, if she gave herself permission to envision it. We didn't need to dig too deeply. Right there, just below the surface, was a bounty of fully formed dreams waiting to be expressed.

There were books and blogs and writing trips to a remote cabin in the woods. There were meditation retreats and a longing to study. And there was a big beautiful dream about a wellness place, where people could gather, gain respite from the busyness of the world, get quiet and go deeper into themselves.

All of the dreams. Purposeful. Passionate. Ready to be born.

But not yet. Because it appeared that there were more lessons for Rose to learn, as she spent another four years going in and out of marketing jobs, each time burning out a little more, yet also gaining more clarity on what she did and didn't want for her future.

And there was a path of transition that needed to unfold as well. It came in the form of deep study into meditation that underpinned her last few years of work, deepening her own practice, sense of self and readiness to act. It was her pathway out of a world she had at times thought she would never escape.

And then one day, she was ready. Recently, Rose had her last day of work in the marketing world. She'd had all the lessons she needed, to be able to release herself from that path and move into her purposeful one.

Purpose comes to us when we are ready for it. As we show up for the work. Learn the lessons. Ride the wave that is our crazy messy life. Don't feel like you have to move too quickly. Let it marinate. Until it's in your bones. Embedded in your psyche. Until it's ready to be released from your soul. Until you're ready.

AFFIRMATION
I keep learning until I am ready to act.

YOU CAN'T EARN YOUR
WORTH WITH BUSYNESS

There are two kinds of people, those who do the work and
those who take the credit.
Try to be in the first group; there is less competition there.

~ INDIRA GANDHI

In my late twenties, I worked for a global professional services firm. I was the marketing director, with a small team, working for the managing partner. Every day it felt like I was hustling to prove my worthiness. Working all the hours, being the last one in the office or online each evening, taking on as many projects as the business could serve up. I was a star performer, part of the inner circle, highly respected.

And even though I was incredibly good at my job, had a seat at the table and delivered results that all my higher-ups raved about, I still thought that my worth was determined by how busy I looked. Now this is a little embarrassing, but I still remember walking fast paced and with a look of intent on my face past my boss' office on more than one occasion, with papers in my hand, because I knew that if he saw me looking busy and intentional he would equate that with value. The sad fact is that he did.

It took me a long time to realise that I didn't. It was completely ridiculous. And I look back now at my twenty something self with waves of compassion for how incredibly hard I worked, and for how much energy I burned doing things that were mean-ingless, all for the sake of looking like I was adding value. The irony is, I was already adding value. The hustle was completely unnecessary.

Here's the truth that can revolutionise how you work: *You are already worthy.*

Your essential nature ensures your worthiness. You don't need to sing or dance for it. You don't need to hustle and grind for it. No act of busyness will add to it.

Do your work with intent and purpose. Make a meaningful contribution. And let the work do the rest.

AFFIRMATION
I am inherently worthy.

FLOW IS THE NEW HUSTLE

*Your work is to discover your work and then
with all your heart to give yourself to it.*

~ BUDDHA

You hear A types and entrepreneurs raving on about the glory of the hustle: how hard you have to work, how much it matters, how your very life and every success depend upon it. People used to wear their busyness like a badge of honour. Now it's about how hard they can hustle. New name, same theme. Work harder, faster, better, more.

If you relate to this type of work and it lights you up in a good way, then go for it. But if the very thought of the hustle leaves you feeling more exhausted than inspired, then I want you to know there is another way.

Let's start with this question: *How would it feel to stop pushing so hard?*

And this one: *What is all that hustling actually for?*

Imagine your ideal way of working. What does it look like? What does it feel like? If the goal is your own version of success, then you have to believe that you can define the way you work to get there. That you can do it in your own way, at your own speed, with your own values and with your own energy.

Flow is the state where we are in the zone. It's how we feel when we have the right mix between the challenge of the task and the strengths we are applying. When we are too stressed, we go into anxiety and overwhelm. Our brains literally start to shut down. Magic doesn't happen in that state. And when we are pushing too hard, hustling too much, we take ourselves out of the game we are trying to win.

Flow is the sweet spot; it's the Goldilocks moment. It's that state where you are at your best, doing your best work, full of inspiration, making the magic. Flow is the new hustle. It's where your greatest work will happen. And you can get there on your own terms.

AFFIRMATION
I work for the flow, not the hustle.

DON'T STOP IN THE MIDDLE

You're not lost in life. You're just early in the process.

~ GARY VAYNERCHUK

Y ou're ready to give up. To quit. To put it back in the box that it came from. You're tired. Dejected. Frustrated. It's just not coming together as fast or as easily as you had planned. *Why aren't I there yet?* is a question on relentless repeat in your brain. This is nothing like what it was supposed to look like. And it's sure not what you signed up for.

You're just So-Over-It-Already.

So you're going to quit. Seems like the easy option. Makes sense really, doesn't it? Cut your losses and all that jazz. I mean come on, you say, I bet it didn't take her this long. Her business is so successful. Her life/project/job/Instafeed/business/insert-crazy-comparisonitis-statement-here looks so perfect.

And then you say this: 'I just don't think I'm ever going to get there. Wherever there is.'

And this: 'It's just so freakin' hard.'

And even this: 'I'm such a bloody failure.'

Ah, yes. Welcome to the middle.

Your journey, your path, your project. You're in the middle. And the middle sucks. It's when the glossy exterior of the new exciting project has worn off. Not so glossy now though, is it? No more shiny silver object. Just dirt and mud and grease stains.

The middle is hard. It's where the real work is. The hard work. The churn and burn and grind. It's where the sweat is required. The kind of sweat that drips annoyingly, ticklishly down your face while you're in a painfully tough yoga pose and there's no way to reach for the towel to wipe it off.

The middle sucks. It's true.

But here's what's also true. The middle is where the magic happens. It's where you do the things you think you cannot do. Where you pull out all the stops. Where the unthinkable can happen. It's Stephen King publishing his breakthrough novel *Carrie* after dozens of rejections. It's Serena Williams excruciating work that was the path to her becoming the best athlete on the planet. It's the artist's fifteenth canvas attempt painted over white because it was so terrible, before the masterpiece happened.

Here's the thing that nobody tells you about the middle. The middle is the path. *The middle is the point.*

So don't quit. Keep going. Rest when the flow isn't coming. Hustle when the grace and ease has abandoned you. Dig deep when you need the grit to see it through. Learn to rest and to allow. Pray if you need to. But don't quit.

Just know that this is the middle. That the middle can be all kinds of horrible. That it will, in fact, suck—guaranteed. But know also that you can find all kinds of magic as you show up for that journey. And that you have to dig to find the gold. So dig as deep as your path requires.

AFFIRMATION

I find the lessons and the magic in the middle.

WAIT IT OUT FOR THE BUTTERFLIES

If people knew how hard I worked for my art,
they would not consider me a genius.

~ MICHELANGELO

S ome days I feel like I'm walking through mud. Nothing seems to be going right with my work. Or perhaps a truer statement would be that nothing seems to be moving fast enough. Everything is moving forwards, but the results seem intangible. Not enough. Too far away from outcomes. Too slow.

Other days, I get the flutter. Somewhere between the pit of my stomach and my heart. Actually, almost in my heart. The flutter. Like the feeling you get when your double shot latte is kicking in. On the crux of anxious and excited. Like anything is possible. Like you could do anything, achieve anything, be anything.

Like the butterflies you get when you're falling in love.

Some days it feels like that. Today was one of those days. Writing this book. Working on *Sacred Living*, a lifestyle site for women seeking more grace and ease in their lives. I had a glimpse today of how magical it can be. Of the potential. Of endless possibilities.

That magical feeling is everything. It's why creatives create. It's why dreamers dream. It's why entrepreneurs start business after business. It's the 'why' behind all of it.

But first comes the work. Wading through the muck. Getting it done.

In those days when it feels like you're moving through mud, hold out for the butterflies. They are always there, somewhere in your gut. Waiting for the right conditions to fly.

AFFIRMATION
I do the work and wait for the magic.

FIND YOUR EDGE

I'm always perpetually out of my comfort zone.
~ TORY BURCH

It's there. Behind the day-to-day. Just out of reach of what you know. Beyond what you think you are capable of. Just past your reach.

It's there. Outside your comfort zone. On the outskirts of the circle, way beyond the box.

Just past the end of your fingertips, even on your farthest reach. It's there.

Your edge. Stretch for it. Find it.

It's where your best work happens. The magic moments. The flow you long for.

But you have to want it. You have to reach for it. You need to get comfortably uncomfortable for long enough to even see it.

You need to feel into it.

What is that thing that would light you up, set your work and world on fire, but that you think is just a step too far? There's no way that you could do that, reach for that, achieve that. You? Not possible.

That thing right there? That's your edge. Play to it.

AFFIRMATION
I am brave enough to play my edge.

LET PASSION IGNITE
YOUR POSSIBILITIES

Let the beauty of what you love be what you do.

~ RUMI

My client Mary was having a really hard time in her career. She knew that what she was doing wasn't lighting her up, in fact she was pretty much hating it. She felt stuck, under-utilised, and just plain bored. There was no purpose or passion in her job, but she had no idea what came next.

As we worked together, the stories of what Mary was really passionate about started to unfold. Connecting with people. Sewing. Entertaining. Crafts. Natural healing. And as we talked more and more, she discovered that she was especially passionate about essential oils and wellbeing.

So I asked her what would it be like to give yourself permission to start playing in these different areas? To play. Not to have to switch careers, make a living, undertake further study, or take it all too seriously. Just to play.

At the same time, Mary had started looking for a new job. In interview after interview, she was told that she wasn't the right fit, or that the role wasn't for her. Then finally, in one last meeting, the interviewer looked her straight in the eye and asked why she was looking for that particular role, when her passions clearly lay in other areas. Mary was stumped. Was it that obvious?

Yes, it was. To everyone but her. She continued to play with the passions that she'd been denying herself and hiding from, because she thought she wasn't allowed to have too many passions, especially with her work and family roles. Once she started to open the door to her diverse interests, she started to blossom. Her creativity was reignited. She felt joyful again. And lo and behold, the right role became available. One that she felt more aligned to, could work part-time in, and that would free her up to start an essential oils business, to further integrate and pursue what she loved doing.

What box have you been trying to fit yourself into? What passions are you denying yourself? Give yourself permission to love what you love and explore it to your heart's content. You never know the journey you might go on, when you allow yourself to pursue whatever lights you up.

AFFIRMATION

I embrace all of my passions simply because they light me up.

MODEL YOUR FUTURE

The greatest danger for most of us is not that our aim is too high and we'll miss, but that it is too low and we will reach it.

~ MICHELANGELO

If you're stuck thinking about what you would really like to be doing and how you could possibly do it, think about this: Someone somewhere is doing what you would love to be doing. The best way to get a taste for what that could be like is to model that very future.

Ask yourself these questions:

- What is it you really want to do? Even small pieces of the puzzle will help.
- Who is already doing this, or aspects of it?
- If you're not sure, think about where you get a pang of envy or a hit of 'Oh, I'd love to do that!' when you look at someone and what they do in the world.
- What is it they actually do?
- How do they do it?
- What's their business model (or other form, like work model or creation model)?
- How can you inch yourself towards this vision?

If you think about people who could inspire the next part of your journey, it can give you a real sense of what could be possible. It can show you the various pathways available, and how they might all come together. And it's a massive source of inspiration and creativity for when you're feeling stuck.

Start a new vision board or art journal. Look on the internet, Pinterest, social media or in magazines and start collecting images that represent all of your potential ideas. Get images of people who are inspiring you—their businesses, their creations or whatever it is about them and what they do that lights you up.

And from this, you can start to build your own unique model, your own vision, for where to from here. It's an exciting process. Stay grounded in the belief that anything is possible. Because it is. You can create whatever you want. And your models are all the proof you need.

AFFIRMATION
I model my future vision into reality.

FIND YOUR LANE

If you have an idea, you have to believe
in yourself or no one else will.

~ SARAH MICHELLE GELLAR

There's a tiny little coffee and chai shop I frequent, just down the road from the beach. It's literally a hole in the wall, no more than two metres wide and about three metres long. They have about ten different types of chai, as many coffees, and all the things you could want in a spice/coffee/chai bar.

As I came off my walk and swim this morning, I ordered my golden spice chai latte with coconut milk and was chatting with the owner, Luke, as he made it.

'You've got a great business going here,' I said. 'I remember when you opened.'

'Yeah, it's good,' he agreed.

'How is business?' I enquired. It's a question I ask nearly everyone I come across. Being a business strategist, I'm always fascinated and curious with the inner workings of people's businesses.

'It's pretty good. We made it through winter. Two businesses nearby closed down. It can be tough,' he told me.

'Yeah, it's not for the faint-hearted, running your own business,' I empathised.

'No, sure isn't. It's funny though,' he continued, 'Now that I've done my own thing, I'd hate to go back to work for someone else. Eight or nine hours of being told what to do? Nah, not going back to that.'

'I know what you mean,' I said, feeling every word. 'I don't think you can ever go back, once you've had the taste of working for yourself. You just have to ride the waves, right? Save in the highs and ride out the lows. But it's worth it.'

I got my chai and headed off, saying I'd see him tomorrow.

It's not for everyone. Some people love the security of working for someone else. They like the structure, or the type of work that you can't do in your own business. Others, like my chai friend Luke, can't imagine doing anything else.

He had found his lane in a tiny coffee chai bar. He was his own boss, and he was making a go of it. And he knew that by choice he would never go back to work for anyone else.

You can end up in the most surprising of places when you pay attention to what lights you up. Even though I worked for big companies for 18 years, never thinking for a hot minute that I would run my own business, things changed. I paid attention. I found my lane. And just like Luke, I never looked back.

AFFIRMATION
I find my own lane.

WHAT WOULD A RADICAL
MOVE LOOK LIKE?

Because you are alive, everything is possible.

~ THICH NHAT HANH

Think radical. Off the charts. Exciting but perhaps mildly terrifying. A definite game changer.

What would it look like?

Is it something completely unexpected, or perhaps something you have been quietly dreaming about for some time?

Feel into it.

We don't often make radical moves. Mostly we skim around the edges. If we want to change something, we play a little, inching to and fro, feeling out the risk and the potential. Mostly feeling out the risk, let's be honest. Change can be scary. We don't want to move too fast or go too deep, you know, just in case.

But what if you did?

What if you leapt into something so radical that it could completely change your business, career or even your life?

What if?

What could be possible if you trusted yourself, your vision, your dream, or even just committed to making a plan to do so?

Just imagine. The whole world could be yours.

AFFIRMATION

I am ready to get radical.

GET REAL ABOUT YOUR FINANCES

I don't know much about being a millionaire,
but I'll bet I'll be darling at it.

~ DOROTHY PARKER

I'd been working with Susan to start her own business. She was still working for someone else and in our last session, I asked her to get a handle on her full financial position. I wanted her to have the necessary information before stepping out on her own, so she could plan accordingly. My questions for her were things like:

- How much money did she currently have?
- What was the amount she needed, to meet her monthly expenses?
- How much could she realistically save between now and the time she wanted to leave her job?

When she came to our next session she was equal parts elated and shocked. She had done what I asked, drilling into every aspect of her finances, and doing a detailed review of her spending.

She was shocked by how much she was spending on superfluous items like clothes, make-up and takeaway food, and she was elated to have found a small amount of money sitting in an old savings account she had forgotten she had.

Mostly, she felt incredibly empowered from the knowledge about where she was at with all aspects of her financials. Her understanding helped us create an exit strategy from her current role, as well as a new business start-up plan, that took her current money picture into account and reduced her financial risk moving forward.

What is your current financial position? No matter whether you work in your own business, a bank, a hospital, an office, a shop or whether you've taken time out to be home with the kids, take some time to work through each aspect of your finances, so you have a clear view of where you're at.

Knowledge is power. Understanding your money situation is powerful. Let it inform the decisions you make, to create a better future for yourself.

AFFIRMATION
I am empowered about my money.

GO TO THE ISLAND,
BURN THE BOATS

The trouble is, you think you have time.

~ BUDDHA

How committed are you to your purpose? How excited are you to do your work in the world? How ready are you to step into your power, to be seen, to really do something meaningful?

If you're nodding and saying 'yes' to yourself, or you feel like you're even on the outskirts of this vicinity, then let me ask you this ...

Are you hedging your bets? Are you dancing around the edges of your work and life, not wanting to fully step in?

Are you just dabbling, playing with the idea of stepping in but only doing it half-heartedly? Are you still invested in your Plan B, you know, just in case? Do you think you're all in, but know in your soul that you aren't even close?

If any of these questions ring remotely true, then I have a message for you. Lean in and listen closely.

If you know in your heart it's time; if you've mitigated all of the risk required; if you've played on the edges and you just know that you really do need to do this thing, and that the time is now.

If you're ready to step into your potential, your power, your purpose.

If you just know. Then here is the message: Go to the island. Burn the boats. And don't look back.

AFFIRMATION
I step fully into my purpose. I burn the boats. I'm ready.

PART 3

Wellbeing

WELLNESS IS WEALTH

*Here in this body are the sacred rivers; here are the sun
and moon as well as all the pilgrimage places. I have not
encountered another temple as blissful as my own body.*

~ SARAHA

The old adage goes that you don't know what you have until its gone. Sadly for so many of us, this is true of our health. We spend our lives pushing and punishing our bodies with too much work, the wrong food, little sleep and toxins like alcohol, then wonder why we have no energy, fluctuating moods, untold stress, and lifestyle illnesses that could be prevented with healthier habits.

We take our health for granted, usually until we can't anymore. I see so many women in my community and among my friends who have become burnt out or ill. Or they've suffered a physical injury like their back going out, which is often our bodies' only way of getting us to stop.

You know how it goes: you work all year for your two-week vacation. You push yourself to the limit getting all your work done so you can go on that break. And then what happens on the first day of your holiday? You get sick. It may be a cold, flu or stomach bug, but again, it's your body's way of saying thanks for stopping (finally), so now let me do some healing.

I've learnt all of these lessons the hard way, believe me. So if this is where you are, you are far from alone. But there is a better way. Our health is our greatest form of wealth, as long as we nourish and nurture it. It can be small steps, not giant actions, which make the greatest difference and most positive impact on your daily vitality.

In Part 3, we will explore many ways you can build wealth in your most important area: your wellbeing.

AFFIRMATION
I look after my health to honour my sacred self.

SLOWING DOWN

Take the gentle path.

~ GEORGE HERBERT

There's an epidemic among modern women. Author and nutritional biochemist, Dr. Libby Weaver, calls it 'rushing women's syndrome'. If you tune in, you might discover that you have fallen prey to it as well.

We often don't realise just how fast we are living our lives, how much we rush every day, or how out of breath we are. We also don't understand the dramatic impact this rushing has on our emotional, physical and mental health, not to mention our spirits.

But rushing sneaks up on you, and bad behavioural patterns are hard to break. The thing about constantly moving so fast is that you often don't realise that it's not normal until you stop.

So I invite you to stop. Right now. Stop for just a few minutes.

Take some long, deep, slow, belly breaths (it might take you a few minutes just to be able to do that, and that's okay, I'll wait). As you sit with yourself and slow down, check in with these questions:

- *How are you feeling?*
- *Do you find yourself constantly rushing from one thing to the next?*
- *Do you move fast throughout your day, even when you don't need to?*

Constant rushing puts us into a fight, flight or flee state, sending our nervous system into overdrive, disrupting our hormones, shortening our breath, pumping our adrenalin, and leaving us exhausted.

You can create more moments of grace and ease in your day by making a conscious choice to slow down.

S l o w   d o w n.

It's not always easy. It requires consistently checking in with yourself, until you have rewired those neural pathways in your brain that are programmed to run at freight train speed. But you can slow it down. The most important thing you can do right now is to just ask yourself: *How much am I rushing now?* and *Do I need to be going so fast?*

Often there is no fire other than the mental loop in our minds telling us to go faster. But you can choose a different story. You can choose space. Deep breaths. Conscious living. Intentional being. And showing up in a way that serves you.

AFFIRMATION

It is safe for me to slow down. My breath guides me home.

YOUR BODY DOESN'T LIE

When one is pretending the entire body revolts.

~ ANAÏS NIN

That knot in your stomach as you walk into the meeting. The clenching of your teeth as you fight back the words you really want to say. The throbbing in your head as you think about your workload. The churning in your gut when that friend calls who you really don't want to talk to. You can't put your finger on it. You can't rationalise it. It doesn't really make sense. But your body knows. And your body doesn't lie.

Those migraines. The upset stomach. The broken foot. The tiredness. The sore throat. The constant bout of the flu. The weight you just can't shift. It's your body's way of telling you something that you aren't tuned into, cognitively or consciously.

When you get a message from your body by way of a feeling or symptom—the way you feel in your body every time you're speaking to a certain person; how you always get sick before a recurring event in your life; or how your energy seems to vanish each Monday morning like clockwork—then at some point it serves you well to listen.

While sitting in your receptive feminine energy, tuning into your knowledge and intuition, and becoming still enough to hear it, ask yourself these questions:

- *What are you feeling in your body right now?*
- *Where do you feel disharmony or discomfort?*
- *Is this a recurring feeling?*

- *What is this trying to tell you?*
- *What action do you need to take to bring yourself back to harmony?*

Our bodies are beautiful, wise vessels that teach us all the lessons we need to learn, if we are tuned in enough to listen and brave enough to act on that guidance. What is it costing you to ignore your own wisdom, or stay stuck in a pattern that is not serving you? What will it take for you to make a shift?

What if you decided right now that you could make any change required with grace and ease? You can. And you can let it be easy.

Tune in. Your body has all the answers you need. Follow it home.

AFFIRMATION
I listen to my body and trust her guidance.

LEARNING TO LISTEN

My candle burns at both ends; it will not last the night.
~ EDNA ST. VINCENT MILLAY

When I was 21 I got really sick, so sick that I was bedridden for six months. Doctors tried to figure out what was wrong with me. I had test after test, but there was no medical explanation for my symptoms: exhaustion, painfully swollen glands, the need to sleep all day and yet be awake with rampant insomnia all night, pain through every cell of my body, no appetite, emotional malaise.

The illness hit me while I was waitressing, as we closed out the lunch shift. I had been pushing it pretty hard: studying for my audio engineering diploma, working in the studio producing bands, waitressing every minute I had to earn money, and going out drinking every night to relieve the pressure of the hustle. I was about to finish my shift when I felt my back stiffen, from the base of my spine to the top of my neck. It was like someone had strapped a brace of steel to my back. I felt the blood drain from my face. At that moment, my manager walked up to me with a look of grave concern on her face, sensing that something was terribly, terribly wrong.

It was a long path ahead of bed rest in between blood tests, herbalists, acupuncturists, naturopaths, more blood tests and endless appointments with doctors. Eventually, they told me that I had something that the alternative health care profession was just starting to understand as Chronic Fatigue Syndrome. Back then, they weren't really sure if it was something that was 'all in the head' or a legitimate medical issue. Of course, it turned out it was the latter and it would plague me, and be one of my greatest teachers, for decades.

I came to understand that my need to drive, strive and succeed at all costs was in direct odds with my body and spirit, which wanted to run at a different, more soothing pace. I wouldn't learn this until I was into my forties. It would be a humbling journey, as I continually went to war with my body, overriding its needs with those of my insatiable mind.

I did learn, eventually. But not until I had many more lessons. A thyroid disorder. A debilitating heart condition that had me in and out of hospital. A series of mini burnouts, which I ignored, leading of course to a major unstoppable burnout that commanded all of my attention.

I would learn through these gifts to find a path of ease. To rest. To treat my body with respect instead of punishment. To nurture it, nourish it, restore it and live at the pace it most desired. To allow my inner creative, that was in desperate need of space, silence and stillness, to safely emerge.

It's an ongoing challenge, listening to what my body needs. In fact, it's one of the greatest challenges of my life (in which I know I'm not alone). Yet it's the journey that has taught me the most about myself, my spirit and my soul.

AFFIRMATION
I listen to the lessons my body is trying to teach me.

BE AWARE OF YOUR
ENERGY LEAKAGES

The ocean is made of drops.

~ MOTHER TERESA

There's a glass vase on the table, holding a beautiful bouquet of roses. But the vase has a tiny crack, almost undetectable to the naked eye. Over time, you notice a small pool of water forming at the base of the vase; as you look closer, you notice a visible crack in the glass. As more water starts to trickle out, you see another crack forming, then another and another, until the vase breaks apart, water gushing out and glass shattering everywhere. What started as a tiny crack that you couldn't even see caused the entire vase to break.

It's the same with your energy. If you observe your energy over the period of a week, in different settings and situations and with various people, you'll be able to witness where you have energy leakages. Where are the tiny cracks where energy is seeping out of you? What detracts from your energy; who leaches your energy; and what leaves you feeling drained? Who or what depletes you?

Your energy leakages may be small: the annoying comment from your sister; the way the barista forgot to put chocolate on the top of your cappuccino; the workman drilling outside your office when you're trying to work. Or they may be more significant: the way your pants feel too snug, making you realise that you've put on two kilos, which makes you constantly agonise over food; or the snarky comment your boss made in front of your entire peer group, that completely derailed you for the rest of the week. Or even bigger: knowing that you can't pay the rent this month without landing that new client or finding a new job; or the call you need to make to the doctor about those tests she ran last week.

Where are your energy leakages? Some are out of our control, so we just have to deal with them and show up the best we can. But we can plug many of them. We can fill those gaps, put putty in them or stop them from happening in the first place.

The first step is to be aware of how your energy feels when full and whole, so you can recognise when it is getting away from you.

AFFIRMATION
I consciously manage my own energy.

HOLDING YOUR BREATH

Pranayama is the practice of breath control. The word
'prana' refers not only to breath, but also to air and life itself.
~ CHRISTY TURLINGTON

B reathing. It's the most natural motion in the world and we do it without thinking about it. Of course, stating the absolute obvious, we must do it to survive. And yet, if you get really conscious with your breath throughout the day, you will experience multiple periods where you are actually holding your breath.

Sometimes I notice it, but only ever after the fact. My chest tightens and I find myself gasping for air, like I am going under water, desperate to take one last breath before I submerge. Often it's when I'm working. Other times it's when I should be at my most calm and serene, like when I'm floating in the ocean. I should be relaxed, but there I am holding my breath. I clench my teeth and constrict my chest and leave it filled with stale air, almost afraid to exhale. And then I gasp, trying to inhale as sharply as possible to fill the void.

I know better, of course. I practise yoga. I'm trained to teach. I do daily pranayama, a yogic breathing practice. But we all get tense, busy and our breath gets short, sharp, high up in our chest or held altogether. This can add significantly to your stress levels, leaving you feeling more anxious and overwhelmed than you would normally be if you were breathing well.

Try this: inhale through your nose for the count of four; hold your breath for the count of four; exhale slowly for the count of four; hold it out for the count of four. That's the four-part yogic breath, and it can change your relationship with your body.

And this: breathe in through your nose, consciously taking that breath deep into your belly. Feel your belly expand, then softly fall, with each breath. If you feel the breath coming straight into your chest, observe it for a few breaths, then without stressing, gently guide your breath down further into your belly. Over time, this will become your natural way of breathing. And being.

Breathing with intention and consciousness (what yogis call pranayama practice) can significantly reduce your stress and bring more energy, ease and calm into your life.

AFFIRMATION
I focus on slow, calm breathing.

WE MUST PARTICIPATE IN OUR OWN HEALING

All you need is deep within you waiting
to unfold and reveal itself.

~ EILEEN CADDY

We want it done for us. The seven steps, the quick fix, the magic pill. Someone to not just tell us what to do or how to do it, but to actually do it for us. We just want it to be easy.

But often it isn't.

We have to participate in our own healing. We have to show up. On the mat, on the cushion, in the temple, on the trek. In the hospital room, in the prison cell, in the church pew on our knees.

We have to show up. Do the work. Feel the pain.

Work the rosary. Pray to Mary. Ask for forgiveness. Redemption even.

Not from anyone else. Healing isn't an extrinsic practice. No-one is watching and rating our progress. We don't get five stars for doing it right.

We heal alone. Even if a million people on the banks of the Ganges surround us during the Holi festival, we still heal alone. One in a million souls on a collective yet singular journey.

We must participate in our own healing. With as much grit and grace as we can find.

AFFIRMATION
I do what it takes to heal.

GETTING THE SLEEP YOU NEED

Sleep is the best meditation.

~ DALAI LAMA

Do you currently get seven to eight hours of sleep a night? If you have little ones at home, are caring for someone, or are working the night shift, you get a pass on this one. But for the rest of us, we really do need to make sleep a priority.

If you struggle with getting to sleep or staying asleep, I feel for you—I have used all the excuses in the book, as I used to live on four to five hours a night. I was always too busy working, or thinking about working, or recovering from my latest burnout, which often included insomnia. But after many years of research into the science of sleep, the conclusions are irrefutable—you need your sleep to function like a good human, and it's essential to your overall wellbeing and vitality.

There are some things that can really help in the sleep department. Set yourself an evening routine to help you wind down from the busyness of your day. Give yourself a curfew for work, email, television, social media and anything that stimulates you and amps up your cortisol and adrenalin levels. Count back from when you need to get up, so you know what time you need to go to sleep to get your (ideally) eight hours in.

Then, the bedtime routine. It could be some gentle yoga, a brief meditation, some light reading, spiritual reflection, journalling time, a lovely cup of relaxing tea like chamomile, some calming essential oils like lavender or vetiver, and perhaps a gratitude practice or whatever else calms and relaxes you. It doesn't need to be long—even 15 minutes is enough to help you switch off and wind down—but the break in your behavioural pattern from these practices will signal to your mind and body that it's time for sleep, not action.

After that, lights out. Sleep really is the best path to restoration, having more energy, a greater sense of happiness and just feeling good. It's also one of our most essential coping mechanisms.

Give yourself the gift of sleep.

AFFIRMATION
My sleep restores me on every level.

LET'S TALK ABOUT YOGA

Only staying active will make you
want to live a hundred years.

~ JAPANESE PROVERB

S o this is the start of a few chapters on yoga. I'm pretty passionate about yoga as a tool for coming back to simple, soulful, sacred living, and one little chapter wasn't going to do it justice. It has been an integral, transforming part of my journey and I want to extend that invitation to you too, no matter whether you have never stepped onto a mat, or if you are regularly getting your downward dog on.

I didn't come to yoga easily. As a former dancer, you would think that it would have been a natural progression I would ease into. But alas, that wasn't to be. As with many things in life, you have to find your place, your poses, your people, and this was the case for me.

It actually took me years to find my yoga groove. One of the first classes I remember taking was a very strict class, where every foot and hand needed to be in exactly the right place. The word 'rigid' comes to mind. It reminded me of my childhood ballet teacher, who used to throw her shoe at me when I stuck my butt out. All I could think was how soon the class would be over.

Then there was a Bikram yoga class that was so hot I nearly passed out. The Pitta in me (my Ayurvedic dosha) was dying and while I loved the practice, it took me about a week to cool down. Literally.

There were many times when I gave up yoga altogether. But there was a knowing in me that I was meant to do this bendy thing and that there was so much more to discover beyond the asana (physical poses). I kept being drawn back.

Then one Friday lunchtime I stumbled upon a studio near my work. The place looked welcoming enough, so I ambled on in and rolled out the mat they provided. In walked a blonde teacher about my age who greeted me with a beautiful smile and a warm embrace. The practice was graceful but challenging: lots of seated poses, downward dogs, forward bends and breath work. She told me later that she taught Hatha yoga. I felt like I had come home.

I started practising with my new teacher a few times a week, and six months later I embarked on the yoga teacher training she was running. This is what I had been searching for. The practice, yes. But I wanted to learn, to know the deep philosophy, thousands of years old, that sat behind the poses. I wanted the spiritual component even more than I wanted to learn what to do with my body.

That was the beginning. And it would change everything.

AFFIRMATION

I find the yoga that is right for me.

IT'S A PRACTICE

*The purpose of a formal practice time is to establish
and sustain the awareness of inner tranquillity
that is always available to us. In the hubbub of
everyday life it is easy to forget that each of us has
this innate capacity to be calm and peaceful.*

~ DONNA FARHI

Sometimes yoga practice feels like transcendence, like you're
levitating off your mat in a sheer state of bliss. You move
through your vinyasa gracefully and with ease, every movement flowing like water through a stream. Your knee is placed
perfectly over your foot at the exact angle your teacher has demon-
strated. Your shoulder stand is strong and straight. Your backbend
sublimely lifted in all the right places. Your closing savasana
beautifully peaceful.

Sure, it happens like that. But mostly, it feels like work. And
some days, that work is hard. I step onto my mat feeling rigid,
even though I only practised yesterday. I forget the pose the
teacher is telling me in Sanskrit, even though I'm a trained teacher
and should know better. My knee hurts like hell in standing side
angle pose, and I can't for the life of me get my hand flat on the
ground next to my foot. My backbend feels like torture, like my
wrists are going to snap off at the joint and my shoulders are
going to break. I keep wishing I was wearing a watch, so I could
see how much more of this I have to take today.

And there are many days in between. But still, there is the
practice. It's not about how flexible you feel, how bendy you can
be, or how close you can get your head to your knee. It's not

about the $80 yoga pants or the fancy mat, or how cute you look in your Lululemon crop top. And it's not about how strong and fierce you look in the mirror in your plank pose.

It's about the practice. Yoga means 'union' in Sanskrit. It's about the union of the body, the mind and the spirit. It's about coming home to ourselves. It's about the ease of the breath while in motion. It's about moving the body before the stillness of meditation. It's about ancient philosophy and internal bodily systems and cleansing and releasing and surrendering. It's about everything that is bigger and more meaningful than the minutiae that fill our days and ravish our minds.

And it's called a practice for a reason. All you have to do is show up for it.

AFFIRMATION
I make yoga my daily practice.

WILL I BE GOOD ENOUGH?

*Real learning comes about when the
competitive spirit has ceased.*

~ J. KRISHNAMURTI

She was coming. One of my favourite teachers, Elena Brower, was coming from New York to run a weekend workshop. The event brief said 'for teachers and dedicated students'. I was a non-teaching yoga teacher and certainly a dedicated student, so I signed up.

As I stepped onto my mat one morning in the lead-up to the workshop, the internal dialogue started. To be honest, it had been chirping away beneath the surface for a few weeks, but with only three days to go the volume had increased significantly ...

> *I wonder if they will all be really experienced yoga teachers and I will be the clumsy one they all look at wondering what the hell is she doing here?*
> *I'll get there early so I can get the spot right in the back corner, so no-one can see me.*
> *I hope I'm not the heaviest person in the room; they will probably all be ridiculously thin and fit with those little crop tops and bare flat stomachs.*
> *Maybe I should just go to the markets on Sunday instead.*

But all the thoughts came down to this one: *What if I'm just not good enough?*

Incessant. Shaming. Blaming thoughts. Why hadn't I practised more? Why hadn't I lost more than the seven kilos I had dropped in the past ten months (*such a slacker*, I thought to myself).

Why can't I get my leg through properly in my vinyasa, what on earth will people think?

Negative. Horrible. So-not-yogic-thinking.

I was in the worst part of my ego. Firmly grounded down into my shadow self. Fearful of not fitting in. Or standing out for the wrong reasons. Of just not being good enough to be there.

I had to get out of my head and shift my energy. I decided to show up and simply be grateful for being there. I walked in a little early to get an inconspicuous place for my mat, and was instructed to place it next to where the last mat had been laid down in the middle of the room. That's okay, I thought, right in the middle, I can hide a little here. Elena, who I had met before and connected with online, saw me with surprise. Her face lit up and she came to greet me with a wonderful warm hug. 'Thank you so much for coming,' she whispered to me generously. 'Of course,' I said, humbled and honoured.

As I was feeling nicely secure in the middle pack of the yogis, Elena decided not to be at the front of the class, but in the middle. And guess where that placed me? Yes, right in the front row, with half the mats facing directly towards me. I just silently laughed to myself. I knew this was a lesson being sent to me from spirit. *Just show up*, it told me. *Leave your ego at the door. It has no place here. You are here to learn. To practise. To evolve. Let yourself.*

So that's what I did, and I had the most wonderful weekend. I was one of the least experienced teachers in the room, and it didn't bother me in the slightest. It actually had nothing to do with the yoga poses. Just the practice of being there.

Our yoga practice is a practice of self-development. Of dealing with our darkness. Bringing our shadow into the light, for the healing that it needs and the love that it deserves. We step onto our mat not because we are perfect, but because we have no need to be so. We belong there, just as we are, with all of our imper-fections. We step onto our mats to heal. To come home to who we are truly are. Or at least to find the path back there.

AFFIRMATION
Yoga requires nothing of me but my presence and practice.

JUST NOT TODAY

Just because you can't today, doesn't mean you can't tomorrow.
~ SARAH WAHIBA SENAN

'Oh, my God. I can't do this bloody pose.'

There was a time when this statement would have sent me into spirals of self-loathing, negativity and scathing self-talk. Of how hopeless I was. How terribly lazy. How I should be further ahead by now.

But after years of practice, showing up to the mat, my inner dialogue when challenged looks so very different now.

'Not today. I can't do this pose today.'

Then this.

'But if I keep practising, perhaps I will be able to do it tomorrow.'

Regardless of where I am with my practice each day, and what my body chooses to do with each pose, it's not a reflection of who I am as a person. It doesn't dictate my worth. The only important thing that matters is that I showed up. I practised today. I witnessed my ego today. I looked upon myself with self-compassion today. I gave gratitude for my body today. I loved myself enough to be present today.

Our practice is an analogy for our life—a reflection of how we are showing up off the mat. The more compassion and grace we can demonstrate for ourselves in our practice, the more we will show in our life. In many ways, it's the greatest teacher there is.

AFFIRMATION
I show up with self-compassion.

BRINGING YOGA TO LIFE

We find that all that we need lies within the content
of the moment, even if that moment is difficult.

~ DONNA FARHI

You could say I was going through a transition. In the space of a few months, a massive amount of change had taken place. I had given up my job as the head of marketing for one of the world's largest tech companies, because I was utterly burnt out and sick. I took two months off work to recover, before coming back in a new part-time role as the head of strategy.

In the two-month break when I was meant to be recovering, I had packed up the house I'd lived in for many years to move my five-year-old son and me into a new house with my then boyfriend and his two teenage children. As it turned out, everything that could possibly go wrong did go wrong. Within the space of just a few more months, I had broken up with the boyfriend and moved again with my son into an apartment at the beach. It was a heartbreaking and challenging time.

The future I had thought was ahead of me—with this new relationship and new work role—changed overnight. It left me questioning everything. What was this job I was in that I really didn't want; what damage had I done to my young child from all of this upheaval; would my heart ever be whole again?

It was around this time that I discovered a book that would change my practice again, along with my view of the world and who I was in it. The book was *Bringing Yoga to Life: The Everyday Practice of Enlightened Living* by renowned teacher Donna Farhi. While on vacation to Canada, journeying on the Rocky

Mountaineer train through the Rockies in the middle of winter, I devoured the book. Page by page, I felt myself unravel, descend, and then slowly come back to life.

Farhi writes that our yoga is a life practice, that it teaches us not only how to be on our mat, but how to show up in the world. As she says:

> *When we begin Yoga practice in earnest, we are signing for a lifelong apprenticeship with our Self and to the Self. And as in any apprenticeship, many skills can be learned only over a long period of time. There are no shortcuts and crash courses, and there is no replacement for the satisfaction and richness that follow in the wake of such wholehearted commitment.*

Yoga has the power to heal us on the deepest levels of our being. Regardless of what your practice looks like, from the most gentle restorative poses to the most vigorous asana, the skills learnt from committing to Self both on and off the mat are life-changing gifts to be embraced and cherished on our journey home to ourselves.

AFFIRMATION

I let yoga bring me home.

THE WORK THAT TRANSFORMS YOU

There is only one journey. Going inside yourself.

~ RAINER MARIA RILKE

I was lying on the table. Nancy Valentine Smith, a gifted medicine woman, was holding her hands above my body, lingering across my sacral chakra. I'd been seeing her regularly for about two years for healing, working on clearing old and deeply held energy patterns that needed to be released for me to step fully into my power.

For the past few months, Nancy had been working deeply into my core. My lower three chakras: the ones that hold the energy for safety, security, personal power, feminine essence and creativity. As she placed her hand firmly on my stomach, she looked at me with a deep knowing. 'This commitment you have to your yoga practice? It's really working. It's transforming you and clearing you on a completely new level to what I have seen before.'

'Hmmmm. Yes,' she hummed, her eyes closed. 'Keep going with it.'

I knew this to be true. I could feel it. I could see it.

When I started working with my new teacher the year before, I felt stuck, heavy, immovable. I held an identity of myself as a yogi, but the reality was very different. I didn't practise often enough, or with nearly enough commitment. I wasn't doing the work.

After six months work with my teacher, I started to feel the shifts. Something was stirring on a soul level. I was ready. Ready to transmute. Ready to transform.

When my teacher told me I was starting the primary Ashtanga sequence, a rigorous physical practice of set poses that came in numbered sequences, in my definition moving from improbable to impossible, I laughed at her. There is no way I can do that, I said to myself. Not a chance.

But as I committed and showed up each day to my mat, to the sequence, to the practice, I noticed many things start to shift. My inner dialogue shifted from extremely negative and disbelieving to thoughts of *Wow, look at what you can do* and *I can't believe you can get your head down to your knee.* As my poses kept progressing, so did my sense of power in my centre. My core felt physically stronger, but on a deeper level my spirit felt like it had solidified within my body. I can hardly explain it.

Transmuted. Transformed. Yes. In a thousand unspoken and unseen ways, the practice was working.

AFFIRMATION
I work my practice and let it work through me.

THE SIMPLE RULES OF
NOURISHMENT

*We may be approaching a time when sugar is responsible
for more early deaths in America than cigarette smoking.*

~ LEWIS CANTLEY, cancer researcher, quoted in *Tribe of Mentors* by Tim Ferriss

When we eat well, it can be the fuel we need to support us on our quest for living a good life. When our nutrition is not so healthy, it can completely undo us and leave us feeling like bingeing on Netflix instead of following our dreams.

You are an individual so what you need to eat to thrive is also individual. But there are some common themes that we can probably agree on that we could all incorporate into our daily life.

Author of multiple books on food and nutrition, Michael Pollan, potentially said it best: *Eat food. Not too much. Mostly plants.*

Eat whole foods from nature, not food that is processed; eat seasonal and organic, or farm fresh, where possible; eat your greens with every single meal; drink pure filtered water; cut out the white stuff in the form of white sugar, flour, rice, starches; limit the amount of meat you eat and increase your intake of plant-based foods (you don't have to cut meat out altogether, just eat plants whenever possible); moderate your alcohol; remove or limit dairy; get rid of your vices.

Be mindful about what you are putting in your body and start to view food as fuel, not simply pleasure. Your body will thank you for it.

AFFIRMATION
I fuel my body with nourishment.

JUST SHOW UP

It is not because things are difficult that we do not dare;
it is because we do not dare that they are difficult.

~ SENECA

Committing to practices that support our wellbeing or spiritual path should be a no-brainer. We all want to feel good. I'm not sure about you, but I don't know anyone who intentionally wants to feel less than amazing. And yet we do all sorts of things to ensure that we don't do what we know will help us.

We get a burger instead of a salad. We go for drinks with the girls, instead of going to yoga class. We check our email, when we know we should be meditating. We scroll endlessly through Instagram, when we'd be better off finishing our work so we can get home. In short, we self-sabotage. We let old habits ingrained in our neural pathways get in the way of our better self. And we suffer for it.

For any practice, the hardest part is showing up. It's the activation energy that it takes—to get on your mat, sit on your meditation cushion, head to the fridge to grab the veggies to cook a healthy meal instead of reaching for the takeaway menu—that stops us from following through on what our better angels know is best for us.

Showing up requires effort for sure. But if you can just get past the initial resistance, that effort will be rewarded. Once you get on your yoga mat, even if you tell yourself it's just for two poses or five minutes, you will usually be rewarded with more energy than you thought you had, end up practising for longer and, of course, feel much better.

If you can show up to your meditation cushion, telling yourself you will do a two-minute session, the Universe will often gift you with the calmness to sit for five, ten or even twenty minutes.

And when we show up to eat more healthfully and nourish our bodies, the way we feel often creates enough momentum to make us want to do it again and again, until it becomes a new habit and way of being.

Show up for yourself. That first few seconds of moving towards what you really want, instead of away from it, will create waves of forward momentum for your wellbeing without you even realising it.

AFFIRMATION

I show up for myself in small moments every day.

THE MYTH OF MEDITATION

*Prayer is when you talk to God. Meditation
is when God talks to you.*

~ YOGI BHAJAN

You've been told to meditate. It will be good for you, they
say. It will help you quieten your monkey mind. It will
bring you peace and calm and make you all zen inside. It will
help you create more space in your life. You will grow to love it.

All of that is true.

And then they say this: 'All of your thoughts will disappear
from your mind.'

That is when your ears prick up like they do when you hear
a lie.

You tried to meditate once or twice. You sat in an awkward
cross-legged position on the floor. You set your timer. You focused
on your breath. Closed your eyes. And waited ... waited for the
calm to wash over you, the monkeys to leave your brain and
peace and calm to prevail.

And then, every thought you ever had came racing through
the mind you are desperately trying to calm:

*God, I'm so uncomfortable. Why do I have to sit on the floor to
meditate, I'm not a freaking teenager? My knees hurt. I have so
much work to do today, how am I ever going to get through it? My
boss is such an ass. He has no idea what I deal with. I think he's
kind of a bully. And Sarah is driving me crazy. I must make sure
I pick up pineapple and broccoli at the shops today. And coconut
water. Oh, and light bulbs. What else do I need? Must write a list.*

And a to-do list for work as well. Must call Mum. And Nancy. And that guy who needs to fix the shower. Jesus, is this medita-tion thing finished yet? I feel like I've been sitting here for an hour! I'm so done with this.

The timer goes off. You've been sitting for an entire two minutes. And for not one second of that two minutes was your mind void of those rabid incessant monkeys.

Welcome to your meditation practice. The number one myth that stops people from meditating is we think that as soon as we start, our minds will empty of the 60,000 thoughts we have on any given day and there will be silence. This is what we are told by well-meaning people who are trying to help. But it doesn't happen like that. And it's not helpful.

Research has been done with the most experienced meditators in the world. They were asked how long into their meditation practice they become aware of the first thought coming into their mind. Brace yourself. Thirty seconds. Thirty seconds! The most experienced meditators in the world. So why on earth would we expect that mere novices like us could sit to meditate and be clear and free of the monkey mind?

They call it a practice for a reason. Your work in meditation practice is not to clear your mind of all thoughts. Your work is to show up, breathe, and when you notice that you've jumped on the thought train, to gently bring your attention back to your breath or your point of focus (mantra, music, guided visualisa-tion, mala beads, candle etc.).

That's the practice in its simplest form. And it's worth persisting with because the research is compelling: meditation boosts our emotional intelligence; brain-imaging research shows that it can help strengthen our ability to regulate our emotions; meditation builds resilience; and multiple research studies have shown that meditation has the potential to decrease anxiety, and potentially boost resilience and performance.

Meditation has also been shown to increase empathy, improve focus, reduce distractions, improve relationships, boost your mood, improve your connections, enhance your wellbeing, lower your stress and make you kinder and more compassionate.

Find five to ten minutes once a day and start a practice. You don't have to sit on the floor if you don't want to, a chair will do just fine. You can use an app like *Headspace* or find some guided meditations online. Or use a simple timer app like *Insight Timer*, which is my favourite. Whatever supports you to build a practice is great. Make it a non-negotiable part of your day. And watch what happens.

Please stop expecting a miracle to happen. Just give yourself the gift of showing up for yourself, taking your seat and finding your breath. And let go of any myths or expectations that stop you from doing that. Then ... simply practice.

AFFIRMATION
I give myself space for my meditation practice.

WORKING WITH MANTRAS

The spirit is created and animated not by light, but by sound.
~ THOMAS ASHLEY-FARRAND

A bout the same time that I picked up the book *Bringing Yoga to Life* by Donna Farhi, I also picked up *Healing Mantras: Using Sound Affirmations for Personal Power, Creativity and Healing* by Thomas Ashley-Farrand. Little did I know that mantras would form such an integral part of my personal and spiritual awakening in the years to come. As the author, a Vedic priest and American expert in the intricacies of Sanskrit mantras, states in the opening to his book: *You can use mantras to help you with any issue and to change your life for the better.*

Mantras, or simple chants, are short phrases that are filled with energy and intention. They are designed to generate powerful soundwaves to promote insight, healing, creativity and spiritual growth. The science and discipline of chanting and formal prayer is practised in every religion around the world. The healing and transformative power of sound is well known, whether passed down from the sages in India, through classical scientists of ancient Greece, or the medieval monks of Europe.

Through using mantras, chanting them out loud or in silence, we activate the power of the word and sound. Mantras, originally in Sanskrit language, can be used for anything: healing relationships and heartbreak, recovering from illness, attracting a partner, improving mental clarity, removing obstacles, overcoming fear, controlling habits and gaining wisdom. You can practise your mantra in a formal seated meditation practice, or repeat it mentally while doing the dishes, cooking dinner, driving the car, or between meetings at work. Any time or anywhere you have a moment of silence, you can practise your mantra.

As Ashley-Farrand explains in his illuminating book: *The vibration produced by chanting the mantra begins to alter our inner condition, both psychically and spiritually, and to break down energy patterns stored in the subtle body. These can be anything from subconscious habits or predispositions to a karmic potential for mishap.* Mantras also allow our chakras to 'switch on' safely and to operate at a higher vibration.

You can choose a complete Sanskrit mantra, or work with what is called a seed mantra or bija. Bija mantras are sounds that contain the essence of a particular sacred energy. Sounds like Om or Aim (ay-eem), representing Goddess Saraswati, are examples of seed mantras that will support your connection and growth, when repeated as part of your spiritual practice.

In the spiritual traditions of India, it is said that you need to repeat your mantra 125,000 times or more to accomplish the objective of the mantra. However, in what Ashley-Farrand calls *worldly problem solution*, you need to repeat it much less. Setting aside a precise time each day to practise your mantra, as well as repeating it throughout the day, is a great way to integrate this spiritual discipline into your life.

I use my crystal mala beads (like a rosary) each morning for my mantra practice. A mala has 108 beads, and I repeat the mantra once for each bead. It takes about 15 minutes as I work with the Ganesha, Durga or Saraswati mantras and it's a beautiful morning meditative practice.

AFFIRMATION
*I heal myself and raise my spiritual vibration
through the power of mantra.*

WHAT ARE YOU REALLY
HUNGRY FOR?

Life itself is the proper binge.

~ JULIA CHILDS

My friend Jasmine, like so many women, is struggling with a weight issue. Year after year she tries to lose the same five kilos, punishing herself with the latest fad diet, cleanse or mad fitness plan. But she keeps coming back again and again to the same place, losing the weight only to put it back on and then some. She knows on some level that if she really wants to create change, she will have to go deeper.

Another girlfriend, Amy, is a workaholic. To make matters worse, she occasionally falls back into issues with substance abuse, fuelled by her never-ending work days, insatiable need for energy so she can keep working, and then her need to come down at the end of the day. She knows it's a life-altering issue that she needs to get a handle on. She also knows that the new therapist she has started seeing is going to make her look at all of her stuff. She is going to have to go deeper too, as she simply can't avoid it any longer.

What both Jasmine and Amy realised, as they showed up to themselves and to the changes they wanted to make, is that when we really commit to creating personal change, there is absolutely nowhere to hide. Jasmine had to face her eating patterns, the weight that she couldn't or wasn't willing to shift, and the emotions that were masked by the food she consumed. Amy's therapist is helping her unpack her drive to work incessantly and harm herself with substances, so that she can start to be free on both levels and get her life back.

They are both having to go deep to remove the layers they were hiding under—the emotional, spiritual, mental and physical layers—to get to their truth.

If you took away everything that masks your emotions, including the food you eat or the addictions you have, what would you find? If you stopped distracting yourself with whatever your fast track to perceived pleasure or avoidance is—television, social media, exercise, shopping, drugs, sex, work, food—what would you discover underneath? What emotions are you running from? Sadness, grief, loneliness, guilt, anger? You may need to breathe into this, and dig deep into your well of self-compassion.

Would you be willing to stop the distractions for just one day, or one week, and see what you are really hungry for? To feel into what you have been avoiding? It's not an easy path, I know. It can be scary and feel much easier and less painful to just keep the food, addictions or endless distractions coming, so that you can keep hiding.

But that is not the life for you. You are worthy of so much more. It is possible to feed yourself on all levels in a healthy, kind and self-loving way.

And here's the truth we all need to learn, even if it takes a lifetime: You can't outrun yourself. Maybe it's time to stop trying.

AFFIRMATION
I am true and honest about how I am feeling.
I honour myself in kind and nourishing ways.

SACRED ESSENTIALS

The leaf of every tree brings a message from the unseen world.
Look, every falling leaf is a blessing.

~ RUMI

Essential oils and the plants they originate from have been used for thousands of years, and are so precious that frankincense and myrrh were given to baby Jesus. They are valued for many things, not least of which is their medicinal and therapeutic healing properties. Just a few drops of these potent, natural, aromatic compounds obtained from the leaves, seeds, flowers and bark of plants, can have a dramatic impact on your physical, mental, spiritual and emotional wellbeing.

Essential oils can help to boost your immunity, invigorate your senses, revitalise your energy, calm your nervous system, enhance your sleep, lead to greater productivity and lead to hundreds of other benefits. I have around 70 different essential oils in my home. I use them topically on my body and aromatically in a diffuser: throughout my work day for energy, focus, creativity, wellbeing and balance; and at the end of the day to calm my mind, relax and create an environment of peace and ease.

Rather than share all of them here, as that's an entire book in itself, I have listed below some of my favourite essential oils and their multiple uses. Note that all essential oils are not created equally. It is critical that you seek out oils that are ethically sourced and produced, pure in quality without fillers, perfumes or chemicals, and that are of therapeutic grade. You can learn more about the oils that I use and how to bring them into your life at sacredliving.co.

Lavender: Perhaps the most commonly used oil in the world, lavender has a fresh floral scent and is powerful yet gentle. For most people, lavender can be used directly on the skin. It calms the nervous system, supports restful sleep, and helps with anxiety and exhaustion. It's wonderful for reducing inflammation, for pain relief and for scrapes and bumps.

Vetiver: Vetiver is a member of the grass family and the heavy, earthy scent of this oil is deeply calming and grounding. It helps ease stress and tension and can bring your mind into the present moment. It puts things into perspective and brings an overall sense of wellbeing. It's wonderful to use at night, rubbed on the bottoms of the feet or chest area, to promote deep relaxation and sleep.

Frankincense: Known as the King of Oils for its potency and breadth of applications, frankincense promotes feelings of peace and overall wellness. A powerful oil for creating grounding, spiritual connection, calming and stress reduction. Wonderful for space clearing and as a meditation oil. It's also a great oil for the complexion, may reduce inflammation and supports a healthy immune and digestive system.

Peppermint: Use peppermint to energise your mind, uplift your spirit and help you feel alert and connected. It can soothe an upset stomach and has significant antimicrobial and antiviral properties. Wonderful for relieving muscle aches and pains, as well for breathing difficulties. I use peppermint every day at my desk and it helps me concentrate and feel buoyant while working.

Lemon: Lemon oil is stimulating and calming and is a versatile oil with a fresh and uplifting scent. Use it to energise, cleanse and detox across the board, from your energy field to your home. Helps boost psychic awareness, strengthens the connection between spirit and soul and releases mental conflict, bringing clarity and calm. Like eucalyptus and other citrus oils, it's a wonderful cleaning agent for a naturally clean home.

Wild Orange: Uplifting and inspiring, this oil relaxes and uplifts, blending beautifully with many other oils. Emotionally, it releases self-judgement and clears fears and obsessions, bringing you back into harmony and balance. Wild Orange will help connect you back to a state of calm and a positive outlook.

Eucalyptus: Distilled from the leaves and young stems of the eucalyptus tree, this oil has a fresh and uplifting aroma. Promoting a sense of wellbeing, it can be used to stay healthy throughout winter or whenever there are germs and bugs around. It is a powerful antimicrobial and immune stimulant, as well as being a great oil to diffuse for mental clarity and an energy boost.

Sandalwood: A wonderful oil, traditionally used in temples, places of worship and for contemplation. Use sandalwood to enhance your meditation, prayer or yoga practice. Traditionally, sandalwood was used as a companion for enlightenment and authentic living. It works to open the third eye chakra, helping you access your intuition and higher self.

Rose: It is said that this oil has the highest vibration of all essential oils. Its sweet, soft floral notes bring a deep connection with the feminine energy within us all. Rose is emotionally uplifting, nurturing and helps us connect to our essential nature. A wonderful skin tonic, rose oil can support a healthy complexion and balance moisture in the skin.

AFFIRMATION

*I use the potent healing qualities of essential oils
to support me on all levels of my being.*

PART 4

Comfort

WHAT DO YOU NEED RIGHT NOW?

You yourself, as much as anyone in the entire
Universe, deserve your own love and affection.

~ BUDDHA

Right here. This moment.

Breathe in deeply. Exhale slowly.

Feel into your body.

Your head, your heart, your stomach, your lungs.

Your root, your base, your spine.

Feel deep into your solar plexus, right there in your power centre.

What do you need right now?

Tune in to your body, your heart, your life force.

Listen. Listen intently.

You may hear the faintest whisper. Or the loudest bellow.

Listen for her. She is trying to reach you.

Right here. This moment.

What do you need right now?

AFFIRMATION

The comfort I need comes from within.

CONNECTING TO THE
GREAT MOTHER

Trees are poems that earth writes upon the sky.

~ KAHLIL GIBRAN

I was in San Francisco for a women's conference. I had spent three days and nights in a hotel conference room, only going outside for a Starbucks visit or for some quick fresh air. By the end of the conference, I was in desperate need of nature. I was feeling ungrounded, run down, and my breath was short and sharp in my chest, instead of long and deep in my belly.

I had a free day before flying home, and I knew that working through it or pottering around the city was not going to make me feel better. I needed space. Clean air. And I needed the earth. I took a half-day trip out to the grand old redwood forest. It was about an hour on a bus, weaving out from San Fran across the Golden Gate bridge and then through the winding roads. As we disembarked from the bus on arrival, I instantly felt it as I deeply inhaled the cool, crisp, tree-filled air: calm, spacious, connected.

I walked through the forest for a few hours in solitude. I stopped to place my hand on the trunks of those ancient trees. I could feel their vibration, like a pulse under my palm. I could feel myself grounding down into the earth. It's called earthing— standing in the earth and connecting to nature. I never wanted to leave.

We can feel a deep spiritual connection to nature, even if we can't explain it in a scientific way. Forest bathing (or shin-rin-yoku, a term that was coined in Japan), literally means to immerse yourself in the atmosphere of the forest. Forest bathing as a natural wellbeing therapy is now practised in many countries around the world. We inherently know the benefit of being among trees. Their ancient wisdom and healing powers emanate from their roots to the tips of the highest leaves. Researchers tell us that being surrounded by trees has powerful benefits, reducing stress levels, boosting the immune system, and improving our mood. You can literally feel it.

Look for ways you can connect with nature. You may not have a forest of redwoods in your neighbourhood, but there are other ways you can earth and ground: go for a bushwalk, head into the mountains or for a hike on a nature trail, sit under a tree in the park or in your backyard. Take your shoes off and feel the grass under your feet. Rub sandalwood, frankincense or vetiver essential oils on the soles of your feet. Ground yourself in whatever ways you can.

AFFIRMATION

I connect with Mother Earth and take refuge in her comfort.

WHAT BRINGS YOU COMFORT?

The master sticks to her tools.

~ LAO-TZU

In those times when you need a little comfort—and for many of us that's most days in some form—it's good to know what will soothe you, ease your emotions, and comfort you.

What might those things be for you? Here is a list of comfort bringers that you might wish to borrow from. Create your own list, your toolkit if you will, so that you always have something simple to draw from.

- A warm bath with lit candles and beautiful music.
- Reading a few pages from your favourite book.
- Applying or diffusing calming and peaceful essential oils.
- A walk in nature or sitting under a big old tree.
- A call with a girlfriend who can hold space for you.
- Listening to mantra or yogic music.
- A lovely cup of calming tea like chamomile or lavender.
- Spending time in the garden.
- A hug from someone close to you, or a cuddle with your pet.
- Clearing space in your home.
- Writing in your journal, drawing or colouring in.
- Burning incense or a candle.

Create your own comfort kit, so that you always have nurturing things you can reach for when the moment arises.

AFFIRMATION

I know how to comfort myself.

OUTRAGEOUS OPENNESS

By allowing the Divine to take the lead, we can finally
put down the heavy load of hopes, fears and opinions
about how we think things should be. We learn how
to be guided to take the right actions at the right time,
and to enjoy the spectacular show that is our life.

~ TOSHA SILVER, *Outrageous Openness*

I met Tosha Silver at a women's conference. She was giving
a talk, and I was in fits of laughter and rapture during the
entire time she spoke. She was one of the reasons I travelled to
the event, having long been a reader of her work. There was
something about her pixie hair, colourful clothes, broad accent
and spiritual vibe that deeply resonated with me. After spending
25 years consulting and advising tens of thousands of people
around the world as an astrologist, she realised that we all have
the same concerns at the end of the day. *How do I stop worrying?*
How can I feel safe? Why do I feel so alone? and *Who am I really?*

In her book, *Outrageous Openness: Letting the Divine Take the Lead*,
she takes us on a journey into her joyful land of living with ease
and joy when we let the Divine take over. I bought the hardcover
book and loved it. But it was the audiobook, on constant replay
on my iPhone that really hooked me in. It brings me a sense of
comfort, a reminder that I'm not alone in this thing called life, and
that I can hand over my worries and stresses to a greater force.

Call it what you will—God, Goddess, Universe, Shakti—
Tosha calls it the Divine. In her words:

What if the Divine is constantly igniting roadside flares to get our attention? What if there actually is a Supreme Organizing Principle with an unbridled sense of humour? And what if we each have this ardent inner suitor who's writing us love letters every day that often go unopened?

Can you imagine? Just sit into the possibility that there is a greater force than our ego and our will at play every day. That there is a cosmic Divine force out there, playing and orchestrating all of the synchronicities and happenings in our lives; and that if we could just get out of the way, it would create more magic for us than we could imagine. We could actually be free from trying to control every outcome, and trust that the Universe really does have our back.

This book, and teachings like it, bring me great comfort. I find myself turning on the audiobook after a hard day, when I feel heavy under the weight of decisions or choices I don't want to make, or when subtle anxiety is racing through my body.

It provides a few simple reminders that I am not alone, that there is a beautiful mysterious source at play in my life, and that if I can just remove myself and my ego from the issue at hand, the Divine will lead me where I am destined to go. It's a comforting and joyful way to be in the world.

AFFIRMATION
I stop trying to control everything. I let the Divine lead.

SIT WITH YOUR DISCOMFORT

For what I really want I can wait.

~ MARYAM HASNAA

I'm staring at the blank screen. Waiting for the words to come. Waiting. I reach for my iPhone to scroll through Instagram, lying to myself that it will fuel my creativity. Realising that I left my phone in another room to save the distraction, and not being bothered to get up and retrieve it, I sit. Stare back at the blank screen. Gaze at the trees in the distance. Ponder my existence. And then, a minuscule spark of inspiration flickers in my mind. I sit. Another spark. I turn to the screen and start to write. I stay with the words even when I'm not sure what I'm writing. And the words slowly but surely unfold.

I'm hungry. I know that I have a photo shoot in four days and I want to look my best. But I'm hungry. In an hour I can have my green smoothie, with the spices and greens and all the things that make me feel good on the inside and glowing on the outside (what you kind of need for photo shoot radiance). But I want eggs and bacon. Even though I'm mostly vegan. On my 5 km walk this morning it was all I could smell as I rounded up through the cafes at the end of my journey. It's Sunday. Everyone's eating. But I wait. Wait for smoothie time. Knowing that I will feel satisfied and nourished. I'm annoyed. But still, I wait.

Discomfort. We want to move away from it as soon as it surfaces. Of course we do, we're human and it's uncomfortable. We live in a culture that provides endless methods of instant gratification to move us from discomfort to momentary pleasure, so we don't ever have to be uncomfortable if we don't want to be. Not on the surface at least.

But growth happens in the discomfort. Creativity happens in the discomfort. Magic happens in the discomfort. So go for the growth. Do whatever you need to do to get uncomfortable. Learn to sit in it. And wait for the magic.

AFFIRMATION
I sit with my discomfort and find the magic there.

WHO'S YOUR PERSON?

Each person represents a world in us, a world
possibly not born until they arrive, and it is only
by this meeting that a new world is born.

~ ANAÏS NIN

A t Grey Sloan Memorial Hospital, Meredith Grey had her person: Cristina Yang. Cristina was her go-to gal. You know, the first call, the always there shoulder, the one who really sees you, gets you, understands everything, will always have your back. Your person.

Do you have such a person? I met my husband-to-be when I was 22. In my mid-twenties we married, and he became my person. As often happens in marriage, especially young marriage, life changed significantly and other friendships fell to the side as his friends became my friends. We divorced when I was 31. With an eighteen-month-old baby, life changed again and became an endless game of survival.

Looking back, I realise that through the toughest period of my life, I didn't actually have a person. I had my family, thank God, who were there in every way they could be. But a 'Cristina and Meredith' person? No, I didn't have that.

Things changed again in my mid-thirties and I developed another life-changing friendship that would see us both through the next decade. Defining. Transformative. Fun. Game changing for both of us. And then over time, that relationship drifted and changed as we each pursued different paths.

In my forties, in perhaps one of the greatest surprises of my life, I've made some of the most intimate female relationships of my life. Deep, soulful, supportive sisters who see me and light me up in the most astonishing ways. As I've changed, deepened, opened and softened into womanhood, these women appeared as if I had specifically called each of them in for their various gifts and powers. The soulful sister who would show me how to soften and experience true sisterhood. The best friend who I would talk to almost every day, who would see every part of me and love me because of it. The creative writer friend who would see my gifts and nurture them in ways I had never experienced. And in turn, I would see each of them for who they truly are at their deepest levels. To their soul.

The comfort that is found in relationships and connections where you are truly seen, accepted and loved for who you are at your core is the greatest comfort of all. If you have found your person, or your people, nourish and nurture those relationships with every part of your essence. If you haven't yet found them, call in your sisters. Join a group where like-minded women (or men) gather. Reach out to start new conversations. Connect with people. You may get the surprise of your life and find the comfort you long for.

AFFIRMATION
I find comfort in my close relationships.

OLD HEADSHOT DAY

*A great life is the sum total of all of the worthwhile
things you've been doing one by one.*

~ RICHARD BACH

It was #oldheadshotday on Instagram. I always loved seeing the images of people when they were younger. The 80s pics of big hair and fluoro *CHOOSE LIFE* T-shirts. The old modelling shots. Baby pictures. Boyfriends and best friends long since forgotten.

I had never posted any for some reason. But this day, as I walked down my hallway, I caught a glimpse of the one photo of me on the wall dedicated to shots of my son when he was younger. It was an old acting headshot, and I had that young, beautiful, full of hope for what would come, vibe going on.

I took a photo of the photo, posted it and wrote this:

This is me. 24.
Still acting, singing and contemplating taking a contract in LA to pursue it all.
I chose a different path.
The next year I'd be married and in the first year of my big marketing career travelling the world.
Poignant to look back at that face and those eyes with all I know now.
With a heart full of self-compassion for all I didn't know then.

Reflections can be so powerful. Looking at the dots that only ever make sense looking backwards. So much youth. So many dreams.

But the Universe had other plans for me. They say we plan and God laughs. They are right. You can never know what lies ahead for you, what lines are already drawn or circled in the sand. You can only trust and pray that life will be kind. That you might make a small difference. And hope for love along the way.

AFFIRMATION

I find comfort in the universal plans for me.

DO THE HARD THING

I see your pain and it's big. I also see your courage,
and it's bigger. You can do hard things.

~ GLENNON DOYLE

Is there a place in your life where you are taking the easy path? I'm a big believer that we can choose the path of grace and ease and it doesn't need to be so hard all of the time. In reality, we can reframe anything, any time we want to. But ease doesn't necessarily mean easy. And sometimes, we need to do what's hard to bring what we want to life.

This is where we can get stuck on our self-development or spiritual path. We tell ourselves that if we really are on 'the path', then everything should flow and there should be rainbows and butterflies and dappling sunlight streaming through the windows. But we live in the real world and life isn't always like that. Presuming that anything 'should be' is where we get into trouble. The expectation. The judgement. The unrealistic assumption that to be spiritual and to live 'in flow' means we don't have to do that thing we don't want to do. Or that we should quash the desire for it all to be somehow different than it is.

So we choose instead to not show up for it. To not work at it. To pretend we don't care about it. Yet we do.

What is the thing that you think you cannot do? What is it, that if you were being really truthful, you would admit you want, but you don't want to show up for the work that's involved in getting it? What's the hard thing that's in the way of you getting to your next level?

It could be anything: getting healthy without wanting to exercise or give up sugar; wanting to write a book without committing to the long hours staring at a blank screen; changing careers without putting in the effort to re-skill in a meaningful way; longing for a committed relationship without being willing to compromise and sacrifice.

What's the hard thing? Where are you opting out of the opportunity to really show up for yourself? Where is effort required, the grit, the resilience to buckle in for the ride of your life to create something truly meaningful and worthwhile? Sometimes we have to choose hard. So choose it. But do so knowing that you can have a side serving of grace and ease right along with it.

AFFIRMATION
I am capable of doing hard things with grace and ease.

REST, DON'T QUIT

When I'm tired, I rest. I say, 'I can't be a superwoman today.'
~ JADA PINKETT SMITH

Tiredness. We all feel it. Sometimes we're tired at the end of a long day. Sometimes we haven't slept well and struggle to get through our to-do list. And sometimes we feel that kind of world-weary tiredness, right down into our bones. The tiredness that makes it hard to wind down, fall asleep and stay asleep, to get the rest needed to restore our spirits.

Most of us have been there. I see a lot of women working through tiredness and restlessness, from some level of malaise through to flat out exhaustion. No matter where you may fall on the tiredness scale, there are some things that you can do right now, today, to bring more comfort and ease into your days, and to embed more restfulness into your life.

We need to learn how to stop pushing so hard, to end the habitual pattern of always driving through with our game face on. We can choose to keep striving. But it's a recipe for disaster and burnout. Learn to stop. Right here, right now. Commit to ending the battle with your exhaustion. The more you push through it, the thicker the forest will become, until you can no longer see the trees in front of you.

So it serves us well to learn how to surrender. To learn how to yield. To let go. Lay down your arms. It's not a form of weakness to give up the fight. It's actually a great sign of courage to say this is enough for now. I'm going to release the struggle. And I'm going to surrender into the journey. This isn't easy I know, it's a continual lesson in grace. But especially when you're tired, learn to find the peace in letting it all go, and seeing what remains.

Once we have surrendered, it's time to get to the real work: learning to listen to our pain. This may be really uncomfortable. When we're feeling any kind of discomfort, the first instinct is usually to numb it. Or distract ourselves from it. Push it down, crowd it out, make it go away. But when we sit with the pain under our tiredness, it has secrets to tell us.

What is your exhaustion trying to tell you? What have you been hiding from with your busyness and to-do list? What do you need to learn here? Get quiet, and hear the wisdom that will speak to you if you listen.

We can seek comfort from resting, not quitting. When we hit the wall of tiredness that can feel like we just ran into a freight train, we may want to throw it all in, think it's all too hard, and quit. Most of us are not so good at resting. At pausing. At drawing breath, reflecting, restoring. But you need to know this: just because you are having a hard time right now doesn't mean that it's forever. It's just this moment, not the rest of your life. Learn to take a moment and know that most things can be recovered. You can work your way to the other side.

Don't make life-changing decisions in those moments when you feel over it. Give yourself the space to breathe. When we give ourselves the gift of rest, it is a beautiful comfort bearer.

AFFIRMATION
I take rest whenever I need to.

MOMENTS OF JOY

We do not count the success of a life by
its length; we count it by its joy.

~ ABRAHAM LINCOLN

Where are your moments of joy? I wonder if you can answer that, in the busyness of your days, the blur of your weeks and in the rush of your life. Can you pinpoint the joy?

In the midst of a business strategy session recently, I asked Suzie, the woman I was working with, this question. She had to really pause and think. And then her answer came, almost shamefully and with tears in her eyes ... 'I actually can't recall the last time I felt joy ... not even a moment of it.' A startling thing to realise. And a reason to pause.

When I asked her to dig a little deeper, the moments were there. Harder to spot perhaps, as they were micro moments, but they were there, as they may be for you. The morning coffee. A moment of sunshine on a gloomy day. The kiss on your cheek from a child. A few pages of your favourite book before sleep. A two-minute meditation.

Where are your moments? Where would you like them to be? Here's a gentle assignment for you, if you are willing. In a notebook you can carry around with you, create two lists:

- List one—throughout your days for the next week, write down any moment of joy you experience, no matter how small.
- List two—create a list of moments of joy you would like to have in your life. Then think about how you can gently and mindfully bring them into your days.

Joy. We can't really flourish without those special moments, and we need to be present to them where and when they show up. You deserve them in your life every single day. A worthy mission, and well worth your time, wouldn't you say? Here's to your beautiful, joyful moments.

AFFIRMATION
I seek out moments of joy in my daily life.

THANK YOU, GRATEFUL,
MORE PLEASE

*Gratitude opens the door to the power, the
wisdom, the creativity of the Universe.*

~ DEEPAK CHOPRA

One of the simplest ways to bring comfort into your day is to turn your attention from what you lack to what you are grateful for. It's impossible to feel sorry for yourself and feel gratitude at the same time. If you're thinking about how grateful you are for your children as you watch them sleep, with their beautiful long eyelashes resting softly on cherubic cheeks, it's unlikely that you are also thinking about how you were cheated out of that promotion at work. Your heart is simply too full of gratitude to have space for resentment in that moment. It doesn't mean you will stay in that heart-centred space, but you know it's a place you can visit whenever you choose.

A daily gratitude practice of noting down three good things that happen during the day is a wonderful way to bring more joy into your life, and much more happiness. Reflect on and write down three specific things you are grateful for. It could be that you made the last bus home, because a stranger asked the driver to wait for you as you ran to catch it. Maybe it was the birds you noticed in the trees on your morning walk. It could even be the really strong coffee that was made just as you like it at the coffee shop. Specific gratitudes. Write them down in a little notebook you keep just for this purpose.

I also love to be mindful as I go through my day about what I am thankful for. I have a little practice of saying 'thank you, thank you, thank you', as I experience things I love. Swimming in the ocean: 'thank you'. My morning yoga practice: 'thank you', as I bow my head in namaste. A great session when a client has a coaching breakthrough: 'thank you'. I also say 'more please' to signal to the Universe that I am grateful and I would like to bring more of that into my life.

Thank you. Grateful. More please. It's a great practice. Feel free to borrow it.

AFFIRMATION

I give thanks for the blessings in my life.

THIS IS WHAT IT FEELS LIKE

I think that wherever your journey takes you, there are new
Gods waiting there, with divine patience—and laughter.

~ SUSAN M. WATKINS

I am walking to the lighthouse this morning, as I do most days when I stay in Byron Bay, my home away home. It's about two kilometres up to the top, passing through rainforest, on roads and wooden paths, past incredible beaches dotted with locals, swimmers and surfers soaking up the magic of the early morning.

I take photos and post them on *Instagram Stories*. I want to share the magic. The crashing of the waves on miles of deserted beach. The light as it dances on the outward curve of the light-house. The rising sun blasting the ocean with radiance. The surfer running into the waves as if towards a long-lost lover. The vastness and wonder of the endless horizon.

As I descend on the other side of the peak, I traverse through more rainforest paths, with the ocean on my right, all the way to Wategos Beach, where dolphins live and surfers ride. The soft-ness and clarity of the aquamarine ocean catches my breath, the beauty literally takes my breath away.

I am filled with such a sense of vitality and overwhelming gratitude that I get to witness this magnificence. I laugh out loud as I simply cannot contain the effervescent energy brimming up in my chest and heart space.

I realise in that moment, with such a sense of clarity, that this is what joy feels like. This is it, in this moment. I stand rooted in place, eyes closed, the wet salty air alive on my skin, the sun beaming down on my face. And I feel complete, incredible, heart-dancing joy. How long can I stay in this moment, I wonder? How can I keep this moment alive? How can I live here in this beat forever?

This is what joy feels like for me. How about you?

AFFIRMATION

I am awake to the moments of joy in my day.

CHANGE YOUR STATE

We are most deeply asleep at the switch when
we fancy we control any switches at all.

~ ANNIE DILLARD

'I'll be fifteen minutes late.'

It was an ominous start. I had that feeling you get in your chest, with a churn in the pit of your stomach, when you dread that things aren't going to go as planned. Twenty minutes later she arrived, rushed, hassled, stressed and clearly ungrounded. Arrggh, I thought, *really?*

We were doing a photo shoot for my various businesses and creative projects. I was a little anxious, hoping everything would go well. Fifteen minutes late was not the way I wanted to start. I could feel the way I do when I start to get annoyed. I get edgy. Short. Snappy. Not the best version of myself. And the start of the process, getting hair and make-up done, was pretty important for the vibe of a photo shoot. And she was late. And frazzled.

As she set up, she enquired, 'So what type of look are you going for?'

'Soft and pretty,' I said. 'Natural and fresh.' They seemed like simple enough instructions.

We were going to be chasing the light all afternoon. It was now 2.30pm and we were meant to start shooting at 3pm. That clearly wasn't going to happen. As she painted my face with a spray gun, dabbed endless things on my eyes, lids, cheeks and lips, drew lines and blurred shadows, the photographer looked on. I could see an increasing look of concern on her face.

'Let me just check on the progress,' I said. Having not wanted to infringe on her artistry, wanting to trust the process and all that, I hadn't felt the need to look in the mirror. But now I did.

As I headed to the bathroom, I caught a glimpse of myself from a distance. All I could see was black. As I got closer, it became apparent that my 'soft and pretty' had turned into 'gothic warrior princess', with more focus on goth than princess.

Heavy black shadow on my eyelids was only worsened by the black shadow under my eyes, like nobody had invented eyeliner. My lips were twice their normal size, not because of some lovely bee sting lip enhancer, but because she had actually drawn liner outside of my lip line and then filled it in, like they do for fashion magazine covers, but without precise execution.

I didn't know quite what to say. I stared at myself, trying to fathom how 'natural' could translate into this horror show in front of me. And we were now 45 minutes behind schedule, with the light deadline closing in.

I could see my poor make-up artist was just having an off day. I knew she was meant to be incredible at her job, and everyone has bad moments. And I knew it wasn't going to get better. So I let her go home. I took to my face with a damp cloth, tissues and powder. I softened, re-outlined and did the best I could. We took a few test shots, then given the brightness of the daylight and knowing we could soften in the post-production process, we proceeded with the shoot.

But here's the thing—when you show up in front of the camera, you have to *show up*. The camera sees everything. We were going for soft, not radically annoyed. Happy, fresh and joyful, not I-want-to-kill-you-right-now-what-on-earth-were-you-thinking?!

I had to change my state. And fast. So I shook it off. Literally. Shaking my arms, hands, head, legs, swishing around a little, jiggling on the spot, shaking my head from side to side. And my beautiful photographer and I laughed. Laughed at the absurdity of what had just happened. And how ridiculous my face was. And how good a story this would be for the book and for teachable moments about personal growth, finding grace and getting into the right place, even when it's really challenging.

The shots remind me of how to show up with grace when I least feel like it. How even a professional with a great portfolio can have an off day. And that we can change our state, whenever and however we choose to, when we set the right intention, get in the moment and go for the joy.

AFFIRMATION
I can change my state at will.

YOUR STRUGGLE IS REAL

We all have it within us to move from struggle to grace.

~ ARIANNA HUFFINGTON

You don't have to keep your brave game face on. It's okay to say that you're having a tough time. To share your pain. To tell those around you that you're really struggling right now. Your struggle is real. It doesn't matter if someone around you is facing something else, something different from you that you may perceive as worse or that inflicts more perceived hardship. It doesn't matter what others think of your struggle, and whether or not you think you are entitled to feel how you feel.

It only matters that you feel it. That you care about yourself enough. That you have enough self-compassion to dig deep into your vulnerability and say, 'Hey, I'm having a bit of a hard time right now' and be heard by a trusted friend, your pastor, your partner or whoever you're with.

I remember years ago I was seeing a wonderful massage therapist. I was having a particularly stressful time over the months that I saw her, with the combination of a busy job and being a single parent to a restless toddler getting the best of me. I was on the massage table one day and she noticed that my shoulders and back were rigid with stress, like my muscles were holding on for dear life. I'm sure that's exactly what they were doing.

'Tell me what's going on, I haven't seen you this tense before,' she asked calmly.

I never wanted to complain to her or mention my seemingly insignificant stressors. She spent most of her time providing massages for cancer patients and those in palliative care. Those people had real challenges, I always thought to myself. Who was I to complain about the general day-to-day challenges of being a single working mother, even though at times I felt like I was on the brink of losing it?

I explained this to her, and with great love she said to me, 'Everyone has their struggle. Yours is no less meaningful to you, or real for you, or stressful for you, than theirs is for them. It's all relative. Don't discount your experiences and life because you think someone else is worse off than you. Your struggle is real. And it's okay to share it and get support for it.'

Whatever you are dealing with is very real for you. It's not discounted by what others may be going through. Your struggle is real. And it's okay and necessary for you to feel into it, own it and deal with it in whatever way will serve you best. Just don't ignore it. Find the grace in the support you will find when you are vulnerable enough to share it.

AFFIRMATION

I accept my struggles and seek the comfort and support I need.

WHAT FEELS LIGHT?

We are not human beings trying to be spiritual.
We are spiritual beings trying to be human.

~ JACQUELYN SMALL

Everything you do, every person you interact with, even your thoughts and the food you eat, have an energy of lightness or heaviness. To live a more simple, soulful and sacred life, we need to move towards that light energy. It makes sense as a concept, right? But how do we do that?

First, we need to be tuned in to how we feel. Moment by moment, mindfulness brings us into a state of mind, body and spirit awareness. From there, we can discern the effect certain people or situations have on us. Does it feel heavy or does it feel light?

The interaction with that client who is always complaining. Heavy.

The way the lady in the coffee shop smiled at you while she held the door open. Light.

Yoga class after a hard work week. Light. The hard work week? Oh, so heavy.

The time spent doing your taxes. Heavy. Creating your new vision board. Light.

Hanging out with an old school friend who constantly reminds you of the awkward teenager you were and all the angst that came with it. Heavy.

Spending time with your new circle of women friends, who help you recall an ancient memory of what true sisterhood feels like. Light.

Tap into the feeling. Heavy? Or light?

Cultivate more moments of light in your day in whatever ways you can. You will begin to notice that the joy in your life is directly correlated to the lightness.

AFFIRMATION

Wherever I can, I go for the light.

WHAT MAKES YOU HAPPY?

Perhaps if one really knew when one was happy one
would know the things that were necessary for one's life.

~ JOANNA FIELD

I'm watching my friend's little boy at the beach. In all his two-year-old glory, he is running up and down the shoreline, chasing the waves, jumping in the little pockets of ocean in the divots of sand. Run, jump, splash, fall. Endless giggles and fascination.

He is happy. This is what pure happiness looks like.

Run, jump, splash, fall. Endless giggles and fascination.

He keeps going until he finds something else to do that will make him equally happy.

Chasing seagulls. Picking up seashells. Then chasing waves again.

It's pure, this type of happy. Just sheer joy.

What makes you happy?

AFFIRMATION
I find moments of pure happiness in my daily life.

CALL IN MOTHER MARY

*All you need to do to receive guidance is
to ask for it and then listen.*

~ SANAYA ROMAN

On top of the old sandstone building in the grounds of my son's school is a large statue of Mother Mary, reaching high up in the sky. It can be seen from miles away and it gives me a great sense of peace when I look at it. It's strange perhaps because I'm not Catholic—my son is, because his father is and it was a choice we made—but I've never read the Bible, nor studied the scriptures.

And yet in recent years I've felt myself being called more and more to Mary. And there have been signs that she is calling to me. The author conference I attended where there were deity cards in the gift bags ... the card I pulled out was Mary and it has been on my wall ever since. The dreams I have had where I've felt such a deep sense of comfort on waking and a sense that Mary was with me. The books that healers and teachers have recommended to me with urgency, without me asking, all heavily featuring her stories.

Mary is the Great Mother; the Mother of all of us, religious or not. In school church services, Father Gavin asks that Mary look out with care for all of our boys—for all those present, and for all in the world. I literally feel her warm embrace as he calls on her, and it always brings tears to my eyes.

Next time you feel in need of comfort and don't know where to turn, say a quiet prayer to Mother Mary. Ask that you receive what you need at that time, that you be supported, and that you receive her loving comfort. Then be open and willing to receive.

AFFIRMATION

I sit in the comfort of Mary's embrace.

IT'S ALWAYS THERE

*Peace is the first condition, without which
nothing else can be stable.*

~ SRI AUROBINDO

It's there. Deep down inside. Perhaps long hidden and forgotten about. Under the everyday stresses and the life-changing disappointments. Beneath the tension, the worry, the never-ending to-do lists and the constant juggle. Buried deep under the crashing waves that may seem like your life.

It's there. Peace. Like the silence and stillness at the bottom of the ocean, that can't be seen from the boat on the surface. Like the beautiful blue sky that sits above the stormy clouds, that you can't see unless you fly up and over them.

It's there. Waiting for you to discover it.

When was the last time you felt peaceful? Content and calm. Not necessarily carefree. But grounded. Relaxed. Deeply connected to your source. Can you even remember?

There is a beautiful saying that I love: *Peace. It does not mean to be in a place where there is no noise, trouble or hard work. It means to be in the midst of those things and still be calm in your heart.*

We sometimes search for peace yet think that we need to be sitting on a mountaintop before we have any chance of experiencing it. Or we need to remove ourselves from our daily life to get a glimpse of it. But that's not the case.

Start by becoming still. Get really quiet. Sit in meditation. Breathe deeply. Take long walks. Connect with nature. Connect with yourself, your passion and purpose. Remember why you are showing up in the world, and who you are showing up for.

And know that no matter what is going on for you, beneath the noise and the chaos, a sense of peace is always with you, deep inside your soul.

AFFIRMATION

Peace is always with me.

STOP FORCING PIECES
THAT DON'T FIT

I've grown most not from victories but from setbacks. If
winning is God's reward, then losing is how he teaches us.

~ SERENA WILLIAMS

D o you ever get the feeling that you are trying to make silk out of sandpaper? Trying to breathe fresh air in a train tunnel? Looking for solitude in the middle of a bustling city?

We all do it at times. But it really doesn't serve us. Seeking an unrealistic or forced outcome often brings tension and constriction, when we are looking for release and expansion.

There may also be times when you are procrastinating more than usual. Procrastination can be a pain. You want to get things done, but you just can't bring yourself to do it. At other times, you're not moving forwards for a reason. Your inner knowing is actually telling you that, for whatever reason, it's just not right.

Here's a revolutionary yet very simple thought: *Stop trying to force pieces that don't fit.* It could be a relationship, a business deal, moving to a new house or even a yoga pose. If it's feeling too hard, then perhaps it's just too hard.

If you can't make it happen, then perhaps it's just not meant to happen. Call it for what it is and if it doesn't feel right, then let it not feel right. Don't force it. Let it go. And find the peace in the release.

AFFIRMATION

I learn to accept what is meant to be, and release the rest.

OM SHANTI

Every breath we take, every step we make, can
be filled with peace, joy and serenity.

~ THICH NHAT HANH

O m Shanti. It's one of my favourite Sanskrit mantras, used as a greeting or a farewell, at the start and end of some Buddhist and Hindu devotional ceremonies, and in meditation and spiritual practice.

The word 'Om' doesn't directly translate as a single word in English, but it represents the sound of the Universe and also the Universe itself. It is believed that Om is the sound that all other sound originates from. Om can sometimes be representative of time itself: Om is everything in the past, everything in the present, and everything in the future.

'Shanti' is a simple and beautiful word and is the Sanskrit word for peace. It's typically recited three times in this mantra, as is the case in many Buddhist chants. Present in both Buddhism and Hinduism, when repeated it's interpreted to mean the Threefold Peace: peace in body, mind and speech.

Shanti represents inner peace, rather than outer peace; the goal of being able to maintain a peaceful, still mind, even when the world around us can seem overly busy and hectic. While we can create an outer environment of peace and calm, it's still highly changeable. Being able to create an inner environment of peace that you can retreat to at any time is the priority when invoking this mantra.

May you always be at peace, or in times when peace alludes you, may you be on the path to finding it.

AFFIRMATION
Om Shanti Shanti Shanti

PART 5

Soulfulness

THE LURE OF OUR BECOMING

*We have this immense interior life inside of us we can call
the life of the soul. Poets and mystics and people have been
trying to figure out what to call this for a long time. But
there is an inner silence in it. And there is an incredible
mystery floating in it. This is where the Divine lives in us.*

~ SUE MONK KIDD

It's a big question: *What is the soul?* You could philosophise over
that single question for a lifetime. Indeed for some people,
answering that question is their life's work. They're called philosophers, mystics, seers, seekers, poets and spiritual teachers.

Jean Houston, an incredibly gifted writer and teacher, clas-
sifies the soul in the exact way that I see it, so much so that I
caught my breath when I heard her say this, as it was the first
time I had heard my knowing sense of the soul articulated so
beautifully:

*I believe that the soul is the essence of who and what we are. It
comes with codes and possibilities and the next layers of who and
what we may yet be. It is often a pain in the neck because it says
wake up, it's time to wake up, don't go to sleep. I think it is also
the lure of our becoming.*

The lure of our becoming—what a stunning phrase. I know
this to be true. I feel it in a very deep part of myself. The soul is
our essence. It is also our potential, and how the endless possibilities for our lives become realised. The words 'the lure of our
becoming' leave me feeling endlessly hopeful with possibilities.

Our soul wants to lead us to our destiny. To lead us to become the best and most realised self we can be. To lure us onto our purposeful path. To raise our hearts, fill our minds with intentionality and help us complete our mission in this life.

Our work, our opportunity, is to tune in, listen and follow our soul's lead. Follow the lure of our becoming. Because our soul will always lead us home.

AFFIRMATION

I trust the lure of my becoming.

THE SEAT OF THE SOUL

Every action, thought, and feeling is motivated by an intention,
and that intention is a cause that exists as one with an effect.

~ GARY ZUKAV

G ary Zukav is the author of *The Seat of the Soul*, a book first
published in 1989 which has sold many millions of copies
around the world. Oprah Winfrey described this book as one that
completely changed the way she viewed herself, her work and her
life. She writes in the foreword to the 25th anniversary edition
that once she read the book, she tracked down Gary's number
and called him, asking him to be on her talk show. First he
asked, 'Who are you, Oprah?' followed by, 'What's a talk show?'
He had been living in a cabin off the grid in the mountains for
many years, and was not aware of the Oprah phenomenon. He
would soon become aware, as his 36 appearances on her show
changed his life, just as his work had changed hers.

Zukav takes us on a unique journey, blending science, spirituality and philosophy. His premise is that the psychological and
spiritual evolution we are on as a human race requires us to shift
from external power to internal power. External power is that
which we can see and experience with the five senses, but he tells
us that this is actually false power, as it can be taken away by
external forces. On the other hand, internal power is authentic
and real, because it comes from us and resides within us.

Authentic power has its source in the deepest aspects of our
being: our soul. The more we can learn about ourselves, our
emotions, karma, reverence and heart, the more power we step
into. Our soul is not limited to this lifetime and is not attached

to our personality. At the source of authentic power is intention: being intentional with our thoughts, our actions, our lives. This is the core essence that impacted Oprah so profoundly.

In *The Seat of the Soul*, Zukav writes:

> *Every action, thought, and feeling is motivated by an intention, and that intention is a cause that exists as one with an effect. If we participate in the cause, it is not possible for us not to participate in the effect. In this most profound way we are held responsible for our every action, thought, and feeling, which is to say, for our every intention.*

Oprah has shared that on reading this book for the first time, she realised she hadn't been doing *The Oprah Winfrey Show* with intention, rather her number one goal was to be liked. After reading the book, she told her team that their goal was now to be intentional with all of their programming—that the primary intention for her show was that they would become a force for good in the world.

It was also her intentionality that led to her leaving the show and moving on to create the OWN network, when she realised that she had done all she could with the platform.

In the book's most recent preface, Oprah writes: *Quite frankly, I don't believe I would ever have dreamed of creating such a network had I not read 'The Seat of the Soul'.*

What is your soul's intention for this life you are living? It's perhaps one of the most important questions you can ask.

AFFIRMATION
I am intentional about my choices and my life.

FOLLOWING YOUR
SOUL'S GUIDANCE

*Between every thought there is a little space. That still presence
that you feel, that's your soul. And if you get really in touch
with it, if you become familiar with this centre of awareness
that you really are, you will see it's your ticket to freedom.*

~ DEEPAK CHOPRA

Inner guidance. Internal GPS. Inner wisdom. They are all
words that describe your soul's communication mechanism
with you. When we are tuned in, we start to receive the guidance that our soul is sending us. The little messages that pop in
through our thoughts. The inklings we get about a new idea. That
feeling in our gut when we meet someone for the first time. The
siren going off in our head when we're about to make a mistake.

If you think back to situations that may not have gone the
way you wanted them to, what were the feelings or thoughts you
were having in the weeks or days leading up to that situation?
Were you tuned in at the time, or were you in full action mode,
not listening to your inner wisdom?

One simple way to look at this tangibly is to think about a
recent decision you made that turned out really well. What were
you feeling just before you acted? Now, think about a time you
made a decision that you regretted and ask the same question.
Can you recall a feeling or inner knowing that guided you either
time? You may recall that your inner sense was different on the
decision that turned out well from the one that didn't.

You are constantly receiving guidance through your feelings
and thoughts from your higher self. Your soul is always guiding

you in the direction that will bring the most joy and lightness into your life, and away from experiences, situations or people that lead you away from your purpose.

Start to pay close attention to your thoughts and feelings before you take action. Get to understand what your normal state of being feels like, so you can understand when your state changes in a positive or negative way. Stay tuned in, so you can follow your soul's guidance every day.

AFFIRMATION

I am tuned into the language of my soul's guidance.

EMBRACE YOUR DIVINE ASSIGNMENTS

The moments of happiness take us by surprise. It is
not that we seize them, but that they seize us.

~ ASHLEY MONTAGU

Not everything that shows up in your life looks like it is meant to be there. But everything is a Divine assignment. The job, project, relationship, move, even the person who sits next to you on the bus, is a Divine assignment in some small or large way.

Next time something seemingly random shows up for you, get curious. What are you being called to do, learn or teach in this situation? Perhaps it's an opportunity to show some kindness to a stranger. There are days when I feel like nothing is on purpose, but then I walk down the street and find myself smiling at everyone with such joy I realise that is my soul assignment for the day. Just to smile at people. Some people look straight through me, busy processing their lives while they rush through their morning. Others look at me like I'm flat out strange, thinking to themselves, 'Is she high? Why is she smiling at me so weirdly.' I bless them as I pass, giggling to myself.

And then there is the elderly man at the check-out counter at the fruit shop, where I'm getting my green juice. I'm about to leave, but as I turn I catch his gaze. And with a warmth that lights up my face, I smile. A moment of connection as he meets my gaze, then his smile reaches all the way to the crinkling at the corner of his eyes as his face lights up like mine. Joy ripples across his face. I have a moment of realisation that this could be the only moment that he truly connects with someone today.

What if that's true? What if, in what can be a lonely world for the elderly who are so often ignored and invisible, this moment was the one that made his day? That made him feel seen. That connected him to the world around him.

I leave the shop feeling connected and uplifted. On purpose. Like this micro moment had been my Divine assignment for the day. I feel it is every day. My son has been known to comment as we walk down the street, 'You and Pa are so weird, you smile and say hi to everyone.' Yes, I always think to myself. Because why not?

Why not connect and show kindness and throw some love towards others in any small way we can? It's one of my Divine assignments. What are yours?

AFFIRMATION

I embrace my Divine assignments in whatever form they come.

YOUR NEXT MOMENT IS UNPRECEDENTED

Do not fear mistakes—there are none.

~ MILES DAVIS

It doesn't matter where you come from. It doesn't matter who you were last week, last month, last year or last decade. It doesn't matter what school you went to, who your friends are, how nice your parents were, or who your boss is. Your past is over. None of it matters now.

What matters is the present. Here. Now. And what comes next.

Your next moment is unprecedented. There is no way of knowing what it will be. Who will be in it. What you will say. What it might mean. You have all the choices right now. Right here. The only thing that matters is what you do now. This moment. This breath. Your next heartbeat.

Unprecedented. Full of possibilities. Entirely up to you.

AFFIRMATION

I live in the possibilities of this moment.

IS THIS WHAT I WANT TO BE DOING?

No matter how difficult and painful it may be,
nothing sounds as good to the soul as the truth.

~ MARTHA BECK

Your soul wants one thing: your truth. In all situations, in all circumstances, with all personal interactions, on every layer of your path, your soul wants your truth.

But it can be hard to get to the truth sometimes, can't it? We tell ourselves stories, we deny what we want, we lie to ourselves, tricking our minds into believing what our bodies know to be false. We sit in the pain of our mistruth, rather than get honest. Because honesty requires that we face ourselves. Honesty means we may have to change.

Our truth reveals everything. And as Gloria Steinem once said: *Your truth will set you free. But first it will piss you off.*

One question that can get you to your soul's truth is this: *Is this what I want to be doing?* Is it? When you're at work answering yet another email. When you're standing in line for tickets to a show you don't want to see. When you're out for drinks when you'd rather be at art class. When you're in the same lifeless relationships you've been in for a decade. When you have to make that potentially life-changing decision.

Is this what I want to be doing? Is it really? You will feel the true answer in your body. Listen to your soul's truth.

AFFIRMATION
I follow my truth, even when it's hard.

DAILY COMMITMENTS
TO YOUR SOUL

Take the gentle path.

~ GEORGE HERBERT

If our soul is the lure of our becoming, as Jean Houston tells us, then the actions we take each day decide how far along the path of our becoming we travel. If we don't take right actions daily, then we can stay at the beginning of that path, ever hopeful that we will progress, but stuck in the being of inaction.

Small daily rituals can be like signs to your soul that you are ready for the next step in your evolution. That you are showing up, making a commitment, doing the work to become the 'you' of your soul. That energy is what can propel you forwards, and keep the soul whispers of synchronicities, signs and guidance alive.

When you make a commitment to yourself, you are making a pact with your soul. You are giving your word. To stand in your integrity, you need to follow through with your word. This is how we honour ourselves.

Today, make a list of soul commitments you can carry out. You can start by choosing one that you will continue for a period of 21 days. It may be starting a daily 10-minute meditation practice, committing to sit every morning with your mala beads and follow your breath. It may be that you will take a 30-minute walk each day, to commune with nature and your soul. It may be spending 15 minutes each day clearing your space, lighting a candle and giving thanks for your day. See what calls to you, and start there.

It doesn't matter so much what you choose, only that it calls to you and that you make a commitment to follow through with it for 21 days. Look at it like a soul contract, binding you in your integrity to carry it out. Then feel the energy in your being shift, as you travel down the path to your becoming.

AFFIRMATION
I commit to my becoming through daily action.

COMFORTABLY UNCOMFORTABLE

The soul often speaks through longing.
It manifests like a restlessness. And when the
soul longs, it's trying to tell you something.

~ SUE MONK KIDD

My girlfriend called me in a panic. She had just started a new business and was in a world of pain. Having worked for someone else for most of her career, this small business game was all new, and she was struggling. Setting up a website, designing offerings, working out pricing, attracting clients, doing everything herself, it was all testing her grit and her grace. Every part of her was telling her to run, to go back to the comfort of having a job, being paid a regular wage and being told what to do.

'It's just so bloody hard,' she exclaimed on the phone. 'What on earth was I thinking? I had that great job, my boss wasn't that bad, and I got paid!'

She was spiralling; I could feel it. But I stayed silent, listening and letting her play out her discomfort.

'I feel like I'm sitting on the spine of a cactus and every time I move, that sharp pointy spike bites me in the bum. It's painful. I don't like it. Help me please!'

She wanted me to give her permission to quit; to go back to the job she had actually hated with the boss who was a toxic bully, and where she was under threat of being let go at any time. She wanted me to soothe her discomfort, to make it go away, to help her become comfortable again.

But even though she was a really close friend and it hurt me to see her in pain, I had no intention of doing that. Because I knew her soul was calling her to walk this new path. I knew she would get through it. And that what she really needed most was to dig in, to get as comfortably uncomfortable as possible, and to sit there for as long as she needed to move through it.

As she waited impatiently for me to tell her to quit, I drew a deep breath and instead told her: 'I think what you need to do my friend is dig in. You need to stay this out. You need to get to work. So why don't you sit on that cactus spine, really feel into it, then wiggle around a little until it becomes more comfortable?'

She was so shocked by my response that she gasped, and then we both dissolved into squeals of hysterical laughter, crying as we laughed out loud. And then she picked herself up and got back to work, carrying her discomfort like a blanket to soothe her soul and keep her warm, as she walked the path she knew she was destined to.

AFFIRMATION

I sit with my discomfort and learn what it has to teach me.

SELF-LOVE IS THE FOUNDATION
FOR ALL LOVE

To love oneself is the beginning of a life-long romance.

~ OSCAR WILDE

When was the last time you acknowledged yourself for all of the wonderful things about you? I would guess it's probably been a while. Most of us are really hard on ourselves. We pick up on every little mistake we make, notice every flaw in the mirror, beat ourselves up for not getting enough done. We're pretty damn mean to ourselves, if truth be told.

What we don't do often enough is spend a few moments in quiet reflection, acknowledging our positive aspects. For example, what a kind and nurturing parent you are. Or what a generous and thoughtful friend you can be. How you bring positivity into your workplace. Or how brave you are for challenging the status quo. How much you have actually done starting that new business. Or how much further you can run in your training practice for the half marathon.

There is an endless list of positive, kind ways to acknowledge all that you are.

Try this: at the end of your meditation practice tomorrow, or before you go to sleep, place your hands on your heart and silently acknowledge five things you really appreciate about yourself. Then the next day, do it again. Continue to do this every day, until it becomes a self-care ritual.

You may find it a little awkward at first. But as you practise this consistently, you will start to build a well of self-love and self-gratitude in your heart that will help you to respect yourself more, set firmer and clearer boundaries, and stop taking yourself for granted.

AFFIRMATION

I acknowledge myself for all that I am.

HOW MUCH PAIN DO YOU WANT?

The soul always knows what to do to heal itself.
The challenge is to silence the mind.

~ CAROLINE MYSS

I was hosting an event on finding your purpose. There were about fifty women sitting in a circle, brought together to have real conversations about things that matter. This question of purpose, calling, doing meaningful work in the world, was one of those conversations.

As often happens when women come together with open hearts and minds, things quickly moved from the surface level questions to ones of a more soulful nature. And one that kept coming up was around fear. How do you move past the fear to get to know what your soul's calling is? How do you move forwards? When do you know you can't ignore it any longer?

One of the women had been reading my last book, *Lead Like a Woman.*

'I've been reading the book, but I'm getting really angry as I read it; so I keep closing it and putting it away,' she told us.

'What's making you angry?' I asked her.

'There are so many things in there that I'm just not ready to deal with. I know they're true. But I don't know what to do,' she said, feeling fully vulnerable, yet safe, in the circle of women.

'You are facing yourself on the page,' I told her gently. 'The book is your mirror, and the words are showing you what needs to be dealt with and moved through. And you know,' I continued, 'the other side of anger is sadness. So asking yourself what's making you sad, is a question I would invite you to sit with.'

Silence. Then a quiet realisation was reflected on her face. A look between us that acknowledged she knew. And then, a softening.

'The question we all need to ask ourselves,' I said to the women, 'is how much pain we are willing to put ourselves through before we face ourselves. How much distraction—whether it's drinking, food, bingeing on TV or social media, sex, overworking, overstimulating or numbing out in whatever way we know how—before we are ready to face the work we know we need to do?'

The work our soul is leading us to do will not go away. It doesn't vanish because we ignore it. It sits, waiting until we are ready to show up. It will get ever more insistent, until we pay attention.

So my question is: *How much pain do you want to deal with?* Perhaps you might consider that it's time to face yourself, to face your soul, to show up and do your work. And to do it with all the self-compassion and love you have inside of you.

AFFIRMATION
I get real with my anger, my sadness,
and the work I have to do.

YOUR SOUL'S TRUTH

In every moment, the universe is whispering to you.
~ DENISE LINN

Trust that you know.

How you really feel.

What you really see.

What you know to be true.

Who you are in your soul.

Beneath your doubts and rumination and endless questions, there is an ocean of silent knowing.

That right there: that's your soul's truth.

Your soul arrived already knowing what to do, how to be, what the answers are.

Stop questioning yourself.

Trust it.

AFFIRMATION
I listen to and trust my soul's truth.

ABUNDANCE IS YOUR
SOUL'S ESSENCE

Ask for what you want and be prepared to get it.

~ MAYA ANGELOU

In his book *Creating Affluence*, Deepak Chopra outlines an A-Z of steps for living a richer life. He writes about building an abundance mindset, of creating a life of affluence, which he says is our natural state. We don't come into this life with a mindset of lack; that's something we learn here. And we can unlearn it.

W stands for Wealth Consciousness, and it's one of my favourite chapters in the book. Deepak writes:

> *W stands for wealth consciousness without worries. Wealth consciousness implies absence of money worries. Truly wealthy people never worry about losing their money, because they know that wherever money comes from there is an inexhaustible supply of it. Once, when we were discussing a world peace project with Maharishi Mahesh Yogi, somebody asked him, 'Where is all the money going to come from?' And he replied without hesitation, 'From wherever it is at the moment.'*

The Universe is infinitely abundant. Start tapping into your soul's essence of abundance to create what you want most in this life. Whether it's an abundance of wealth, love, work, positive thoughts or peacefulness, your soul's calling is for you to have it. Cultivate your wealth consciousness without worries.

AFFIRMATION
I live in an abundant Universe.

LIVING WITH AN
ABUNDANCE MINDSET

Every time you praise something, every time you appreciate
something, every time you feel good about something, you are
telling the Universe, 'More of this please. More of this please.'

~ ABRAHAM

Do you ever wonder why some people become fraught
with anxiety when the economy experiences a downturn
and others seem to be completely unfazed by it? Why some
people have a stream of abundance in their lives, while others
are always scratching around for the next piece of work? I see
people watching the fluctuations of the share market every single
day, constantly worried they are going to lose their money if the
share price goes down. But it always goes down eventually. The
stress and constant fretting is unnecessary, because if you play
the long game, it usually goes up again.

One of the secrets to keeping a calm mind and an optimistic
spirit is this realisation: *You are the source of your own abundance.* The
thoughts you think, the feelings you sit with, the intentions you
set, the books you read, the commentary you engage in, all have
a direct influence on whether you live your life with an abundance mindset, or a mindset steeped in scarcity and fear.

We all have negative thoughts, and they are nothing to feel
bad about. But you can choose to wallow in them, or to simply
say 'next' and bring in a positive thought. One positive thought
cancels out a hundred negative thoughts. Next time you catch
yourself in a negative thought pattern like, 'I never have enough
money', simply replace it with the positive thought, 'I always have

an abundance of money'. Over time, you will change the neural pathways in your brain, along with your energy vibration, to go directly to the positive, abundant thought.

Choose the books you read wisely. Fill your mind and spirit every night before you go to bed with a few pages of uplifting positive messages. As you close your eyes before drifting off to sleep, repeat positive affirmations to yourself like: *I live in an abundant Universe* and *I have everything I need* or *I always draw towards me what I love and need in any moment.* These are the thoughts your subconscious will then be working on as you sleep, constantly seeking out the experiences you need to fulfil that affirmation.

Keep your mindset focused on the abundance you have and seek, and you will attract it to you. Then simply show up and do your work and trust that you do, truly, live in an abundant Universe.

AFFIRMATION
I am the source of my abundance.

YOU CAN AFFORD TO BE GENEROUS

Do your little bit of good where you are; it's those little
bits of good put together that overwhelm the world.

~ DESMOND TUTU

When we live with a scarcity mindset based on fear and lack, we keep things to ourselves—money, information, even love—for fear that there won't be enough to go around and we will be left with less than we need. But if we actually believed that we live in an abundant Universe, then we would know that there will always be enough of everything to go around. We could afford to be generous. With our time, money, affections, knowledge, and especially with our love.

Practise small acts of generosity and see how you feel. You will likely notice that your act of kindness or sharing will bring more kindness and sharing back to you.

Smile at strangers on the street. Open doors for people. Give money to the homeless person (always, even the smallest amount). Donate to a charity. Share the information you have just learnt at work with that person who hoards information as if it's power. Be the first to say 'I love you'. Plant seeds in the garden. Give your time to a friend who needs it, even when you are crazy busy.

Whatever you think you don't have enough of, give it. There is an infinite supply of everything you could possibly need. And you can afford to be generous with all that you have.

AFFIRMATION

Generosity is one of my core values. I live it every day.

REMEMBER WHEN

Perfectionism is the voice of the oppressor, the enemy of the people. It will keep you cramped and insane your whole life.

~ ANNE LAMOTT

R emember when you wanted what you have now? When who you are, where you're at and what you're doing was just a dream? Pause for a moment. Feel where you are. Look at how far you have come. It doesn't matter if you're not 'there' yet—that mythical place where you will think you have finally arrived.

You are here.

You did so many things you said you would do. Look at it. Feel it. Appreciate it. Wonder in the amazement of it. Revel in it. You are here. And just for now, for this minute, there is nowhere else you need to be. Be grateful for it. And for yourself. For all you have done, and all that you are.

And be happy. Right here right now. For who you have become.

AFFIRMATION

I celebrate my being.

WHAT DOES YOUR SOUL
SAY ABOUT MONDAY?

*Darkness has a hunger that's insatiable, and
lightness has a call that's hard to hear.*

~ INDIGO GIRLS, FROM *Closer to Fine*

'Ugh. I'm just going to have to do it. I really don't want to, but I should. People are counting on me. I said I would, so I will. I have to. But I really, really, really don't want to.'

As I was driving home from my beach walk this morning, thinking about what was on my calendar for the week, I had a flashback. It was from a certain period in my life and the thoughts I used to have at the end of the weekend, as I contemplated my week ahead. I used to called it Sunday Night Dread and it descended like a dark storm cloud, enveloping my body and emotions with cyclonic force. It started at about 4pm. Churning stomach. Rising anxiety. Checking emails. Writing endless to-do lists. Sleepless night. And then the Monday morning hell. Rushing around, stressed out mess, constricting suit jacket, tortuous pantyhose, and those bloody high heels! Oh, and the super fun, start of week, office commute. I had come to dread it. All of it.

I recall so vividly putting my son in the car one morning to do the school drop-off after a particularly harrowing morning, and muttering to myself under my breath, 'There is no bloody way I am doing this for the rest of my God damn life.' I was angry and exhausted, and underneath all of it sat a profound sadness that this was the treadmill of my existence—and there was no off ramp in sight.

It was like that for a long time, until I really started listening to my soul crying out for more. More peace, more joy, more purpose, more soulfulness in my life.

If you also have a sense of dread before your week starts, know that it doesn't always have to be like that. Next time the dark cloud starts to envelop you, gently ask yourself these questions:

- *What are you looking forward to this week?*
- *Where can you add in some moments of joy?*
- *If you could make a change towards what you want most, what would your soul call you to do?*

When we force ourselves to do what we think we should do, rather than what we long to do, we are out of touch with the life our soul is calling us to live. Buried deep down under those shoulds is your happiness. Move towards it in small ways every day.

AFFIRMATION
I intentionally live a more soulful life.

SEE THE MIRACLE IN EVERYTHING

Every blade of grass has its angel that bends
over it and whispers, 'Grow, grow.'

~ TALMUD

We get to choose the way we look at the world. Part of that is how we choose to look at the small things that happen in our everyday lives. We can just see the mess, the to-dos and the drama. Or we can choose to see the miracles that are all around us. Because when you start looking for them, they are everywhere.

The miracle of being able to open your eyes in the morning and see the new day. The miracle of being able to place your feet on the ground and give thanks for the earth we live on. The bloom from a rose in your garden, that represents the never-ending cycle of nature doing its Divine thing. The miracle in the food we eat, the people we love, the work we are blessed to do in the world. The pure miracle of being alive, and the privilege of growing older.

There are miracles everywhere, in everything around you. Choose to see them and sit in gratitude for the blessings you have.

AFFIRMATION
I choose to see miracles everywhere I look.

BE GRATEFUL FOR WHAT YOU HAVE

Perhaps loving something is the only starting
place there is for making your life your own.

~ ALICE KOLLER

One of the greatest ways to tap into the 'you' of your soul is by being grateful for what you have. We are so endlessly busy that it's easy to lose touch with all that we have today, in our pursuit of what's next. Gratitude and counting our blessings are the key to not only being happy in the present, but also creating abundance for the future. Imagine the warmth of your bed as you wake up in the morning and the feeling of your feet touching the floor. The lighting of incense before your morning meditation; the beautiful coffee before you start your day's work. As you move through your day, notice all of the small and large ways you are blessed, and express appreciation and gratitude for all that you have in your life.

It's also giving thanks for what you have, even if you are still wanting something more or different. You may want more clients. Start with feeling deep into your heart for the clients that you do have. Even if you are starting a new business and have only one client, love that client so much and give so much gratitude for them that the Universe will not be able to help but respond with more abundance.

You may want more time to write. You know you have a book in you, but you bemoan the fact that you can't take time off to get it written, because the boss won't let you, or you have too many family commitments to be able to take a break. That's okay. What time do you have? Ten minutes in the morning before the kids get up or thirty minutes once a week in your lunchtime break is enough to get started. Be grateful for the time you have.

Perhaps you are longing to move apartment or house? You really want more space and a quieter environment, as your neighbours are really noisy. While waiting for a new home to come into your life, clear out your home and create more space, being grateful for the roof over your head and safe space to reside in. Get to know your neighbours a little, so you are less irritated every time you hear them.

The path to abundance and having more of what you want is being grateful for what you already have. Turn your attention to soulful gratitude today.

AFFIRMATION

My life is blessed and I am appreciative for all I have to be grateful for.

USE THE WORDS OF YOUR SOUL

Things do not change; we change.

~ HENRY DAVID THOREAU

If you tuned into your inner dialogue, what would you find? Over the past ten years, my inner narrative has changed dramatically. Whereas I used to have a constant stream of comments berating myself—I messed up that presentation, I shouldn't have eaten that chocolate, I'm too judgemental—I now speak much more kindly to myself. I'm more compassionate, loving, softer, encouraging. My narrative has gone from evil high school frenemy to beautiful best friend soul sister.

Rather than have the devil incarnate screaming in my head thousands of times a day, it's now like my soul is whispering, 'You've got this, you can do it, keep going, you're so great.' It's not perfect and I still have my moments, but the inner critic voice has faded. In her place, a helpful friend often appears.

Think about your own inner dialogue: is she harsh and fierce, always complaining and criticising? Or soft and nurturing, cheering you on? Perhaps she is somewhere in the middle. Focus in on her. Feel into what your soul would sound like if it were leading the conversation. What words would be used? What would the tone sound like? Then start playing that record on repeat as often as possible. Because it's the only soundtrack you need to step into your best possible life.

AFFIRMATION

I speak kindly to myself.

RELAX, IT'S GOING TO BE OKAY

In the end, only three things matter: how much you
loved, how gently you lived, and how gracefully
you let go of things not meant for you.

~ BUDDHA

If there was a core message from our soul to us on this plane
called life, it might just be this: relax, it's going to be okay.
It may not be okay today. You may be going through a terrible
ordeal. You might be sick, a loved one may be in trouble, you
might be fighting with your spouse, or you may have just lost
your job. These are all terrible things to endure.

But. There is always a 'but'. If we could see all of the things
that show up on our journey as lessons from our soul leading
us to our highest path, to our most fulfilled self, then we would
know that everything is going to be okay. That we are, really,
just being lead back to love. Because love is all there is. And
everything else is only there to show us that. To teach us that.
To lead us back to that. To love.

No matter what is happening in your world right now, know
that it is only happening to teach you the lessons you need
to return home to who you truly are. To grow into whoever
your soul knows you are meant to be in this life. You will
endure. You are strong enough to move through this. And
there really are brighter days ahead, no matter what you are
currently facing.

Someone once said everything will be alright in the end. If it's not alright, then it's not the end. So relax. It really is going to be okay.

AFFIRMATION

I trust my path.

PART 6

Consciousness

THE DOOR TO CONSCIOUSNESS

When an inner situation is not made
conscious, it appears outside as fate.

~ CARL JUNG

S ages from the ages, philosophers, psychologists and spiritual gurus have explored and debated what consciousness is since the beginning of time. We all experience it, yet it is difficult to explain. You could literally sit and endlessly ponder the question if you were so inclined, and never reach a definitive answer.

Everyone has a doorway that leads them to conscious awakening. For some it's an illness, a tragedy or the death of someone close to them. It could be a burnout, a breakdown or a break-up. For others, it's a breakthrough, an aha moment, something that transcends them above the noise of their daily life. However it happens, wherever it happens, it's an opening. It's when we realise that there is something bigger than ourselves at play in life. That we aren't alone. That there is more to this life than what we can see with our eyes, more than what appears in physical reality.

For many, there is the moment of before and after. Before stepping into conscious awareness ... and after. Before, when things feel grey and routine. After, when the world becomes full of colour and alive with possibilities. It's when our spiritual life begins.

In many ways, we are always at the start of this continually unfolding journey, which challenges us to higher levels of our conscious being. But walking through that first door, or the door that really grabs us by the shoulders and says, 'Hey honey, it's time to wake up,' is the start of our spiritual life. Our entrance into the life that matters.

AFFIRMATION

I walk through the opening doors into my conscious awakening.

THE PATH TO AWAKENING

A woman's spiritual life is an evolution.
She must build it herself.

~ SARA AVANT STOVER, *The Book of SHE*

It had been a busy morning. The call from a girlfriend fuming and venting because she'd just been fired (even though she secretly knew she needed to move on). The client exasperated by the behaviour of a toxic colleague she could no longer tolerate (even though she knew it kept happening so she could step into her power). The sighs of despair from another about a change in path that was unexpected and sure to be challenging (even though her instincts told her it had to happen).

They may not have chosen them, these events that were unfolding. But they all knew, in their heart of hearts, that they were happening to help them wake up. To become more conscious. To get more intentional with their lives and their choices.

In addition, they were all having this realisation: the path to awakening is awkward. It can be a rough road, filled with peaks and troughs and deep, dark valleys on the way to the light.

There is a universal truth I invite you to hear on your path to spiritual and personal awakening: *Transformation is messy.* It just is. Ask anyone who has been on a real path to waking up, to becoming more conscious in their lives. Ask them what it really feels like to descend into their own depths. Then really listen for the answer.

They will tell you, unquestionably, that it's hard. Challenging. That it can upend your life and your thoughts about who you thought you were in the world. That it can unsettle you to your very core, forcing you to question everything—from what you eat, to who your friends are, to the work you are truly called to do in the world. That it can unearth issues in your relationships, and that some will make it and some will not. That you won't be the same person coming out as you were going in, and you may not want to relinquish some of the parts of yourself that just won't cut it anymore.

That it will be nothing at all like you thought it would be.

But remember this: The path to awakening is *everything*.

It's not only that you wake up and become more conscious. It's how you get to the light. It's how you even get to see the light in the first place. Awakening can be tiring, confusing, infuriating and exhausting. But be sure to stay tuned in for the magic among the mess. Because beneath all of it there will be moments of joy, and a knowing that awake is where you want to be.

AFFIRMATION

I commit to my evolution.

YOUR LEVEL OF CONSCIOUSNESS MATTERS

We are the ones we have been waiting for.

~ ALICE WALKER

History unfolds as a product of our level of consciousness. We look around us at the world today and wonder how we got to be here. If we are awake, we're staggered and speechless at the events around us, both close to home and far away. We wonder how God or whomever we pray to, how the government or corporations or the 'one percent', could have let the world get into the state that it's in.

While there are powers that be that have responsibility to take care of the world and its people, that responsibility is not absolute. It also falls on every one of us, a truth that many are not willing to either hear or act on. We got here, to this place where things seem so out of control, because this is the level of our collective consciousness. The refugee crisis, corrupt politicians, closing the borders, a profound lack of humanity, starving children, preventable illnesses, human and sex trafficking, the environmental crisis, inter-racial and gender wars, discrimination, racism, sexism, misogyny, hate crimes, ageism, gun violence—all of the things that ail us come from the collective 'us'.

Raising our consciousness, individually and collectively, through self-awareness, spiritual development, reflection, transformation, activism and action, is the way out. It's the way through. It's the only way to literally save the world and all of us in it.

As Jean Houston teaches us: *We are in the time of renaissance, a time of radical new possibility. We are in the time or either grow or die.*

Raising our consciousness matters. It matters for our own development and for the evolvement of self. But it is also so much bigger than we are, and the contained world we each live in. It matters for all of humanity, for all of the people who cannot fend for themselves. It matters for animals and the environment, for the poor, the downtrodden, the forgotten, for minority groups, for the persecuted, for the old and the sick—and, most importantly, for the children.

As women, we have long been the healers, the teachers, the unifiers, the community leaders, the activists, the revolutionists. The Dalai Lama has said: *The world will be saved by the Western woman.* I believe the world will be changed and saved by women, period. It is up to us. And the time is now.

AFFIRMATION

I take responsibility for raising my level of consciousness and taking action where I am able.

BECOME CONSCIOUS OF
YOUR OWN THOUGHTS

The one who's watching is the gateway to spirituality.

~ MICHAEL SINGER

Perhaps one of the most powerful spiritual and developmental lessons I have ever learnt is about becoming conscious of my own thoughts. It took me a long time to wrap my head around this truth: *I am not my thoughts. I am the thinker of my thoughts.*

Sit with that for a moment. You are not your thoughts. You are the thinker of your thoughts. That's a little mind-boggling.

What does it really mean? Simply that you can become more aware of the thoughts in your head. Once you realise that there is an endless stream of thoughts parading through your mind every moment of every day, and that you can in fact become the observer of the thoughts rather than be in the stream of them, your consciousness changes. You actually become more conscious.

But in practice, it's not so simple to do. In fact, we can spend a lifetime of spiritual practice unravelling ourselves from our thoughts. Becoming 'untethered', as author Michael Singer teaches us in his bestselling book, *The Untethered Soul.*

Where do you even start? Today, begin to notice your thoughts and find some separation from your identity, your being and your thoughts. Start to observe them, instead of being in them. Be the witness. If you find yourself getting caught up energetically or emotionally in the stream, take a breath and come back to the knowing that you are not your thoughts.

You are not your thoughts.

Separate yourself from them. Observe them. Be the witness. And by so doing, open a little more into your conscious self.

AFFIRMATION

I am conscious and aware that I am not my thoughts.

CHASE THE LIGHT

Travel light. Live light. Spread the light. Be the light.

~ YOGI BHAJAN

We live in a world filled with duality. Rain and clear skies. The moon and the sun. Love and heartbreak. Calm and chaos. Light and darkness. Striving and letting things be.

Just as each new day brings light after the darkness of night, we all have a choice about how much light we bring into our lives.

It's inevitable that we will have periods of darkness in our lives. It could be the loss of a cherished partnership, a job ending unexpectedly, financial troubles, or dealing with grief. In such situations, our only choice is to move through them with as much grace as we can muster, and to reach the other side with our sanity and soul intact.

In the normal run and hum of daily life, however, there is a greater choice we can make in each moment, whether we know it or not. Whether to sit in the darkness, dwelling on everything that isn't how we want it to be, or to choose the light, focusing on the positive? When we look for the light it is everywhere, even in the smallest moments. The love heart the barista drew on your morning coffee. The wet noisy kiss your child planted on your cheek. The fresh flowers grown in your garden that now sit on your kitchen bench.

We need both the light and the dark, just as we need rain to make the flowers grow. And we can acknowledge and respect the darkness, but we don't have to live there. Look for whatever brings the light into your life. Seek whatever casts out the shadows. And chase the light that illuminates your life in every way possible.

AFFIRMATION
I seek out the light.

RAISING YOUR VIBRATION

Desire, ask, believe, receive.

~ STELLA TERILL MANN

You hear healers, teachers and authors in spiritual circles talking and writing about raising your vibration. It sounds fancy, intriguing and a little strange to many, especially those in the early stages of their spiritual journey. What they are really talking about is expanding your level of consciousness.

The entire Universe is made up of vibrational frequencies and energy. Without getting into the quantum physics of it, everything is energy—literally. As we expand our consciousness and raise our own vibration, we also raise the vibration of the planet, and it becomes an essential part of our role as light workers.

When our vibration is high, our life seems to flow. Our cash flow is good, our relationships are strong, our health can feel vibrant and our work is on purpose. When our vibration is low, we can feel like we're walking through an obstacle course all day, struggling to get on track with our efforts.

This entire book is an exercise in raising your vibration. As you simplify your life, step into your purpose, unlock your creativity and get sacred in your womanhood, your vibration lifts. With every page you read and every suggestion you try, you expand your conscious state. It's all part of the process of becoming whole.

One of the most potent ways to raise your vibration is to attune the thoughts that you think. Aligning with positive and uplifting thoughts is important, because our thoughts, just like everything else, hold an energy frequency. The more positive the thoughts, the higher the frequency. Higher vibrational frequencies carry more light and spaciousness, while lower energies feel more heavy, dark and dense.

High vibrational intentions like love, kindness, hope and compassion have been known to change the matter and make up of everything—from a glass of water or an apple sitting on a window sill, to the mood response from drinking a cup of tea. Lower vibrational energies like hate, fear and anger can do the same.

Raising your vibration starts with being more intentional about your thoughts, words and actions. Thinking and acting more positively, even without saying a word, changes your energy. People around you feel it and respond to it. This is what it means to live with light and love. You can literally step further into the light every day and project that light into the world, with the higher vibrational energy created by your intentions.

AFFIRMATION

I focus on raising my vibration through my
positive thoughts, words and actions.

STAY IN YOUR OWN ENERGY

*You must learn to be still in the midst of activity
and to be vibrantly alive in repose.*

~ INDIRA GANDHI

How often do you find yourself voyeuring into someone else's life? We live in the era of social. We can look into the lives of practically anybody and see everything, from what they had for breakfast to their romantic life. Granted, it's most likely not real life, rather a meticulously curated feed of perfected images and Instagram-worthy stories making up their highlight reel. But it's still a way to enter into someone else's existence. And, importantly, into their energy field.

This is something we don't often think about, as we mindlessly scroll away or hit play on a video. We're not just in someone's life or business. We are entering into their energetic space.

Try this out for yourself. Think about someone you follow religiously on your favourite social platform. How often do you look at that particular feed and how do you feel when you do? For some, the feelings are uplifted, energised, happy, inspired. For others, it's envy, feelings of being less than, demotivated or even just plain sad.

As I was writing this book, I noticed that the more I stayed off social media, the more deeply I could dive into the energetic essence of this work and the feelings I wanted it to represent. I needed to stop opening up the stream into people's lives. I needed to get out of other people's energy.

Everything is energy. Be careful of how and where you pick up what other people are putting out, and how that makes you feel.

ARE YOU CREATING
CHAOS IN YOUR LIFE?

What a gift of grace to be able to take the chaos from
within and from it create some semblance of order.

~ KATHERINE PATERSON

How often do you feel like your life is one giant chaotic mess? Like you're part of a bad 1980s soap opera that you don't remember being cast in, and you're constantly swirling from one drama to another. When you next find yourself amid the swirl, pause for just a moment. Take a deep breath and ask yourself: *How am I contributing to this situation?*

It's easy, perhaps even habitual, to feel like everything that happens to us is the result of external forces. We feel caught up in other people's stories and dramas, through no fault of our own. Perhaps that's true. But perhaps it's also true that the chaos is caused (at least in part) by our own stories, projections, patterns and habits.

If you stopped and really looked at the chaos with clear and objective eyes, what would you see? Drama is a great distraction. When we're busy dealing with the chaos, it stops us from having to look at the important things that need to be addressed in our lives. Like our relationships. Our terrible job. Our unhealthy habits. How unhappy we are.

What could you change, and how much drama and chaos could you release, by changing yourself, your mind or your patterns? These are questions worth asking. Dwelling on. And answering.

AFFIRMATION
I release the need to create chaos in my life.

~ 211 ~

YOU CAN UNSUBSCRIBE

Saying 'no' can be the ultimate self-care.
~ CLAUDIA BLACK

The 'friend' who triggers you every time you see her face on Instagram. That weekly email newsletter you get in your inbox, that makes you feel like you're doing nothing with your life. The endless tweets about the state of the world that pain you every time you look at them. The Facebook group that constantly sends messages which bug you, even though you don't want them to.

You think you should be able to deal with it. It's just technology after all. You should be bigger than that, you tell yourself, and not get annoyed or triggered because you are up in your comparison zone, judgement vortex or insane cycle of overwhelm.

But you don't want to deal with it. And guess what? You don't have to. Your technology or social media feed doesn't need to be your path to enlightenment. You don't need to deal with those things or people that trigger you, if you don't want to.

Unfollow. Unsubscribe. Unlike. Unfriend.

Just like that. You are in control of what enters your consciousness. You can choose to align with what empowers you, not what takes your power away. Just like that, you can take back the real estate in your mind, your heart and your energy field.

AFFIRMATION
I get to choose what I consume and interact with online.

THERE IS NO 'THERE' THERE

Only infinite patience produces immediate effects.
~ FOUNDATION FOR INNER PEACE, *A Course in Miracles*

Sahara was a wonderful coaching client who I'd worked with for many years. When she came to me she was a senior executive, feeling like she was stuck in her career. She was lacking confidence, creatively stifled and completely void of any spiritual life. She was getting through it—the job, her marriage, parenting—but she wasn't feeling fulfilled by much of it.

As we journeyed on our coaching path, she made incredible progress. She was a diligent client, who showed up prepared for each session, had a list of questions, had done her homework thoughtfully and was really present for each of our discussions.

A year into our work, and after a few months of steady sailing, something happened that really rattled her. As we worked through it in one of our sessions, I could sense a frustration that had nothing to do with the issue we were discussing. I paused and asked her, 'What's really going on here?'

Sahara sighed. It was one of those sighs that seemed like it had come from deep down within her soul. 'I just thought I was done already.'

'What do you mean by done?' I asked.

'You know, done with all of the work. We've covered so much. So much personal development and deep stuff. I made so much progress. And now I am back here.'

I waited. I knew there was more.

And then this: 'I thought I was *there*. That the hard stuff was over. You know, I thought I had arrived.'

Her level of heartfelt disappointment was palpable. And I tried to break it to her as gently as I could. The work is never done. We never actually arrive. As long as we are alive, we keep journeying. There are always more lessons, more truths, more soul searching and discovery. More liberation. Deeper levels of empowerment and freedom.

When we accept this, then we can surrender with an open mind and heart. Because the truth is that's all we can ever really do. Show up. Be open. Be kind. And do the work.

AFFIRMATION
I celebrate how far I have come.

CHOOSE PEACE OR
CHOOSE JUDGEMENT

*Am I looking through the eyes of peace or am
I looking through the eyes of judgment?*

~ GABRIELLE BERNSTEIN

If you tracked your thoughts and words for the entire day
tomorrow, how many would be peaceful and loving, and
how many would be filled with judgement of yourself or others?
I recommend trying and witnessing this for yourself.

If you're like most of us, you'll find that you spend a massive
amount of time being judgemental. We are constantly putting
things into categories of good and bad, should have and shouldn't
have, and various other narratives about how we see the world
around us.

When we live more consciously, we begin to realise that it's
actually not necessary to judge everything we see and experience. When we stop judging everything as right or wrong, we
start to experience something that seems hard to fathom among
the thousands of thoughts we think and the countless words we
speak every day: we start to have more space and silence in our
consciousness. We find more energy inside ourselves, as we feel
the need to speak less. Our internal narrative and chatter begins
to quieten, when we don't feel required to put a label on every
single thing that passes us by.

To live with more connection to our soul, to our essence, we
must choose to become more discerning with our thoughts and
words. We can choose to move away from the need to describe
everything, have an opinion about everything, and evaluate,

label and judge everything in our life. We can choose peace. With every thought, with every word, and with the silences in between.

AFFIRMATION
I create inner and outer space when I
choose peace over judgement.

GO DEEPER

Learn to get in touch with the silence within yourself
and know that everything in this life has a purpose.

~ ELISABETH KÜBLER-ROSS

It's New Year's Eve, and the sun is starting to lower in the sky. I'm standing on the edge of the ocean, toes in the water, hair dripping wet down my back. I have no plans for the evening, preferring to welcome the new year in solitude.

As I stand here, my thoughts turn to the year that has been and what may come to pass with the coming months. I say a silent prayer of thanks for the blessings I have received. Even though the year has had its challenges, there have been ample gifts to be grateful for.

As I release the dreams of the past year that weren't yet ready to be birthed, I slip into a soft meditative state.

Tuning in. Surrendering. Releasing. Listening.

Surrendering. Releasing.

Listening.

And then I hear these words as clearly as if someone were standing to my right, whispering them in my ear:

'Go deeper.'

Listening. 'Go deeper.'

As I hear the words, I feel myself grounding down into the sand. My feet are welded to the earth, as if my bones, veins and blood are penetrating down into the soul of the Universe.

Anchored. Solid. Here.

'Go deeper.'

And I know it's time. I'm ready. To let go of anything that isn't serving my life, my work, my purpose. To release anything or anyone who isn't contributing to me being of greatest service. To walk away from practices or people that are keeping me stuck.

But most importantly, it's time to listen. To listen more intently to the wisdom that is trying to reach me. Ancient wisdom. Knowings. Voices that have been stirring for eons and are finally ready to be heard.

There is only one way to hear the guidance that directs our most purposeful life:

Surrender. Release. Listen.

Go deeper.

AFFIRMATION
I release. I listen. I go deeper.

BE WHERE YOU ARE (EVEN IF IT'S NOT WHERE YOU WANT TO BE)

The ego asks a thousand questions for
which there are no answers.

~ FOUNDATION FOR INNER PEACE, *A Course in Miracles*

You may not want to be here.

You have big beautiful dreams. You want to *be there already.*

But you're not there.

You are here.

So be here now.

Be here fully.

Be present to the magic and the mess that is around you, for better or for worse.

Just be where you are.

By being here, you increase your chances and energetic propulsion to get you there.

They say that you need to love what you have, before you can release it and let it go.

That you need to be fully where you are, before you can get to where you want to be.

There is truth there.

Love where you are. Express gratitude for it. Be present to it. Live it.

AFFIRMATION
I am present to the life I am living now.

WHAT DO YOU ALREADY HAVE
THAT YOU WANT MORE OF?

*Whatever work we attempt cannot be perfectly
done unless our minds are tranquil and calm.*

~ K. PATTABHI JOIS

I was in the ocean this morning, in the joyful state I'm usually in when frolicking around. On my walk to the beach, I'd been thinking about my plans for my business: where I needed to take action, and the things that would move me towards what I wanted most. In a word, that was 'freedom'.

As I played in the water, I had this stark moment of realisation, like lightening had literally struck me where I was swimming: I already had freedom. This, this right here in this moment, this was freedom.

It was 9.30am on a Thursday morning. I'd allowed myself to sleep in a little, switching my alarm from 6am to 7.30am, as I was feeling a bit tired and run down. I eventually left the house at 8am to wander down to the beach, have a walk and then swim.

I wanted to be at my desk by 10.30am, but I had some flexibility in that. After all, I was setting the schedule. I had no boss to answer to, no clients booked in, as I was in book writing mode. So there was no pressure to rush. I could take my time. I ended up spending almost an hour in the water, it was just so good—warm and clear with small undulating waves I could float around on. As I wandered back to town to grab a smoothie and a chai latte, I realised that I already had what I craved the most.

I ran my own schedule. I answered to myself. I chose my clients, my projects, the amount of work I took on, what I said 'no' too. I set my own hours. I got to choose my team, my collaborators, my business partners. I picked my speaking gigs. I had a publisher who let me decide which book to write next. I had enough money to pay the mortgage, the school fees and the essential needs for my son and me.

I didn't need to search for or yearn for freedom. I had it. I was living it. Sure, there could be more. More creative freedom, which meant more time to write—my ultimate dream. And sure, there could be more financial freedom. I would love to pay off my mortgage, be debt-free and not ever again have to worry about money. But I had enough.

It's easy to get caught up in the cycle of focusing on what we think we don't have. Exhausting ourselves with thoughts of what we lack, what's missing, what we need more of to be happy. That can be a vicious, self-defeating cycle. But I know from personal experience that when we focus on what we already have that we want more of, more of it is what we get.

Perhaps you can take a look at your own life, just as it is right now. What is it that you want most? Where does this already exist? Even if it's in the smallest pockets, identify it. Celebrate it. Express massive amounts of gratitude for it. And watch it expand into the more you long for.

AFFIRMATION

I have what I am seeking.
The more I celebrate it, the more it grows.

THANK YOU

I don't believe. I know.

~ CARL JUNG

To every door that has ever closed on me, thank you.

For there were other doors I was meant to walk through.

To every failure I ever anguished over, thank you.

For you taught me the grit and grace for what came next.

To every dream that was never realised, thank you.

There was something so much better waiting for me.

To every person who didn't see me, value me, love me, thank you.

For the ones who came after you honoured me deeply.

To everything I have ever wanted and lost.

Thank you.

Thank you.

Thank you.

For in your loss, you set me free.

AFFIRMATION

I let go and set myself free.

RAPTURE

One day you finally knew what you had to do, and began...
~ MARY OLIVER, *The Journey*

I have a piece of art on my desk by artist Alberto Sanchez. A woman is standing in a stream of water up to her mid thighs. Her head is tilted back, her eyes are closed, her chest is open and her arms are extended at both sides, with her fingertips grazing the water behind her. She's wearing an ethereal cotton dress; it falls off her shoulders and her red hair cascades down. You can see a beautiful tattoo across her chest, which looks like angel wings and roses in a large intricate design.

The artwork is called *Rapture*.

Rapture, noun, a feeling of intense pleasure or joy.

What I see when I look at this woman is freedom, rebellious-ness, wonder, a woman completely in the moment like nothing else matters. She is a wild woman, a wise woman, a woman unto herself, untamed and with her power unleashed. She has ancient wisdom inside of her that the world needs. And she has a seriously badass tattoo.

As I look at her, I wonder what it would be like to fully live like I imagine she does. To live a life in rapture. Free. In intense pleasure. Joyful. Sovereign.

I look around at the women in my life. The mothers, workers, healers, nurturers, entrepreneurs, lawyers, nurses, artists, teachers, leaders, travellers, coaches, speakers, strategists, doctors, bankers, yogis. All trying to live on purpose, make a difference, show up in a way that matters, and take care of those close to them.

And I often wonder as I look at all of our lives, where is the rapture? Where is the unleashed power? Where do we find joy and intense pleasure? Where do we give of our wisdom without worrying how it will be received, just because we know we need to share it?

Here is the truth of it: Rapture is wherever you choose to experience it. The freedom is wherever you create it. The sharing of wisdom happens whenever you are brave and bold enough to stand up, speak out and use your voice. And pleasure and joy can be experiences that we have to make space, time and moments for. It is within our power to do so, if we care enough to make it matter.

We worry too much. We worry about how we look and how we sound; how we'll be perceived and what people will think; how many likes we do or don't get, and what we think it says about us; how we aren't doing enough, being enough, achieving enough, striving enough; how nobody sees us or really cares about our gifts. We worry that we're worn out by it all, and we long for a time when we could just be, instead of always trying to become.

Because becoming is exhausting. It puts us firmly in our masculine energy and leaves our feminine dying on the vine. It makes that softer part of us, who just wants to be received and seen and acknowledged and loved, yearn for a different life. It leaves our feminine crying out for peace and space and longing to run away from it all—to a place where she can simply be.

Let's make a pact to stop becoming and just start being. Being who we truly are. Real, gritty, honest, unpolished, unfiltered, uncensored, unconcerned with anything other than coming back home to who we truly are. In this moment, this day, this time and this place.

Let's just be. Let go of the striving to be anything other than who we are. Drop the chains that bind us. Take off the mask that hides us. Let the light shine on all that is good and true and whole. Let's choose to be wildly enraptured with ourselves and in our own lives.

AFFIRMATION

I find my rapture every day.

CATCHING UP

How much of the world had I missed
while living in my head?

~ GLORIA STEINEM

Life moves fast. Sometimes we need to slow down to catch up. To literally catch our breath. Slowing down is a conscious choice, but often not an easy one. It's hard to make yourself stop when you feel like you're running a marathon. What if everyone passes you? What if you become irrelevant? What if you lose?

Slowing down can be hard. To slow down you have to surrender a little. You have to trust a lot. You need to be okay with people moving ahead. Of course people will pass you, if you are standing still for a moment.

But they are on their own path, not yours. They are running their own race, in their own way. And here's the thing about slowing down. Or even pausing. You won't miss it. This thing you are chasing so hard? You won't miss it.

If it's for you, it will wait for you. Trust that. Catch your breath. Stand still for a moment and breathe. Your life will slow down as much as you allow it to. For now, just for now, allow yourself to catch up.

AFFIRMATION

I allow myself to breathe, stand still and surrender.

WHEN THE DISTRACTIONS ARE GONE, IT'S JUST YOU

Hell is the place where nothing connects.

~ T. S. ELIOT

Endless distractions. Work. Social media. Friends. Family. Parenting. Email. Television. Clutter. Drama. Responsibilities. Food. Incessant talking. Habitual scrolling. Any form of addictive behaviour only compounds the issue. Normal and somewhat manageable distractions become compulsive, potentially driving us to the brink, causing all manner of havoc in our lives.

But what if you removed the distractions? What then? What if the brink could become your edge? Some people can remove distractions from their lives when they really need to. Others, especially those with addictive personalities and tendencies, find this impossible without some level of support.

I have friends who take themselves off to ashrams in India for weeks or months at a time to dress in robes, wake at 4am, meditate with a guru or take a vow of silence. Others have checked into rehab, desperate for isolation and structure, penance if you will, for their self-perceived sins. Others have tried to tough it out with willpower, which can end in defeat, even in self-sabotage, when the limited supply of self-regulation runs out.

However, what we find at the bottom of the distraction pile, when the pit is empty and we are all done, is the same, no matter the method used: we are left alone with ourselves. When you strip it all away, it's just you. The you without a phone in your hand, the tenth chocolate biscuit in your mouth, your fifth vodka martini or the fifteenth hour sitting at your desk.

Just you. Alone. This place can feel vast. Like an endless desert of nothingness.

The time seems to last forever, a single hour like the longest week. When will you get your next hit? The dopamine rush from the next message, email, sugar high or pressing deadline. When will it come? You feel almost desperate for it, like an addict craving the next cocaine hit.

When it's all gone and it's just you with yourself, you can feel horribly alone. Lonely even. Like you're the only person who is going through this, the only crazy one. But you're not. We're all there at some level. Whether it's a technology distraction or a seemingly uncontrollable sugar addiction, we all have something we are dealing with.

You're not alone. Even though I know it can feel like it.

When you make the choice to move through the darkness that comes with just being with yourself, a revelation happens with every moment of success, every little win. You can do this. Even when the craving rises and you think you will concede, you remember you made a choice. You chose something different for yourself. You want to be better, to do better, to live better. You *decided*.

You can breathe through the distraction. Through the addiction. Through the process of change. And there is more waiting for your life on the other side of yourself.

AFFIRMATION
I choose to release myself from my distractions and addictions.

CONSCIOUS PARENTING

It is what it is. This means we parent our children as
our children are, not as we might wish them to be.

~ SHEFALI TSABARY, *The Conscious Parent*

I've been a single parent for most of my son's life. His father and I separated when he was 18 months old, and divorced a year later. We agonised over the decision; went to counselling and patched things up for a while, only to have them fall apart again. We could both see that everyone would be happier if we split up. But it was an incredibly hard time.

I struggled through as a single mother with my game face on. I didn't have any close friends with children nearby, nor any good role models at work, so I did what I thought women do—I just got through it. When I look back now on my first five years of being a mother, I realise they were definitely the hardest of my life.

No-one really prepares you, do they? They hand you the baby in the hospital and wish you luck. Nothing prepares you for that first baby—the crying, endless sleepless nights, sickness and all that comes with it. Especially if you are doing it on your own.

If you combine work outside the home with motherhood, you'd better strap yourself in for the ride of your life. I was always there doing the things you are meant to do. I tried to work flexibly, so I could pick him up from school some days, walk him home and have afternoon time together, while juggling the phone, emails and work commitments. I did the reading groups, was a class mum, did tuckshop, helped with school events. I tried as hard as I could to be present. But behind closed doors I was a mess:

stressed out, exhausted and worried that I was constantly doing everything wrong. Mother guilt is real. And it's debilitating.

It did get easier, especially once he hit high school. I often laugh with him that I was born to raise teenagers, not little kids. I've hit my stride and it's easier now for many reasons: I run my own business, have control of my schedule, we're an incredible team and he is a really amazing person.

But perhaps more than anything else, it's easier now because my intelligence as a parent has increased. I think that in the first ten years of his life I was in survival mode, just trying to get us both through the ride without anyone getting hurt (or needing a lifetime of therapy). You wouldn't have known it to look at me, or him. He was a happy child and always had his emotional and physical needs met. And yet ... I could have been more present. I could have been more conscious.

I look at my son now as an 18-year-old—a six foot two gorgeous young man with incredible qualities like humility, generosity, humour, grit and a spirit that only comes from an old soul—and I realise that for all I got wrong, I did some things right. I always wanted to be attuned to him, to create space for him to develop into his own person. I made a decision when he was young that I was going to let him lead, not the other way around. I didn't want to control who he could or couldn't be.

If he wanted long hair, he could have long hair. He chose his friends, sporting or creative activities, how hard he worked, which high school he went to. I never placed emphasis on his grades or report cards, only that he was working to his level of ability, so he could be proud of himself. It was about the effort, not the outcome. I always told him to remember who he was, to focus on his character above all else.

I've now discovered this is what psychologist, bestselling author and parenting expert, Dr Shefali Tsabary, calls 'Conscious Parenting'. I didn't know it had its own term, but I guess that's what I've always tried to do.

Parenting is hard. Being a mother is hard. It can be excruciating. Yet we hardly talk about it. We all show up with those game faces on and our perfect children on our Instagram feed and then silently scream behind closed doors, because we're frustrated and exhausted and think we are ruining our kids for life. Secretly, we're questioning whether we will ever get our lives back, knowing we can often be a shell of who we thought we were before. And we expect our kids to fulfil us, to please us, to grow up in our shadows and likeness, and put all the pressure in the world on them to fit in, meet our standards, to represent us well.

We need to give ourselves a break and be a little bit kinder and gentler with ourselves. It's okay to admit that it's hard raising little humans. It can be terribly hard. But it's also the honour of a lifetime to be chosen to be their parents. We need to loosen the reins and let them become who they are destined to be. To become who they are in their soul. Their journey is predestined. They came here with a purpose. Our role as parents is to let them fully grow and blossom into who they truly are, with as little interference as possible. To be attuned to them, to support them, and to simply love them in both their being and their becoming.

AFFIRMATION
I choose to parent consciously.

SEE WHAT'S POSSIBLE

Whenever I have to choose between two evils,
I always like to try the one I haven't tried before.

~ MAE WEST

As children, we have an unlimited consciousness—we spend our days dreaming and imagining all that can be possible in worlds both real and imagined. Pronouncements of being an astronaut, a dancer, a doctor or famous actress flow from the mouths of little ones as easily as asking for food when they're hungry. It's natural, intuitive, fun and creative for them to think about all of the possibilities in their lives. And they don't give it a second thought.

And then we grow up. Our consciousness of what's possible and who we might become becomes smaller, contracting rather than expanding. The big dreams of childhood turn into the perceived realities of adulthood. So we wade on through our lives acting like we don't have the freedom or permission to dream of something better for ourselves.

But in reality, we do. We still have that same imagination that we had as children. It may be dormant and dusty, but it's there, buried under the busyness and perhaps boredom of our lives, just waiting to be ignited back into our consciousness.

When I was young, I had big dreams of becoming a famous actress and living in Hollywood. I never questioned it. My son used to rave on and on about how he was going to cycle in the Tour de France, while also playing for Manchester United. He never spent an ounce of energy wondering why this couldn't be possible (and I never pointed it out to him either).

As children, we have unlimited thinking. And it's such a travesty that we lose it. We can reclaim this as adults by bringing our imagination back to life. Think back to a dream you may have once had. Resist the urge to jump on the well-formed neural pathway lined with all of the reasons why it can't happen. Sit in the possibilities. In a quiet place, hold the dream in your mind. With the full power of your imagination, think about all of the pathways and possibilities for the best scenario available. When you think you have it, as good as it could possibly get, dream bigger. If you want a job that pays a certain amount, double it. If you are after a new home, make it even dreamier. If you want a book deal, think about the massive book advance and best promotion and publisher you could ever dream about.

Think as big as it comes. Feel into it. Imagine how your world will change once it comes to fruition. Use your unlimited thinking to zoom into the best possible outcome that could occur. Write it down daily in the present tense, as if it's already real, then sit in that vision. Fine-tune the picture. Feel the emotions and joy.

Come back to that vision multiple times a day, every day, continuing to expand into the grand consciousness that is your most abundant life. Live out your dreams in your mind, making them so real you can literally see and feel them. Then every day take the small, discrete actions to bring them to life.

Come back to the emotions you felt in the dream as your anchor: the more you feel the emotion, the quicker you will bring the vision to life. And use that energy to continually see what's possible.

AFFIRMATION

I use my unlimited thinking and expanded
consciousness to see all that's possible for my life.

PART 7

Sacredness

SEEKING WHAT'S SACRED

The ache for home lives in all of us, the safe place
where we can go as we are and not be questioned.

~ MAYA ANGELOU

The word 'sacred' has two main meanings: it can relate to spirituality or religion, or it can describe something that you cherish, revere or are dedicated to, like being a good parent, being honest, or protecting the environment. You can relate to one meaning without relating to the other, and by no means need to consider yourself religious to find sacredness in your life.

Seeking what's sacred in life is about finding what you hold most dear, what stands apart from other things in their meaning to you, and then to cherish it. It may be something that frequently holds meaning for you, like protecting family time every day as sacred time. Or you may not think about it often and are only reminded of what is most sacred to you at certain times, like the birth of your child, the passing of a loved one, or family celebrations.

What meaning do you associate with the word 'sacred'? Does it invoke happy or peaceful thoughts, or perhaps there are some associations from childhood that you may want to let go of. Are there places that are sacred to you—perhaps the ocean, a favourite holiday destination you visit with your family, a tree in your backyard, the place where you meditate each morning, the room where your baby used to sleep?

Sit with these questions: *What is sacred to me? What brings me peace? What brings me a deep sense of reverence and connection?* There may not be words, but simply a feeling, that connects you to something sacred that you can't express, and that is fine too.

How could you deepen your commitment to what is most sacred in your life? It could be time, energy, space. Seek out where you can find refuge and solace that, at times, only the things we hold most sacred can bring to our lives.

AFFIRMATION
I understand what is most sacred in my life.

WOMEN ARE SACRED

*A woman's work is to define herself. There is an urgency
for women. When you have inherited a construct that
names, describes, and practices an ideology that women
are somehow less important, less necessary, then the work
of defining yourself carries with it a kind of fury.*

~ DOMINIQUE CHRISTINA, *This Is Woman's Work*

As women, long ago we lost our place as the revered beings
we once were. Grandmothers from eras past used to be
the head of the tribe. Women's cycles were sacred, with red
tents created for us to retreat to during our moon cycle, to be
nurtured, to rest and sit in circle together. Being born female at
one time in history was the ultimate honour, as women alone
were able to give life, nurture life, and preserve the life of family
and community.

Before women were killed as witches for being healers and
wayshowers, they were revered for their Divine feminine powers.
Women weren't shunned from society because of their fading
beauty and disposability. They were cherished and honoured.
They were sacred.

We are so far from that today. You only have to turn on the
television or click on social media to see stories of domestic violence, murder and the mistreatment of women at the hands of
men—often men close to them. We see football players, musicians,
movie producers and executives being prosecuted for harassment,
sexual and otherwise. Ending violence against women has become
a platform and a cause, but there is no end in sight.

At the core of all of these issues is the place women hold in society. This is a vastly complex issue, mirrored and layered on millennia of history, centuries of patriarchy, and cultural, racial and gender issues that would take an entire library to make sense of. But here, today, we can start with us. With women holding themselves as sacred, and believing one another to be sacred. By treating ourselves and all other women as sacred. And by showing the men in society and in our lives, especially the boys that we raise, what it means to treat a woman as sacred.

It's not the end we are hoping for, but it's a start. And it's a starting line we can all front up to and walk across together.

AFFIRMATION

I value and honour myself, and all of my sisters, as sacred.

WALK GENTLY ON THE EARTH

This is the core of our task: to respect and revere
ourselves, and so bring about a world in which women
are respected and revered, recognised once again as
holding the life-giving power of the earth itself.

~ SHARON BLACKIE, *If Women Rose Rooted*

A prayer for sacred living …
May we live our lives as sacred journeys and respect ourselves and all who grace our path. May we know and cherish our earth as a sacred place and honour those who came before us. May we walk through this life gently. May we treat all of life, Mother Earth and all people, with kindness and respect. May we only take what we need, and give back seeds to the ground to grow into life whenever we can. May we walk in peace, lightly, joyfully for all the days we are given. May we do no harm and only bring light, treading carefully in and out of places, relationships and environments with as much as love and laughter as we can muster.

May we be humble, not arrogant. May we be filled with love, rather than fear. Peace, not hatred. May we dissolve our anger and develop empathy through questioning and listening, to understand, not just to speak, our own words. May we really hear each other. May we appreciate the beauty and bounty that is around us in every moment, from the food on our plates, to the blooms in the garden and the moon and stars in the night sky. May we know how wonderful and magical it is to be alive, and to have the miracle that is this life. May we be audacious and gracious enough to live it fully. May we always journey well.

AFFIRMATION

*I walk gently, humbly and with great
love for this beautiful life.*

YOUR NEXT SACRED STEP

We are what we believe we are.

~ C.S. LEWIS

What is that one thing you are yearning to do, if only someone would say that you could and you should? What is your heart and soul longing for? What desire have you squashed so small that it now fits in a ring-sized box and sits in the farthest corner of your mind?

What have you given up on, because you felt like you didn't have the one thing you needed to at least try and make it happen for yourself? What are you missing? Have you been waiting for someone to say those magic words to you?

Okay. Here they are: *You have permission.*

Permission to follow your dreams. To be who you really are. To create something you love.

To throw off the shackles.

To leave the man who you know will never love you the way you want to be loved.

To take your kid out of that stuffy private school and send him to performing arts college, so he can follow his dream.

Permission to quit your job, sell your house and go to Paris to attend culinary school.

To get that tattoo, dye your hair pink or write that novel you know is inside you.

Permission to tell the world that you hate your impressive job in finance and really want to be a jewellery designer. And to actually go and do it.

Permission to want what you want and be who you are, and have that be okay. That it's enough. That you are allowed to, even destined to.

And to know that you will survive. That you will even have the audacity to thrive.

And here's the thing that no-one tells you in your pre-programmed life, already laid out with expectations of who you should be and what you should become. You don't need anyone else to give it to you.

This is your life. Your world. Your creation. And you can do whatever you want to in this life. You just have to say 'yes'.

Yes, I want that. Yes, I deserve that. And yes, I give myself permission to own it.

You don't need all of the answers. You don't need to know how the story ends. You just need to have the courage to begin.

Just say 'yes'. Say 'yes' to yourself.

AFFIRMATION
I give myself permission to want what I want.

YOUR SACRED VOICE AND MESSAGE

Tell your story. Share it with the world.
Your medicine is needed.

~ ELENA BROWER

If you had just one message for the world, what would it be?
We all have a sacred voice and message to share.

Some of us find it early, becoming deeply connected to it as we grow up, hearing it more strongly as the years pass. Some of us come to it late in life, as we enter our crone years, our elder years, when our wisdom comes through so we can finally share it. Sadly, many women never find their voice, even if they know they have a message to share.

Your voice is needed. Your message is needed. They are both medicine for a frail world. You are the medicine. Your voice is how you create change, no matter how large or small you consider that change to be. Tell your story. Share your message. Use your voice.

AFFIRMATION

My voice is sacred and I share my message with the world.

SACRED FEMALE FRIENDSHIPS

The best thing to hold onto in life is each other.
~ AUDREY HEPBURN

When growing up, I really struggled with female relationships. Like many girls, I was bullied at school. The freckly redhead seemed to be an easy target. Back then though, in the 70s and 80s, we didn't really talk that much about bullying. It was just kids being kids. No social media to highlight it, no media campaigns to stamp it out. It was just part of life.

It was always the girls who bullied me, never the boys. And even though I developed some strong friendships and even had that 'best friend' we all long for, they were always pretty fluid and easily disentangled.

As I went through my rebellious teen years, my best friends were all guys, musicians mostly, and we would hang out endlessly listening to music, playing in bands, recording songs in bedrooms and drinking beer. They were good times,

But I had a skewed view of what true female friendships looked like all the way into my late thirties and even my forties—when I finally found my women. I think you know them when you find them. Some were coaching clients who turned into beautiful friendships, after we had finished working formally together. I met my best friend when she showed up to a writers' circle I was running. As I looked at her, I just felt something click. It was like a door suddenly opened or a veil was lifted. I could really see her, even though we had just met. Years later, she would tell me that I was the best friend she had waited many lifetimes for. I felt exactly the same way.

It's a sacred friendship, as are many others I have formed with women throughout the years. As I sit here now and think about the circle of women I am passing through this stage of life with, I finally know what sacred female relationships look like. They are connected, strong, kind, loving, fierce, knowing, supportive, nurturing, real, gentle, spiritual, honest, trusting, fragile, defining and true. And very, very sacred.

AFFIRMATION

I develop and nurture my sacred female friendships.

YOUR SACRED PLACE

Your sacred space is where you can find yourself again and again.
~ JOSEPH CAMPBELL

D o you have a sacred place, a specific space or area that is reserved for you to think, work, practise devotion, or just be? In these busy times, it's essential that we have a space to retreat to. While my entire home feels like sacred space to me, the area at the end of my bed where I have my yoga mat, meditation cushion and altar is deeply sacred, as is the small landing at the top of the stairs that is my office, filled with things I love that inspire me and that I hold sacred. It's where I do the vast majority of my work and writing.

In *The Power of Myth*, Joseph Campbell writes beautifully about this:

> *A sacred place is an absolute necessity for anybody today. This is a place where you can simply experience and bring forth what you are and what you might be. This is the place of creative incubation. At first you may find that nothing happens there. But if you have a sacred place and use it, something eventually will happen.*

Where might your sacred place be? It may be a room, or a spot under an old oak tree in your backyard. Find a place you can deem sacred and visit there as often as you can, to come back home to yourself.

AFFIRMATION
I create a sacred place to retreat to, tune in, create or just be.

SACRED SELF-CARE

There must be quite a few things a hot bath
won't cure, but I don't know many of them.

~ SYLVIA PLATH

You could say that this entire book is about sacred self-care. It's about getting to know yourself more intimately, understanding your needs and learning to honour all parts of yourself.

How we care for ourselves ripples through every part of our being and our life. When we're nurturing and loving, we feel that love through every layer of our vibration. We also show others how to love and care for us, by how we love and care for ourselves. If we put our needs at the bottom of the list, we may find that other people will put our needs there too. This is especially important for the carers, the nurturers, the doers and the strongest among us, who may know how to take care of others but rarely look after themselves.

There are a thousand different ways to practise self-care. Here are some beautiful and nurturing sacred practices you can bring into your days. Choose what calls to you, and use these or other practices to support you on your path. Perhaps bring one new ritual into your life each week and luxuriate in really loving yourself on a sacred and soulful level.

Grounding and earthing

Many of us have lost our sacred connection to the earth, always being indoors or, when we are outside, having our feet covered. Earthing is the Ayurvedic practice (the ancient healing system of India) of connecting to the rhythms and cycles of Mother Earth.

Walk in a garden, your own or one nearby; sit under a big tree with your hands on the roots or your back against the trunk; enjoy the beauty of flowers; walk barefoot in the grass, feeling the soil beneath your feet. Feel the vibration of the earth pulsing through you, as you connect with the Great Mother.

Bathing

The art of bathing is a beautiful way to relax at the end of the day, or any time you really want to nurture yourself. You can turn any bath into a spa-like experience, creating a sanctuary at home. Bathing is a wonderful way to clear your energy, as well as replenish and calm your body and mind. Gather a few candles, some essential oils, flowers in a small vase, and healing bath salts like magnesium or sea salt. Add the oils to the salt, then add to the running bathwater. Use calming oils like lavender, chamomile or rose for a blissful self-care experience.

Self-massage

It's wonderful to receive a massage from someone else, but not always possible to have one regularly. However, you can indulge in the practice of abhyanga or self-massage, which is a beautiful way to nurture your sacred self. Stemming from Ayurveda, it's not only a beautiful experience, it also helps to release toxins from our systems, is relaxing, helps ease joints and muscles, and helps our skin glow. Using a carrier oil like coconut, sesame or almond, place it in a small bowl together with a few drops of your favourite essential oil. Working your way from your feet upwards, use long strokes and work in circular motions up and across your entire body. Let the oil soak in before getting dressed (wipe the bottoms of your feet so you don't slip) or do this before bed in the evening.

Beauty rituals

Taking care of our skin can become perfunctory in the busyness of our days. But taking a few extra moments once a week to really nurture our skin through a beauty routine can be good for the soul, as well as being calming and relaxing for our spirit. Create your own natural beauty products (like face masks) using avocado or oatmeal, or use a favourite product that you have. Steaming your face, applying a nourishing serum and then a face mask (which you can leave on for a few hours while you are at home) then finishing with your favourite moisturiser is a simple yet indulgent ritual you can practise at home as often as time allows.

Tea rituals

From spending years in Asia, I've come to appreciate the simplicity and beauty of a tea ritual. Rather than rushing to prepare your tea and then drinking it while you do other things, the ritual of a tea ceremony encourages the practice of mindfulness, silence and connection to self. Tea is incredibly healing and I always have an array of organic loose-leaf tea at my home. My friends and clients love coming over, and always delight in the simple ceremony of gathering the small tea cups and a beautiful teapot, making the tea and then sitting together, communing and enjoying it together. Anytime you feel like a moment of respite, mindfully make yourself a cup or pot of herbal tea and simply sit and savour the moment while you enjoy it.

AFFIRMATION

I practise sacred self-care to nourish and nurture myself.

SET A SACRED ALTAR

Simple rituals are a smoke signal to the Universe that
we are ready to work and play and make some magic.

~ AMANDA GIBBY PETERS, *Simple Shui*

D o you have an altar space in your home? An altar sounds
fancy, but it's simply a place where you can gather objects
that are meaningful and sacred to you. It's a place where you
can pause, breathe, perhaps meditate, reflect on things, or pause
for a moment.

In my home, I have a number of small altars throughout my
space. One on the small entrance table with a candle, ceramic
cross box, Ganesha statue and some shells from my travels, with
some small art pieces and cards in frames hung above. When I
enter, it reminds me when I enter that I am coming into a sacred
place. It helps my guests' pause as they enter, and get an instant
sense of calm and joy.

I have another in my bedroom, my main larger altar that
supports my spiritual practice. On top of my wooden chest of
drawers, I have some favourite spiritual books; current cards
from decks on Goddesses or wellbeing that I'm working with;
ceramic tiles of Hindu deities Lakshmi, Saraswati and Durga
that I lovingly bought at a favourite market; crystals, mala beads,
sage and palo santo for clearing the energy; and other beautiful
objects that I hold dear to my heart.

When I host events in my lounge room, bringing women
together in circle, I create an altar on the table in the middle of
the room. I'll gather things that are meaningful for the day or
evening, typically a deity statue, flowers, crystals, affirmations,

art work, essential oils. It becomes a focal energy point for our work together.

When I travel, I create a small altar in the room wherever I am staying, to create a sense of home, connection and sacredness when I am away. I always have my diffuser and essential oils in this space too. They both help to ground me, no matter where I am.

Altars help focus the energy and bring a place of peace, surrender, practice and connection. They can be small, large, permanent or highly changeable. We can change our altar at every full or new moon, releasing the old or welcoming in new energy, as well as setting our intentions for the next cycle.

Items you can include on your altar include fresh flowers, crystals, affirmations, cards, quotes that inspire you, a favourite book, personal mementos (photos of loved ones, teachers, meaningful objects), things collected that you love (feathers, sea shells), incense, essential oils, candles, images of deities or Goddesses and so much more. The list is very personal and will depend on what you relate to and what's meaningful and sacred to you.

Spend some time collecting your own objects, find a sacred space and a surface like a small table, then create your own altar. You will find that as you tend to it, make offerings there like lighting incense or placing a fresh flower, and meditate in front of it or sit in reflection or journal, you will start to build up a beautiful sacred energy, and want to return again and again to nurture and replenish yourself.

AFFIRMATION
I create a sacred space for myself.

LOVE THEM AND LET THEM GO

Love is just a tool to remind us who we are
And that we are not alone when we're walking in the dark.

~ RUDIMENTAL, *These Days*

R elationships are sacred. Not all of them of course, but most have some sacred message for us on our path to becoming whole. And some change us, deep down into our soul, like the one I had a few years after my divorce. It lasted many years, and there were special and transformative moments. But looking back, we were two broken people coming together, having found one another in the darkness after marriage breakdowns. It never had a chance of working. But back then in my thirties, I was still naive about what it really meant for two whole people to join together to make each other happy, rather than try to fill each other up and plug the gaps left in broken and damaged hearts.

His kids plus my son, at different life stages, just as we both were. It was destined for disaster. And devastating heartbreak. We held on for too long, neither of us wanting to let go of the love that ran deep, that had lit something in both of us that we didn't want to extinguish. So we stayed, while both scratching around for something else to fill the hole. For me, freedom. For him, peace. And we both knew that neither would be found with the other.

Sometimes we find pieces of ourselves in another sacred soul, and knowing them helps us reclaim a little of what we have lost. The connection soothes us, like putting balm on an itch we knew we needed to scratch but could never reach. But we also need to be wise enough, whole enough, to let go of whatever isn't meant for us. To take the lesson, pack up the pieces of ourselves that remain, and walk away. Being grateful for what was. And hopeful for what can still be.

He moved on quite quickly as it turned out. I was standing in my mother's kitchen the day I found out he had remarried. It was less than six months after we parted; the vision of tears streaming down his face as he left for the last time was still a scorching memory. I was beyond shocked, my hand clasping over my mouth as I gasped out loud. I felt heartbroken all over again. But I also knew somewhere beneath the shards of glass in my heart that my future was not tied to his, that my path was too brightly lit for him to walk with me, and that my most sacred path, at that time, needed to be walked in solitude.

When we spoke a year later, when I rang to wish him well and congratulate him on becoming a father again, I asked how it was being married for a second time. 'It's comfortable' he said, a settled tone in his voice. He was seeking a comfortable relationship. I was seeking to light the world on fire. It was a miracle that our paths had crossed in the first place—only because of a post-graduate class and two adjoining seats in the same study group. Fate. Destiny. Further steps along the unveiled path that is our mysterious life.

This passage always makes my breath catch in my throat when I hear it, and then makes my heart soften. It's a song called *These Days* by Rudimental:

I know you moved on to someone new. Hope life is beautiful.
You were the light for me to find my truth. I just wanna say, thank you.
Leaving to find my soul. Told her I had to go.
And I know it ain't pretty, when our hearts get broke.

Too young to feel this old. Watching us both turn cold.
Oh, I know it ain't pretty when two hearts get broke.

Our hearts do get broken. In the words of Leonard Cohen: *There is a crack in everything, that's how the light gets in.* Sometimes we have to love them and let them go. Let them be the light that helps us find our truth. And just say, thank you.

AFFIRMATION

I release what is no longer meant for me along my sacred path.

LOVE WHERE YOU LIVE

The ordinary acts we practice every day at home are of more
importance to the soul than their simplicity might suggest.

~ THOMAS MOORE, IRISH POET

We don't always get to choose where we live. Circumstances can dictate our living arrangements, who we live with, or the location. But we can make the most of where we are at any given time. Think about your current home, then make a list of the things you absolutely love about it. It could be the light that comes in through the kitchen window, or the hardwood floors. Maybe it's the space at the end of your bed where you meditate, or the fact that you have parking in a really busy street. Write it all down. It will help you appreciate it all the more for intentionally noticing it.

What don't you love so much? Maybe it's noisy, or you have neighbours who talk all night on their deck. Perhaps your home is really small and you would dearly love more space for the kids to run around. You might have family staying and not have a lot of space of your own right now. Or your place may be really run-down, needing a good coat of paint and some extra love.

During the next three months, what could you do to make your home more like you want it to be? Make a list of the small things, the medium effort things and the major projects that would enhance what you love and improve on the things that need some care.

It's so important that we have a sacred home to live in. Whatever your current situation, you can always create small ways to love your space more. Fill your home with positive energy, radiant white light, flowers or house plants, positive affirmations, crystals, beautiful images and positive intentions. And watch your home become more sacred every day.

AFFIRMATION
I create a home I love.

SEEING YOUR MOST SACRED SELF

Perfectionism is self-abuse of the highest order.
~ ANNE WILSON SCHAEF

There's a question that's guaranteed to set us up for failure. While it's often asked with good intentions, in reality it often leads us to feel bad about ourselves. Here's the question: *How can I be my best possible self in every moment?* You see the problems right away, don't you?

Best possible self. Every moment. It's got failure written all over it. In a world where you are probably already too hard on yourself, why would you want to set up a scenario where you're judging yourself by an impossible yardstick, every day?

Let's be more gentle with ourselves. You will have good moments, where you're closer to a version of who you want to be. And you'll have many moments where you are far from it. We all do. It's called life. Just like our journeys with confidence and purpose, we don't leap to self-acceptance in one great bound. We're not Superwoman. But we can inch ourselves closer, with daily actions that can set us up for our own version of success.

Practise softening into your most sacred self. Sit into your feminine energy. Realise the truth of who you are in your essence. Tune in to the vision of the woman you are when you are fully aligned. This is the only version of yourself you ever need to be. And you don't have to travel far to meet her. You just need to come back home.

AFFIRMATION
I soften into my sacred feminine essence.

GET SACRED WITH YOUR
BOUNDARIES

Only through skill does balance come.

~ DONNA FARHI

Think back to the last time you felt resentful, annoyed or that someone was trying to take advantage of you. You probably experienced one of your boundaries being crossed. As women, our boundaries are really important. They're a core part of putting limits on how we interact with others, what is and isn't acceptable, what we will and won't stand for. Once we are clear about what's most important to us—our life vision, purposeful work, relationships, and other aspects we cover in this book—then we can determine where we need to set our boundaries, and how we will go about holding those lines.

Our boundaries can be emotional, psychological, energetic or physical. People placing demands on your time, energy or emotions can cause you to lose track of what you really want or need, causing you to get sucked into their agenda. It can leave you feeling stressed, overwhelmed and can cause major issues in relationships.

The key is to not only work out where you need boundaries in your work and personal life, but to make those boundaries sacred. This means that you don't simply set and forget them, or let them be crossed easily because it's too hard to keep them in place. It's about setting your intention about why they matter to you, and how they protect what is most sacred in your life. That could be time with your children or family, energy you are keeping for your creative pursuits or spiritual practice, precious time with friends, or time alone to reset and recharge.

You don't have to explain to others why your boundaries are important, as they really aren't anyone else's business except your own. You get to choose where you need them. You get to decide how you will design them. And you also get to decide how and when you will negotiate them, if and when you choose to. Keep them sacred.

AFFIRMATION
My boundaries protect what is most important to me.

LIGHTEN UP

Everyone shines, given the right lighting.

~ SUSAN CAIN

How much pressure do you put on yourself to be the best version of yourself? Be honest. I bet it can get pretty intense in that head of yours. And I would wage money that it's the cause of a lot of your stress and anxiety, and those feelings of 'less than' and 'not good enough' that you carry around with you everywhere.

I'd love you to give yourself a break. Cut yourself some slack. Go just a bit easier on yourself. Realise that you are doing the very best you can. That you have a lot going on. And that reading all those magazine articles, looking at social media all day, or reality TV where people look like they have their lives altogether and wrapped up in a pretty bow is feeding your sub-conscious with pictures of the impossible. It feeds your insecurities. It sends you into judgement and comparison. And it keeps you stuck.

So lighten up a little. Take a break from the full-time job of self-improvement and personal development. Take a step back. Take a long deep breath. Then work on the small ways to step into the woman you are wanting to be. Do it with grace and ease. And know that as you show up with more self-compassion, you're creating the space to tap into your most sacred self, and also creating space for the women around you to do the same.

AFFIRMATION
I create space to lighten and step into my sacredness.

UNPACK YOUR DREAMS

Look and you will find it—
what is unsought will go undetected.

~ SOPHOCLES

If you opened up an imaginary drawer where you had placed your dreams over the course of your life, what would you find? Think all the way back to your childhood. Even as I write this, I get a sense of sadness and longing in my heart. All of the hopes that were abandoned for so many reasons: dreams of being a working actress that I focused on for the first 23 years of my life but gave up on too soon, without really pursuing them; dreams of a family with three kids and as many dogs in a rambling home, that died along with my divorce; and countless other dreams that never saw the light of day, because they were pushed aside before they even had a hope of being born.

What would be in your drawer? Are there a few poignant dreams, or is your drawer jam-packed, stuffed so full that there are corners poking out through the closed drawer? If you opened that drawer and started to pull out the scraps of paper that represented each dream, what would you find?

Are they old dreams or recent dreams? What are you putting in the drawer right now? This year, this month, this week, or even today?

And here is the real question to ask yourself: *Are you happy to leave those dreams where they are, or are there dreams in there that you would really love to dust off, and finally bring to life?*

For me, the actress and family dreams are ones that have long been replaced with the reality of my life. My career took me in a different and fulfilling direction, and the family I longed for turned into the smaller and irreplaceable unit of my son and me—more than I could have ever dreamed possible. And yet there are others that I am still trying to bring to life: being as brave as my fifteen-year-old self, before I learnt how to conform and fit into the mould of what society expected of me. Dreams of the next phase of my career and business. Giving myself permission to dream all of them in the way that suits me now. And dreams for other people that are becoming more important than my own.

What will you give yourself permission to dream about at this point in your life? Take those dreams out of the drawer. Pin them to the wall, write them on your mirror, tattoo them on your arm if you need to. It's time. To dream all the dreams. And to bring them to life.

AFFIRMATION

I give myself permission to dream my dreams.

EVERYTHING IS PROGRESS

The prize is in the process.
~ BARON BAPTISTE

Sometimes we feel like only the big steps matter. That only when we achieve a major milestone are we actually moving forwards. But in truth, every single thing you do is progress. The smallest thing you tick off your to-do list today is inching you closer to your goal. And whenever you are being intentional with your actions, however tiny or monumental they are, then you are honouring what is most sacred about you, and to you.

Every time you eat a little bit healthier, you are supporting your body to become more vibrant. Every moment you take a conscious breath, you're supporting your nervous system to be calm and your spirit grounded. Every time you achieve a micro goal, you're moving further towards that dream you hold so dear.

Don't overlook the little things. They all add up to help you create the life you most want to live. Keep taking small steps and realise and celebrate that as long as you keep moving forwards, you are making progress. And all progress is sacred.

AFFIRMATION
I keep moving forwards.

ALLOW THE BEAUTY IN

The human heart yearns for the beautiful in all ranks of life.
~ HARRIET BEECHER STOWE

In the hustle and bustle of life, slowing down enough to see the beauty around you can be an afterthought, if a thought at all. But noticing the beauty in everyday little things is a wonderful way to bring peace, contentment and joy into your life.

It doesn't take much effort at all. Cut some fresh flowers from your garden and put them in a vase beside your bed, so you see beauty as you wake up. Print out and pin up beautiful images from Pinterest or magazines on your walls. Look at the stars in the night sky and marvel at the moon. Admire beautiful fabric in a store, the smile on your lover's face, the glimmer of the ocean.

Beauty is around you all the time. It makes us feel more alive, more connected, and more sacred. Create a daily habit of drinking it in.

AFFIRMATION
I pay attention to and soak up the sacred beauty all around me.

SACRED FEMINISM

I am not free while any woman is unfree,
even when her shackles are very different from my own.

~ AUDRE LORDE

We're living in a time when feminism is going through a new uprising. Global women's marches, fighting for equality for all, for women's rights, children's rights, human rights, *Black Lives Matter* and many other causes are being supported not only by women who identify as feminists, but by all genders, ages and races, who see themselves as part of the feminist movement. Because really, at the end of the day it's about human rights, and none of us can rest until we are all free and safe.

As women at this time in history, one of the critical questions for us all to ask ourselves is: *Who is our feminism for?* Is it for women who just look like us and have the same issues as us, perhaps the ones we fight for in workplace diversity and inclusion, as we aim to close the pay gap and get more women into leadership? Or is it also for refugee women, homeless women, women suffering domestic abuse or living in shelters? Is it for the woman fleeing her homeland for fear of death, or for the woman working in a cafe on the minimum wage, one of four jobs she works to feed her three children who she hardly sees as she works around the clock? Is it for gay women, queer women, transgender women?

Is your feminism of the militant kind, women fighting against men, backlashing against the patriarchy? Or is it an inclusive feminism, intersectional feminism, fighting to unite all people, to help everyone who needs it rise up with the belief that when one woman rises, we all rise, and the whole of society is uplifted?

Who is your feminism for? This is a time to open our eyes, open our hearts, and expand our consciousness and feminism for all who need it. This is a time to make our feminism sacred. The very future of humanity depends upon it.

AFFIRMATION

My feminism is sacred and for all.

AUTHENTIC ACTIVISM

The world will not be destroyed by those who do evil,
but by those who watch them without doing anything.

~ ALBERT EINSTEIN

It can be hard for many women to think about becoming activists. Life is busy and often stressful. That's not an excuse, just a reality. For so many women, just getting through the day, dealing with work, family responsibilities, child raising, relationships and health challenges—all while managing to pay the bills and keep everything moving—is an overwhelming amount to deal with.

Add to that the fact that activism sounds like a scary word. What does it mean? How would I become an activist? What would I actually do? They are all valid questions. There is also a lot of judgement and shame around how much people are doing, how they are helping, what their particular brand of activism looks like. Is it social justice for Black, Indigenous and People of Colour; is it fighting for women's rights, workplace equality and equal pay; perhaps you're an activist for saving the environment; maybe it's rescuing children from human trafficking or from the hunger crisis; or perhaps you're passionate about refugees, people in political asylum or getting homeless people off the streets? It can be overwhelming and you may want to fix everything, but not knowing where to start, you go back to the noisiness of your everyday life.

Some people aren't built for the frontline. Instead they are light bearers, prayer bringers, healers, teachers, spiritual activists, seekers, mystics, meditators, yogis and others who want to be peace bringers, who wish to be part of the solution in other ways.

The bottom line here is that we are all being called to act. To get off our yoga mats or out of our church pews and into the world. Because the world needs saving, perhaps now more than at any other time in history. And the world will be saved by us, women who are awake or awakening to their power, and are ready to be active in bringing solutions, not looking away from the problems because they seem too large or too scary to deal with. Not looking away because we think that someone else will fix them, deal with them, address them. That someone else is now us. We need to become the conscious leaders, to stand up and say, 'Enough, not here, not anymore.'

It's yoga teacher, Seane Corn, co-creating *Off the Mat, Into the World*, 'to help people bridge the gap between yoga, transformational work, social justice and activism from the inside out.'

It's Dr Jackie Huggins, Indigenous Australian author, historian and Aboriginal rights activist of the Bidjara and Birri-Gubba Juru peoples, and her work with Indigenous people, particularly in reconciliation, literacy, women's issues and social justice.

It's Malala Yousafzai, human rights activist, youngest Nobel Peace Prize laureate, and founder of the Malala Fund, fighting for the right for every girl to go to school.

It's teenagers in America saying 'no more' to school shootings and creating a movement to change gun laws.

It's Glennon Doyle and others including Brené Brown, Cheryl Strayed and Elizabeth Gilbert, creating *Together Rising*, using their platforms and voices to raise awareness and money for areas of crisis.

And it's also small, local, everyday actions that make a difference.

It's my friend Sarah, who donates her time to the local women's refuge whenever she can, between school drop-offs and her day job.

It's my girlfriends and I taking clothes to the charity that helps women get back into the workforce, after being homeless or being victims of domestic abuse.

It's donating to the local op shop; helping out at the local soup kitchen for homeless people; creating inclusive spaces so that marginalised people have an opportunity to speak and be heard. It's participating in your local area clean-up day, collecting rubbish and plastic in the park or along the coastline. It's donating small amounts to youth charities, to provide a bed or hot meal for a homeless teenager.

It's having conversations. Listening. Helping out in whatever small way is possible. It's raising awareness if we have a platform. Calling out injustice. Amplifying the voices of others, wherever we are able. It's being conscious global citizens. It's looking, rather than turning away, when we see something painful.

We each need to find our own authentic path to becoming an activist. It looks different for everyone, and some have more capacity, more resilience, more time, money or energy than others. But the bottom line is that for all of us, no matter our colour, race, gender, age, ability, sexual preference or situation, it's time to become fully awake, to stand up and to share our voices for those who cannot stand up for themselves.

As Jean Shinoda Bolen says in *Urgent Message from Mother: Gather the Women, Save the World*: 'I believe that the thought that women together can change the world is emerging into the minds and hearts of many of us, and that the vessel for personal and planetary evolution is the circle with a spiritual center.'

May we journey together for the good of all. May we understand our privilege and use it to help others who need it. May we refrain from judging how others show up, and rather play whatever small or large part we can. As women, may we be conscious, awake, inclusive leaders, who will indeed change the world. And may we all come to recognise that our work here is sacred.

AFFIRMATION
I am awake, ready and willing to play
my part in healing the world.

COME HOME TO YOURSELF

If you travel far enough, one day you will recognise yourself
coming down the road to meet you.
And you will say YES.

~ MARION WOODMAN

When it all comes down to it, our only real role in life is to learn how to come home to ourselves. It's less about who we want or need to become, and more about remembering who we actually are. Less doing. More being.

It's about uncovering all we have lost, and coming back to who we know we were before everyone else told us who to be. It's stripping away the layers and the masks and the roles and the expectations and giving yourself permission to be who you truly are. The you of your soul. It's about remembering the truth and depth of your sacredness.

Go gently with this. Breathe more deeply. Practise quiet contemplation. Listen to your intuition. Learn to trust yourself. You have all of the wisdom inside you to return to your truest nature. It's time to come home.

AFFIRMATION

I am home when I am my most sacred self.

PART 8

Courage

WHY NOT YOU?

*When I stand before God at the end of my life, I would
hope that I would not have a single bit of talent left
and could say, 'I used everything you gave me'.*

~ ERMA BOMBECK

S it and think about your biggest, craziest dreams for a moment.
Really feel into them. What are you doing? Who are you
with? What difference are you making? How does it feel? Now
think about all of the stories (thoughts) that just came up right
alongside those dreams. I bet they were thoughts like: *That will
never happen. I couldn't possibly do that. No-one would buy it, listen to
me, or let me. I can't afford it. It's all been done before.*

And this one: *Those dreams are for other people, not for me.*
Not for me.

If you suspended your self-judgement for just a moment, and
thought of the very best possible outcome for your life, what do
you see?

Now think about who else is doing something like what you
want to be doing. Unless you are a scientist or doing PhD research,
there is nothing really new, so someone somewhere has gone
before you. Think about who that someone is, or multiple people
who have done or who are living what you dream of being.

Sit into that. Feel into it.

Now I want you to lean right into this next question. Come
even closer. Come all the way in. Are you ready?

Here is the question: *Why not you?*

I want to know, really know, why not you?

Why can't you have this dream you are dreaming about, if you're prepared to do the work? If you're willing to show up for it. If you're willing to claim it and then go after it every day. If all of the 'ifs' are answered. If you just decide to be brave and go for it, with a healthy dose of planning and support.

Are you still listening? *Why not you?*

Let me answer that for you. There is no reason.

This thing is for you. We only receive whispers of inspiration for dreams that we have the capacity to manifest.

So go. Go do that thing you're dreaming about. Go now.

AFFIRMATION
I am the chosen one. I bring my dreams to life.

LOSE SIGHT OF PERFECTION

The greatest thing I ever did was lost sight of perfection.
Forgot it existed. Stopped trying to gather it with my
hands. Stopped thinking it was tangible. Definable.
Something I could buy. Something I could be.

~ L.E. BOWMAN

It's one of the leading things that robs us of our happiness: forever trying to grasp for perfection. Our constant grappling with questions about whether we are enough—strong enough, pretty enough, smart enough, good enough—leaves us with a constant feeling of seeking, never relaxing into our being, like we're constantly scratching on the closed door of our most sacred self.

Author Anne Lamott describes perfectionism as: *the voice of the oppressor, the enemy of the people. It will keep you cramped and insane your whole life.* When we're chasing perfectionism, a quality that can only ever elude us, we can never be whole, always cramping ourselves (as Lamott says), squeezing and shapeshifting until we finally feel like we fit. The problem is we never do, so long as we deny ourselves our truest self.

If you've wondered why you can never relax, or be happy with what you have, then you know you're in the perfectionist zone. The promotion you worked so hard for, the children you longed for, the fitness you finally gained, the number of awards you won, the amount of charity work you dedicate yourself to. But you never have a sense of arriving or of it being enough, because you're always still striving for the next thing, the one that will finally be the bandage for the scab you have been forever picking at that won't heal.

Our perfectionist selves live in fear of never being enough, of failing, of being seen as less than we know we are. But when we live in fear, our choices and actions are misguided. We spend our time scratching around in our heads, instead of leading and living from our hearts. We focus on external achievements, rather than intrinsic meaning and satisfaction. We burn ourselves out striving, instead of loving ourselves with self-care.

In the following chapters on Courage, we look at many of the ways we can let go of our perfectionist beliefs and behaviours, to stop running and seeking approval, and to soften into what we need to finally arrive home to ourselves. For now, simply start to notice where you are being a perfectionist. When you do, gently breathe yourself into the present moment, feel into your body and breath, and repeat to yourself today's affirmation. And remember what Jane Fonda shared after a life-long battle with perfectionism: *The challenge is not to be perfect ... it's to be whole.*

AFFIRMATION
Wherever I find myself right now, I know I am enough.

EVERYTHING DEPENDS ON
HOW MUCH YOU TRUST

Don't be surprised at how quickly the Universe
will move with you once you have decided.

~ JORDAN BACH

If you just knew. Knew that everything you are working for is going to work out. That it will all come to light in the best possible way. Better than you could even dream of.

What would you do? Would you get clearer, try harder, show up more, be bolder? Would you back yourself in ways that just don't seem logical from what you can see now?

If you just knew. Knew that you were the best in the world at what you do. That people cared about it. That they were watching. That you were seen.

What would you do? Would you commit to your work, nurture your art, take yourself more seriously, make it matter? Would you get up earlier, be more present, say 'no' to what doesn't matter, or just care more?

If you just knew. If you simply trusted. That you were being guided. That it was all divinely timed. That what is for you will not pass you by. That if it is here with you, then it is meant for you. That you really can, honest to goodness, trust the journey.

If you just knew and trusted that you were going to be okay. That it will all go to plan. That everything will work out just like it's meant to.

What would you do?

AFFIRMATION
I trust that everything is working out for my highest good.

THE PERMISSION GAP

The way you tell your story to yourself matters.
~ AMY CUDDY

I've always wanted to ...
I've stopped myself because ...
What I needed was ...

We all have things that we want to do, dream of doing, or secretly long for. But a lot of those things, big or small, never see the light of day. Take a moment and think about how you would complete these sentences. Just one minute. Go on, I'll wait.

I've always wanted to ...
I've stopped myself because ...
What I needed was ...

This right here is what I call The Permission Gap—that gap between the things we've always wanted to do, and the things we've actually done.

There are typically three reasons we get stuck from moving forward with the things we really want:

1. We need someone to tell us that it's going to be okay.
2. We need support for our choices, so we know we aren't totally crazy.
3. We want someone to stop us, because it's generally easier not to jump.

We want to be validated. We need to be validated. We want to know we are going to be safe, that it's all going to work out. That our world won't fall apart. That we won't, God forbid, fail.

Here are some common desires that can put women firmly in the permission gap:

- Quit a job
- Start a business
- Leave a relationship
- Be more creative
- Move countries
- Get a tattoo
- Write a book
- Ask for more support
- Start a side hustle
- Completely change careers
- Speak the truth
- Be more real

We get lured into the permission gap by our stories. Not our real stories, not the truth. The stories we tell ourselves about what will happen if we show up, act, be ourselves, take a risk or do what we really want to.

Perhaps some of these stories will sound familiar:

- People won't like it
- People won't like me
- It will be too hard
- I'll be judged
- People will think I'm crazy
- My partner/parent/kid/boss/friends won't approve
- I'll look silly
- I won't fit in
- People will be upset

- They will say 'no'
- *I will fail*

But here's the question I want you to really sit with: *What's the cost of living your life in the permission gap?*

What is the cost of your inaction? What are you missing out on? Adventure perhaps. Following your true passion and living your life on purpose. Meeting your soul sisters or life partner. Being the person you were put on this earth to be.

Maybe just living your life with more freedom and lightness and joy, because you aren't being constantly weighed down with the heaviness of the thoughts, fears and irrational stories that keep you stuck.

What if you just said 'yes' to yourself? What if you picked one thing that you currently want to do and, instead of deliberating in the permission gap, you just went ahead and did it? What if?

I dare you to pick one small thing. Or pick one crazy big thing. And take the action you are longing to take.

Write the book. Start the side hustle. Leave the relationship. Book the holiday. Ask for the promotion. Build your brand. Sell your house. Become an artist. Kick out your toxic flatmate. Dye your hair red. Get the tattoo. Volunteer in Nepal. Become a vegan. Speak truth to power. Just say 'no'. Finally, say 'yes'!

The permission gap is not a place you can live your one big glorious life from. It's a persistent safe zone. It's too comfortable. And nothing great happens there.

Be brave, dear friend. Give yourself permission to not only want what you want, but to take action. Because greatness is in the doing. And the only permission you need is your own.

AFFIRMATION
I give myself permission to fully live.

THE JOURNEY TO BRAVE

Bravery is rarely about doing something bold. The most brave act is often a quiet, internal moment when we sit in great discomfort, close our eyes and gently whisper, 'I will stay'.

~ LAURA MCKOWEN

I was on the phone to one of my best friends for a long-awaited catch-up. We lived in different cities and though we saw each other every few months, it always seemed far too long between visits.

Sharing stories back and forth of our recent trials and adventures, a common theme emerged among the happy tears and laughter. Deep inner transformation was being reflected by massive outward changes in both our businesses and personal lives. We were showing up to do the work and, as often happens, our worlds were shifting in response. And it wasn't always comfortable.

As we were soulfully sharing our respective journeys, I paused, suddenly realising just how far we had both come on our path to wake up as women.

'Hey, what's going on here?' I laughed. 'So much is changing so quickly for both of us.'

'You know,' said Bec, taking a deep breath and with a long poignant exhale, 'We're just getting really fucking brave.'

There. Right there. The truth spoken.

We were just getting really, truly, profoundly brave.

AFFIRMATION
I am brave.

SHE PERSISTED

If God gave you the vision, God will give you the provision.

~ IYANLA VANZANT

I saw Oprah Winfrey on an old television interview. It was around the time she was about to embark on hosting her first talk show.

Only in her early thirties at the time, here was a woman who had such deep-seated confidence and self-belief that it seemed to emanate from her very soul.

Poised. Articulate. Sure.

The interviewer asked her, in a somewhat patronising tone, what she would do if she didn't succeed. With a steeliness in her eyes and conviction in her voice Oprah replied, 'I will. I know I will.'

No doubt. No question mark. Solid, grounded certainty.

When she closed up her talk show after 25 years and took a major risk to start her television network OWN, she again faced potential failure.

Her show was the hallmark of her success. It created the woman, the self-made billion dollar fortune, the legend that Oprah became.

Oprah had risked everything to walk away and OWN had a few shaky moments. The critics gathered and salivated. She battled that potential failure. And yet, she moved forward anyway. Because she had a vision of what was next for her.

She knew that she was destined to create an even greater platform for her message. And, with that same steely determination, she persisted.

AFFIRMATION
I persist in the face of failure.

HAVE THE COURAGE TO QUIT

*Fear is the cheapest room in the house. I'd like
to see you in better living conditions.*

~ HAFEZ

You've invested years working on a project. So much money, time, energy, passion and tears have gone into it. And yet you just know it's not working, that it will never be what you had hoped for. Do you keep pushing forwards, relentlessly trying to make it into something? Maybe. But perhaps the smartest and bravest thing you can do is walk away. Cut your losses. Learn the lessons. And move on to something that has the potential to be all you want it to be.

Your relationship has seen better days. You used to be so connected, so in love, couldn't get enough of each other. And then slowly over time, so slowly and subtly you didn't realise it was happening, the walls came up. Small at first, little annoyances you could brush off like flies, but they grew into an impenetrable barrier to your connection. To intimacy. It wasn't like there was a betrayal, but in a way there was. A betrayal to the truth of the relationship. To the soul of who you both signed up to be. Do you stay, soldier on, push through and try to reclaim what it was? Or not.

Courage isn't always just about perseverance. Sometimes, the most courageous act is to know when it's time to stop.

Walking away is hard. It can be painful.

But when the last fight has been fought and all the words have been said, courage tells us to bless the situation and move on.

Pushing through may seem like the most courageous move. But if you know in your truest heart that it's over, then have the courage to quit.

BE JUST 10% BRAVER

*Fear is the chasm between where you are right
now and where you want to be. Courage is
the bridge that will help you cross it.*

~ REBECCA RAY

I was on the phone with one of my long-term coaching clients.
We were talking about the new role she had just stepped
into—a position she had earned based on years of hard work,
proving herself, and achieving great results. Finally she was being
recognised with this promotion.

She was feeling good about it; excited and energised by all
of the possibilities. Yet as we were speaking, it was clear she was
still questioning herself. Did she really deserve the role? Should
she ask the questions that were on her mind during initial meetings, when she thought the wrong decisions were being made?
Should she share her ideas yet? Did she know enough? Should
she even be there?

All questions based on stories, self-doubt and limiting beliefs.
And at the bottom of it all was the question that haunts many
of us women —am I really good enough?

We worked our way through every issue, question, story and
scenario and closed many things out, so she could move ahead
in a positive way.

And then I asked her, 'If you could be just 10% braver
tomorrow, what would you do?'

'Hmmm, great question' she said, as she pondered her answer.
'I'd speak up in the meeting. I'd ask the question. I'd put forward
the idea. I'd step into just a little bit more of my power.'

And with that, I could feel her relax, breath more easily and sit more deeply into the possibilities of what she could actually do in this new role, if she gave herself permission to really show up.

10% braver. It's not that scary. Not too far outside your comfort zone. Doesn't require any life-changing or heroic efforts. Mitigates your risk. Keeps you safe. But still inches you towards the best and most powerful version of yourself.

At the end of the meeting, the end of the shift or the end of the day, it still leaves you feeling like you showed up for yourself. That you didn't diminish yourself, that you owned your worth and backed yourself just that little bit more.

10% braver. What would it mean for you?

AFFIRMATION
I inch myself towards my bravest self.

STOP FIGHTING

She was powerful not because she wasn't scared,
but because she went on so strongly despite the fear.

~ **ATTICUS POETRY,** *The Dark Between Stars*

In her creative treatise *Big Magic,* Elizabeth Gilbert gave us a new take on fear. She shared how she deals with fear by telling it that it can be along for the car ride, but it must sit in the backseat; it cannot give directions and it will never, ever, be allowed to choose the music. The most important thing she says about fear is that we need it. It keeps us safe. Alive even. And all of this BS about getting rid of our fear and living a fearless existence? Well, that's just rubbish.

Overcoming fear is so overrated. Imagine if we took all of the energy spent trying to be fearless, and channelled it into constructive energy towards what we are trying to create. Take this book for example. There is a lot of fear in writing this book— well, any book actually. Every time I sit down and stare at the blank screen I have a dialogue in my head that goes something like this:

> *Do I have anything to say? Will this be interesting? Does anyone care? Will anyone even read this thing? Why am I bothering, it's all been said and written and read before. I'm going to spend all of this time and effort and will it actually make a difference? Will I even be able to finish it?*

Right there. Fear staring back at me, screaming at me from inside my head, laughing mockingly that my ego even thinks I can get this thing done, let alone that it will matter.

That fear could keep me stuck. I could spend all of my time trying to make the fear go away, squash it down, ignore it, mock it right back. But that takes so much energy. So instead, I take a really deep breath, and in my calmest, most mothering voice I say this:

Hello there. Please settle down! I know you're here for a reason and I respect that. You want to make sure I'm on my A game, that I'll give this book the attention it deserves, that I'll make it great. I get it. I appreciate that. Thank you. But really, I don't need you swirling around my brain every minute. It's distracting, annoying and it's not doing either of us any favours. So it's time to settle. I'll come to you as needed for a check-in. Until then, put your head-phones on, play some music and chill out.

Stop fighting your fear and acknowledge it. Deal with it as you would a small child. Then get back to your work, never forgetting that the world needs the gifts that only you can bring—whether you're scared or not.

AFFIRMATION
I manage my fear so it serves me. It does not control me.

THE ANTIDOTE TO FEAR

We cannot escape fear.
We can only transform it into a companion that accompanies
us on all our exciting adventures.
Take a risk a day—one small or bold stroke that will make
you feel great once you have done it.

~ SUSAN JEFFERS

Fear is a contraction. Fear wants you to stay stuck. It wants you to think about all of your mistakes, the skills you think you don't have, the reasons your ego tells you shouldn't take the next right step. Fear wants to strip you of self-confidence, because it knows that you can't move forwards without it. Fear wants to take away your faith in your own power, and in any higher power you are connected to. Fear wants to keep you firmly grounded in your small self, because it secretly knows (but doesn't want you to know) that your true self is powerful beyond measure. And fear is terrified of you in your power.

The antidote to fear is action. Once you move ahead and engage, fear loses its grip on you. It tries really hard to hold on, grasping and clutching at you as you start to shift. You get slippery as you fidget a little, settling into the possibility that yes, you are going to take that step. And once you start moving? Fear will try hard to grab you, shouting in your ear that you can't possibly do it, this thing you are moving into, and who on earth do you think you are anyway? Because it knows. That once you start to move, once you sit into your faith and build into your self-belief, once you replace your crippling worry with even the smallest action, that it will have lost its power over you. That you will be finally, or at least for this small moment of momentum, beyond its grip.

So move. Go. As gently as you need to. Take even the tiniest palpable step. But act. Move forwards, in the direction you wish to head. Dispel the worry. Keep your eyes ahead, your heart open and your mind focused on what's next. And watch your fear slouch down and slyly slip away. Or at the very least, get very, very quiet. And in that quietness, keep going.

AFFIRMATION

I take the next right action, not in the
absence of fear, but in spite of it.

YOU CAN LET IT GO

Sometimes letting go is a far greater act of
power than defending or hanging on.

~ ECKHART TOLLE

Stick with it. Tough it out. Dig in. Dig deeper. Go the distance. Play to win. Race to the finish. Get it done.

We're told in a thousand different ways to hang in there, to never quit, to always keep going, no matter what. Even when it no longer serves us.

But you know what? You can let it go. Truly, you can. For whatever reason you want. If it doesn't feel right. If the passion has died. If it was never meant to be. If you no longer love it. If your heart has moved on. If you just don't care anymore.

If you're forcing yourself. If it's just okay but you want amazing. If it's become a 'should do' or a 'have to'. If you just don't want to do it, or be it, or have it, or suffer through it, for even one more minute.

Then here's what …

You can let it go.

Right here. Right now. In this very moment.

You can release it. Walk away from it. Say goodbye to it.

You can. I promise you, you can.

If you choose to. You can let it go.

AFFIRMATION
I let go of what no longer serves me.

REJECTION WON'T KILL YOU

Nana korobi ya oki.
Fall seven times, rise eight.
~ JAPANESE PROVERB

It won't kill you.

You think it will. You think that if you ask and you are rejected, it means something bad about you. That you are less than: less than worthy, less than others, just less.

So you don't ask. You choose not to go for it: the job, the client, the project, the deal.

It's safer where you are. Right?

Actually, no. It's not.

Not safer. Not more satisfying. And certainly not more gratifying.

It's just you, stuck for fear of failure. For fear of someone saying 'no'. For fear of the dreaded rejection.

But here's the message that will set you free: *Rejection won't kill you.* It won't.

It may sting a little. It may feel like a setback. It might even hurt for a while.

But you won't die. You will survive it.

If you keep moving and trying and hoping, it will get you to your next thing, your next opportunity, your next 'yes'.

The rejections you receive along the way to your dream are exactly what you need to become who you're meant to be.

Pile them up. Pin them on the wall. Celebrate every single one them. Say a quiet 'thank you'.

Stephen King's first published novel *Carrie* was rejected so many times that he collected the rejection notes on a spike in his bedroom. It was finally published in 1974 with a print run of 30,000 copies. When the paperback version was released a year later, it sold over a million copies in twelve months. To date, King has sold more than 350 million books!

Kathryn Stockett, author of *The Help*, was rejected by more than 60 literary agents before finally gaining representation. Her debut novel has since been published in 42 languages, sold more than ten million copies and spent more than 100 weeks on *The New York Times'* bestseller list.

Sara Blakely, founder of *Spanx*, was taught by her father that failure is required on the path to success, a lesson that served her well. When she was 27, she developed a new concept for hosiery but was rejected by every company she approached. They didn't see the value in her idea. Then one man said he would back her and the rest, well, you know what they say. Sara should know about success: the net worth of Spanx is more than a billion dollars.

Failure is part of the process. It's required learning. So what will you do? You could just choose to go for it. Regardless of the outcome.

Rejection won't kill you. Failure won't stop you. Unless you let it.

AFFIRMATION
I see every 'no' as a pathway to the right 'yes'.

SHOW UP ANYWAY

You can't be that kid standing at the top of the waterslide,
overthinking it. You have to go down the chute.

~ TINA FEY

We were sitting at the helm of a 40ft yacht in the middle of the harbour, legs dangling over the edge. It felt like pure freedom. Eight years old and with a new friend, the daughter of my Dad's business associate whose yacht we were on. It was one of those days that stays with you, yet for unknown reasons.

When it was time to go home, I turned to my new friend and said, 'I'll write you a letter. As long as we make it home.'

'What do you mean?' asked my new bestie.

'Well, it's a long way back to our place and, you know, we're *driving*,' I said, completely serious and with a slight tremor.

That was a constant concern in my young life. Driving on the 22-hour road trip with my family every year to visit relatives interstate, this conversation would take place the morning of our departure:

Me: 'Dad, you're not going to drive through the winding hills are you?' My voice would shake but I was ever hopeful that a road had magically been cut through the side of the mountain during the past year.

Dad: 'You just put your head on the pillow, honey. Have a nap and we'll be there in no time.' Dad would speak calmly, avoiding the question.

I knew what that meant. Mountains. Endless winding roads, bends, hills, trucks, speed, hell. It all added up to terror for me. I would put my head under the pillow and count and pray until we miraculously reached the other side, then read voraciously for the rest of the journey as a distraction from my catastroph-ising thoughts.

For as far back as I can remember, I've had an irrational fear of being a passenger in a car. I can't explain it and neither can my parents. Nothing of note happened in my early years to bring it on. I can only think that it was something I brought in from another life; that's the only explanation that makes sense to me, woo-woo as it sounds.

I've carried this fear with me my whole life, using various techniques to manage my anxiety. Essential oils, Bach flower remedies, meditation, breathing techniques, positive visualisa-tion, jade crystals for protection, chanting mantras, praying to deities, you name it, I've done it.

And then my son turned sixteen and needed driving lessons—a single parent's nightmare. Because guess what? Tag—you're it: driving teacher! It took me five months after he got his learner's permit to summon up the courage to get in the car with him. I still remember the exact feeling: sweaty palms, heart racing, doused in lavender oil, trying not to have disastrous thoughts, praying to the angels to keep us safe.

As it turned out, he was and is a great driver. And I surprised myself. I was remarkably calm. Composed. Guiding his driving with sound instruction. No sharp intake of breath. No freaking out. Having deep insight into my passenger antics (in LA when he was eight years old, I gripped his hand so tightly in the taxi on the expressway to the airport that I nearly broke it) even he was shocked.

The fear didn't abate; it was still there under the surface every time I got in the car. But I did it anyway. I chose to do it. Because he needed to learn. Because it was my role to teach him.

Because I was more invested in him driving well and safely than I was in my anxiety. Because fear is just a story we tell ourselves, real or not. Because fear, just like courage, is often a choice. And because we can invest in a different, more positive story, and act in spite of fear—if we choose to.

AFFIRMATION

No matter how difficult it is, I move through my fear.

BE TOO MUCH

Bring all of yourself to life. And if you're
told you're too much, smile and think: Maybe.
Or maybe their capacity is too small?

~ GLENNON DOYLE

How often do you dumb yourself down during the course of a day? How many times in a week do you dim your light, so that you can shine less brightly? How many times in your life have you been told that you're 'just a bit too much' and that you need to bring it down a notch?

If you're like most of us, it's innumerable. As women, we dim ourselves every day, so many times without even noticing it. We'll be just a little bit less of ourselves, of who we really are, for fear that if we are too loud, too bright, too much, then we'll be scolded, laughed at, despised even. That there will be consequences for being who we really are and being seen for it.

This has happened since the beginning of time. They used to burn us at the stake, remember? We do remember. That's the point. We remember all too well. It's burned into our conscious-ness, scarred deep into our collective feminine memory. The warnings are there every day: don't be too brilliant, too beau-tiful, too outspoken, too talented. Don't be too much. Because the price you will pay is potentially the highest price in the land.

It may just cost you everything.

To hell with that. We are so done with that patriarchal thinking. It's time for you, for me, for all of us women to stand up in all our glory. To embrace our 'too muchness' for all the world to see. To be loud and proud and opinionated and sassy and strong and vibrant and challenging and powerful. To be all the things we know we are, but have perhaps been too afraid to even witness for ourselves.

Go out into the world with all of your pieces gloriously on show. And revel in as much of your 'too muchness' as you possibly can.

AFFIRMATION

I own all the fabulous parts of myself.

NOT EVERYONE WILL SEE YOU

You can be a juicy ripe peach and there'll still
be someone who doesn't like peaches.

~ DITA VON TEESE

We all want to be seen. Not just noticed and glanced at. But truly seen. Every part of ourselves. Seen for who we truly are.

But not everyone will see you. Not everyone will get it.

One of the greatest lessons in life is that it's okay not to be seen. Not every person is your person. You don't have to belong to every group. Not everyone has to be your friend, or even like you for that matter.

You don't need everyone to get you. You just need your people.

Just because they don't see you doesn't mean that you're not valuable.

It doesn't mean you need to shrink, or hide, or become 'less than'.

It doesn't mean you need to morph, or change, or bend to become something or someone that they will see.

Their lack of witnessing you doesn't change you. It actually has nothing to do with you.

You may have a deep longing to be seen. And you will be. By your people. At the right time. And for the right reasons. Keep being you.

AFFIRMATION

I am seen by those who are meant to see me.

WHAT DO YOU WANT TO SAY?

*It took me quite a long time to develop a voice, and
now that I have it, I am not going to be silent.*

~ MADELEINE ALBRIGHT

Gloria Steinem's book, *My Life on the Road*, was a revelation to me. I'd studied many aspects of feminist history in my early PhD research, but reading the stories of actual events firsthand was like being there, in many moments that defined history. I was reflecting on the book while writing about women finding and using our voices, and one of Steinem's stories leapt out for me to share.

She recounts the story of being at the Lincoln Memorial in 1963, when Martin Luther King Jr. was leading the march on Washington in a campaign for jobs and justice. As he finished his remarks, Gloria Steinem heard Mahalia Jackson, the Queen of Gospel, call out, 'Tell them about the dream, Martin!' And one of the most famous speeches in the history of the world, 'I have a dream ...' commenced.

What if Mahalia hadn't spoken up on that day? What if she hadn't called out, 'Tell them about the dream, Martin'? What if her voice, a black woman's voice so frequently silenced, had not been heard? We will never know. But we do know that she made a profound difference to history on that day.

As I reflect on this, I think about where I need to raise my voice. Where I need to speak out. Where I need to be brave about starting conversations that matter, to do the work I want to do in the world. And I think about all the times I've stayed silent. In boardroom meetings, where I waited for the man beside me to raise the issue I wanted to raise. In discussions with my male boss, any number of them, where I disagreed and wanted to say so. In relationships, where I bit my tongue instead of speaking my truth.

And I think about you, in your work and life, and I ask you this: Where are you not speaking up? Where are you staying silent? Where do you want to raise your voice: on what issues, on what projects, in what settings? What do you really want to say to your boss, your team, your partner, your best friend or your kids? Where are you holding back? And why? What are the stories you are telling yourself about what might happen if you truly showed up, spoke up, and were seen? How can you challenge those stories, knowing that 90% of them, if not all of them, just aren't true?

What if we pushed past the limiting stories in our minds and just said what we wanted to say? What if we believed that we have just as much right, just as much intelligence, and just as much value to offer as anyone else? What if we really found our voice and stopped looking around for those who might shut us down for speaking out?

What if we just decided to speak?

Ask yourself this question: *What do I want to say?*

Stepping into our true confidence starts with finding the courage to speak our truth. From speaking up in a meeting, to speaking out on social justice issues, to speaking up at home, your voice matters.

Make a commitment to yourself to speak up. To honour yourself, your intelligence, your power. To have your voice be heard.

AFFIRMATION
I use my voice.

FOLLOW YOUR ENVY

*Owning our story can be hard but not nearly as
difficult as spending our lives running from it.*

~ BRENÉ BROWN

Envy is often seen as a very negative state, one where you can feel inadequate or less than others. Actually, it gets a pretty bad rap. But it can also be an indication of what you really want. If you see something in another person or in a piece of work that makes you envious, it can open you up to a need or want that you may not be in touch with.

Here are some simple examples. You might look a picture of a beautiful women in a magazine while thinking, *I really wish I had skin like that.* Or you could look at the pool in a friend's backyard and wish that you had a pool for your kids to play in too.

But go deeper. The woman in the magazine ... your desire to radiate vitality and health. The kids and the pool ... longing for family time. I look at successful business people, entrepreneurs who are doing amazing things, and I can feel a twitch of envy. It's not that I want to replicate their success, but rather that I want that level of creativity in my growing business.

Trigger. Right there, that twitch, is a signal of what I need to work on. I look at writers who are doing magical things with their words, book marketing or community building. *Trigger.* I need to be looking at those things for my next major work too.

I watch people who have glowing health and happiness and a sense of vitality that I long for. Envy? *Trigger.* Get thee to the yoga mat, meditation cushion and green smoothie maker. Pronto.

Next time you look at someone or something and feel a sense of envy, don't panic. Don't brush it off. Look a little closer and see what that envy is there to teach you. Take the lesson and leave the rest. Write it down. Play with it. And take those desires and longings and put them to work in helping you create the life you truly want.

AFFIRMATION
I look deeper at what my envy has to teach me.

QUIETEN YOUR INNER CRITIC

*If you are willing to look at another person's
behavior toward you as a reflection of the state of
their relationship with themselves, rather than a
statement about your value as a person, then you
will, over a period of time, cease to react at all.*

~ YOGI BHAJAN

Y ou know who she is. You know what she sounds like. And
she's just mean. She rabbits on incessantly with her diatribe
of insults and injuries about everything that you do.

She is relentless. She is your inner critic. And she is not your
friend.

Perhaps your inner critic sounds something like this: *Oh my
God, you are just hopeless. Why on earth did you say that in the meeting?
Everyone thinks you're so stupid. Don't wear those jeans, you look horrible.
You really need to get to the gym, honey. Don't think you can create anything
good. Everyone is better than you. You will never, ever, be good at anything.
You will never be good enough.*

As I said, she is mean. And relentless.

But here's the thing. She is not you. She doesn't speak the
truth. And you can learn to quieten her down. She may never
disappear completely. But she can be silenced to the decibel of
a whisper, instead of a roar.

First, become aware. Start to really listen out for her. Tune in
to the stories she is telling you. We sometimes become so accus-
tomed to her being there that we think it's a normal part of our
consciousness. It's not. Don't tune out, tune in.

As you hear the stories and lamenting comments, start to observe them. Be the witness to them. Instead of getting emotionally hooked, simply listen as you would if an acquaintance was talking to you. Be objective. Passive. Emotionally disengaged.

Breathe through it. Let her burn herself out. Like a fire with no wind, her flame will flicker out if it's not being fed with your energy, reaction and resistance.

Then tell yourself a better story. When she's raving on about how terrible you look in those jeans, check yourself in the mirror and say to yourself, 'Wow, my butt looks good today!' She won't know what to do with that, I can promise you.

Keep replacing the negative dialogue and stories with little snippets of positive ones. Tell yourself how smart you are, point out your positives, say 'thank you' to compliments and add, 'I know, right!' Write down little mantras and stick them where you can see them, or post them as alerts in your phone.

Also (and you can't miss this) meditate. The more you learn to quieten your mind, the less space your inner critic has to run wild and free. Learn to sit. Breathe. Find the space between your thoughts and be still there.

Remind yourself how amazing you are. Tune in to your inner best friend who loves you, adores you, respects you and sees you for the fifty kinds of wonderful you truly are.

AFFIRMATION
I feed myself wonderful thoughts that nourish me.

IS THAT TRUE?

Every day, every minute, you have the power to choose.

~ LISA NICHOLS

Every day I have clients tell me about the situations they find themselves in, the actions they wish they'd taken and how they are now stuck and regret the outcome from their inaction. The first question I always ask them is this: *What stories were you telling yourself at the time?*

It's not the situation we find ourselves in, it's the stories we tell ourselves about the situation that stop us from taking the action we want to take, or using our voice in the way we want to. And our stories are what lead us to living smaller lives than we dream about.

One of the most powerful questions I use personally and teach those I support is this: *Is that true?*

Is that true that everyone will think you're stupid, if you ask that question in the meeting?

Is that true that your new start-up will be rejected for funding, because your idea isn't sound?

Is that true that you can't lose weight, get fit, or run a half marathon?

Is that true that you can't start a blog, write that article, or complete the research for your Masters degree?

Is that true that your boss hates you, because she walked right past you without saying hello?

Is that true, all of the stuff that goes around and around in your head, every minute of the day?

When we ask this question, we aren't seeking lies. We're not searching for a truth that isn't there. We're breaking the rumination cycle, and seeking out alternative scenarios to the one playing out in our mind.

There may be five reasons why your boss didn't acknowledge you when she walked past. Sure, she may not like you. But is there actually any evidence of that? Or could it be because she'd just had a bad meeting, lost an important client, or perhaps had a stressful call from home? Highly likely that it's one of these alternate scenarios and not the worst case one playing relentlessly in your head.

What are your stories? Learn to catch them as they come up. Once you tune in, you will realise just how active your monkey mind is, and how much absolute rubbish it carries on with all day long.

Ask yourself, 'Is that true?' Seek out the possible true answers to demystify the story you are telling yourself. Then reframe the story. Write a new story that is true and that will help you take the action you long to take.

Confidence is the ability to turn our thoughts into action. Our stories can be what prevent us from getting there.

Use this technique to get yourself unstuck. My clients tell me this can be life-changing. So try it—it works.

AFFIRMATION
I challenge my stories and reframe them into
helpful truths that move me forwards.

LIFE IS NOT AN INSTAGRAM PHOTO

The sunrise, of course, doesn't care if we watch it or not.
It will keep on being beautiful, even if
no-one bothers to look at it.

~ GENE AMOLE

Recently, I was having a conversation with my friend Georgia. She was talking about Mary, a business competitor in the same social circle, and lamenting that her life looked so perfect, that her business seemed to be going so well and that everything she was doing looked amazing. This comment came just as we were discussing her own current cash flow, potential new business model, and how she could take things to the next level. Georgia was feeling a little vulnerable with her progress and, as happens, she was looking around at everyone else to see how successful she should feel. As she looked at Mary, largely evidenced by her perfect Instagram feed, her assumption was that Mary's life was perfect, her business was booming and there was absolutely nothing wrong with her existence.

Georgia had fallen into the trap that we all fall into, often on a daily basis: the comparison trap. While we know that life is not reflected in an Instagram photo, nor in a Facebook post, a perfect tweet or that beautifully designed image on Pinterest, we still get sucked in. We particularly get triggered when things aren't going as well as we hoped, when we feel a little down, or when we're in transition. We look around, comparing our insides to everyone else's filtered outsides, and wonder why we constantly feel 'less than'. And yet, we can't seem to switch off that nagging need to compare and then rank ourselves, according to our perception of how well (or not) we're doing.

It's only when you peek behind the curtain and see what's really going on beyond those velvet drapes that you get a sense of reality over mystery. The entrepreneur posting about their latest blockbuster business concept, who is actually on the verge of bankruptcy. That blogger you envy for their massive following, who sits at home every night stressing over the next day's posts, until she is sick with fear of losing her audience. The woman who seems to have the perfect job and life, who secretly wants to quit because she hates every minute of it.

We can love social media and use it as a distraction, a source of inspiration, for connection, creativity and fun. But it becomes dangerous and self-limiting when we use it as a tool to compare our life with others. We are all real and human and everyone has their own battles. When you look at another's success, know that there is always a good dose of the unglamorous that will have accompanied it. And when you do see someone's vulnerabilities, be sure to celebrate and honour them, because more often than not, that's more of the true story than the perfect picture will ever be. Most importantly, stay in your own lane, focus on your own gifts, and celebrate all that you have to be grateful for.

AFFIRMATION

*I will not compare myself to strangers
or friends on the internet.*

PART 9

Womanhood

LET'S TELL THE TRUTH
ABOUT OUR LIVES

The truth always creates an opening.

~ DANIELLE LAPORTE

If women told the truth about their lives, the world would shake. We would wake up. We would all recognise that we really are in this together, in this life where we are all trying to thrive (or survive). That none of us is perfect, and thank goodness we can stop pretending that we are. That the patriarchy has had us all so very busy worrying about our thigh gap and getting rid of our wrinkles and fitting into the skinny jeans and being perfect mothers and competing with each other over everything under the sun, that it's kept us from our real work in the world. It's kept us small and in our shadow. It's kept us out of our true source of power, our feminine power.

Can we just tell the truth about our lives?

We do see some women telling the truth about their lives, both online and offline. The unfiltered images. The real stories. The truth. And what happens when they do?

When women do stand strong in their vulnerability and say, 'This is me in all my messiness and this is how I live my life,' something radical happens. Women collectively exhale. We breathe in a little easier. Our shoulders drop. Our bellies release. The pressure to be perfect eases. Doorways to what's possible open. We look at other women and say with relief, 'Me too!' and feel like we're a little less alone in what can be a lonely world.

We find sisterhood. Community. Belonging.

Let's make a pact. Let's tell the truth about what it really means to be a woman today. Let's show the struggles and the successes, supporting and celebrating them all. Let's just be real. Because like it or not, we are all in this together. So let's be together on this.

AFFIRMATION
My truth opens up possibilities for myself and others.

I'M FINE THANKS

Try to say nothing negative about yourself for three days, for forty-five days, for three months.
See what happens to your life.

~ YOKO ONO

Here's a revolutionary thought: *There is nothing wrong with you.* And another: *You are not broken. You don't need to be fixed.* Do you believe me? I'm not sure you do.

I'm not surprised. You have, after all, been told what to do for your entire life: who to be, how to act, how to dress, what you should look like, how to behave. You've been conditioned to please, to serve, to support, to obey, to conform, to fit in, to concede, to compromise. You've learnt how to be unassuming, to be quiet, to speak when spoken to, to hush, to let the boy go first, to not be bossy, to be gracious, to wait your turn. You've discovered how you need to behave to be liked and to get ahead. Mostly, you have learnt why you're just not quite right, simply as you are.

The path to freedom is paved with awareness, awakening and loads of self-compassion. And it starts with an acknowledgement of this simple truth: *You are utterly fine just as you are.*

Roll that up and smoke it for a while. Savour the scent of it. Chew on the remnants. Spit out the lies and unhelpful guidance you've been served your entire life, like a cowboy spitting out an old piece of tobacco he no longer has the taste for.

You don't need it anymore. You don't need any of it. There is nothing wrong with you. You are not broken. You don't need to be fixed.

You are on your own beautiful, challenging, unique path of coming home to yourself. You are waking up, seeing yourself as you always were, before they told you who and how you should be. You can just do you. Every day. In every way. And know that you are enough. Right here, right now, and for all eternity.

Breathe into that. Soak in it. Lather it up. Let it sink deep within you. And let that knowing soothe your soul, enliven your heart, invoke your wild, and open up all that is possible for your beautiful life.

AFFIRMATION
I'm fine thanks, just as I am.

THAT NIGHT AT GLORIA STEINEM

I say if I'm beautiful. I say if I'm strong.
You will not determine my story. I will.

~ AMY SCHUMER

I'd been waiting months for this night to come. Gloria Steinem, the iconic writer, feminist activist, trailblazer and changemaker was speaking, and I was going to be there. I had followed her work for as long as I could remember, especially in the previous few years as I conducted early parts of my PhD research. I was in awe of her, and couldn't have been more excited.

Waiting for Ms. Steinem to take the stage, chatting with my girlfriend, I heard someone clearing their throat behind me. 'Excuse me, are you a writer?' she asked and then continued, 'Are you Megan Dalla-Camina?'

'Yes I am,' I replied. Could this night get any better? As an author, connecting with readers is always a moment to be cherished.

'I saw you speak at that writers conference. You were incredible. I just love your book,' she continued, referring to my first book *Getting Real About Having It All*. She was a woman perhaps in her late fifties, slim with soft grey hair.

I was feeling great about myself that night, confident, happy, vibrant. This just took me to a whole new level.

And then she continued, 'Here's my card. I'd love to talk to you about your weight, and share the details of the doctor who helped me lose all of mine.'

Wait, what? *What did she just say to me?* It was like I'd been hit by a train. Bam! Just like that, my heart started racing, my stomach plummeted and my face turned beet red.

She wasn't done yet though. She continued, oblivious to my horrified reaction, 'You're amazing, and you were so incredible speaking at that event. You could be even more amazing if you lost the weight.'

I was speechless. I took the card from her hand, mumbled something politely, then turned back in my seat. My girlfriend hadn't heard the exchange, but she could see the look on my face. As I told her what had happened, it was all I could do to keep her from lurching behind to strangle the woman.

As her words played over in my head, I felt myself shrinking into my seat. I tried to pinpoint the emotions I felt. I was embarrassed. Mostly, I felt shamed. As if all of my fears about myself were labelled across my back for all to see. My confidence plummeted and the enthusiasm I had for the night vanished. I wanted to leave. To hide myself and my extra kilos somewhere where no-one could see me.

And yet the irony didn't escape me. Here I was waiting for the most famous feminist in the world to speak to us about women and power, self-worth and our place in society. And there was a woman telling me that I could be so much more fabulous and powerful if I wasn't heavy, if I looked different, if I better fitted the mould of what a 'successful' female author looked like. Who does that, I thought?

I would later see a 1985 video of Oprah Winfrey being interviewed by Joan Rivers. Joan asked, 'How did you gain the weight? You said you gained 50 pounds. You shouldn't let that happen to you, you're very pretty. And you're single. You must lose the weight!'

If you look closely at Oprah's reaction, you can see she is shocked, as she fumbles through a response on live TV. She would, years later, recount to Dr. Oz that she felt shamed by Joan. That all she heard as Joan was speaking was a siren screaming inside her head, 'She's calling me fat, she's calling me fat, she's calling me *fat!*'

That is exactly how I felt and I learnt a lot about myself that night and in the months to follow. We decide who we are as women: what we think, what we believe, how we look, the clothes we wear, the size we are. We decide how we parent, how we partner, the jobs we take, the choices we make and how we show up.

It's taken me a long time to realise, even after losing the excess weight, that I will not be dictated to by anyone else as to what my version of womanhood looks like. That I will not be shamed for my choices, and nor should any of us. Our worth will not be defined by other people's opinions of who we should be. For how slim or heavy we are. For our age, our colour, our bank balance, our job title or the lines on our face. We define our own worth.

AFFIRMATION

I stay grounded in my power. I define my worth.

WOMEN'S PATHS ARE DIFFERENT

Turns out that the fabled Hero's Journey is a bunch of hooey when you're writing about Heroines.

~ JILL SOLOWAY, WRITER/DIRECTOR

We have long known about the Hero's Journey, whether we've called it that or not. The concept was developed by Joseph Campbell, an American professor of literature working in comparative mythology and religion, well known for his book, *The Hero with a Thousand Faces* (1949). In this book, he shared his theory of the journey of the archetypal hero and the mythical cycle of man's journey to victory in his own life—the model of the heroic quest. This has underpinned many notable stories in our era, from *Star Wars* to *Top Gun* to *The Wizard of Oz*.

In her desire to understand how a woman's journey related to the journey of the hero, Maureen Murdock, a psychotherapist working with women in private practice, spoke about it with her teacher, Joseph Campbell, back in the 1980s. She felt that while a woman's journey incorporated aspects of the hero's journey, there were key elements related to feminine spirituality that were missing from Campbell's model.

She was stunned and dissatisfied with his response to her assertion, as he stated that women don't need to make the journey. Campbell maintained that: *In the whole mythological tradition, the woman is 'there'. All she has to do is to realize that she's the place that people are trying to get to. When a woman realizes what her wonderful character is, she's not going to get messed up with the notion of being pseudo-male.*

Murdock found his answer deeply unsatisfying. That the women she worked with did not want to be 'there', or as she put it: *be handmaidens of the dominant male culture, giving service to the Gods; they need a new model that understands who and what a woman is.*

And so Murdock went about creating the model outlined in her groundbreaking book, *The Heroine's Journey: Woman's Quest for Wholeness.* It explained so much about women's psychology, their lives and how they become whole by reclaiming the feminine aspects of themselves.

AFFIRMATION

I honour my unique journey as a woman.

THE FEMININE BETRAYAL

It is easier to fight an enemy outside than an enemy within. It is important for women to know that an Inner Patriarch exists within them, that patriarchy is not just an enemy to be battled on the outside.

~ HAL STONE

In the opening lines of *The Heroine's Journey: Women's Quest for Wholeness,* Maureen Murdock writes about her work as a therapist. She details the cry of dissatisfaction with outward success she heard from women, particularly those between the ages of thirty and fifty. That dissatisfaction would often show up as a feeling of emptiness or sterility, even as a sense of self-betrayal.

Many women were left questioning what all this success—financial, academic or artistic—was for, when it left them exhausted, suffering from stress-related illnesses, overworked and overscheduled, with little inner fulfilment or joy.

In Murdock's words: *This was not what they had bargained for when they first pursued achievement and recognition. The image they held of the view from the top did not include sacrifice of body and soul.*

She concluded that the reason women were experiencing so much physical and emotional pain on their heroic quest was that they had chosen *to follow a model that denies who they are.*

When I first read those words many years ago, I was stopped in my tracks by their enormity. They explained so much to me. My mind was swimming with realisations about so many aspects of my life, my career, my work, my health. They left me reeling but elated, with these resounding thoughts thumping through my brain like an incessant beat on a heavy metal track: *It's not just me. There is nothing wrong with me.*

I reflected back on my career. I thought about the endless struggle to succeed. The excruciating workload, decades of suffering through twelve to sixteen-hour days, always being 'on', never showing vulnerability or perceived weakness. Cramming every waking moment with work, more projects, meeting more deadlines, achieving more goals, getting higher degrees, striving for more financial rewards. And endlessly ignoring my body and the signs of tiredness, then exhaustion, illness and the inevitable burnouts. The moulding, sacrificing, struggling. If only I worked a little bit harder, was a little bit more like the men, removed more of my perceived womanly weaknesses, fitted in better, delivered greater results, then all of those feelings of emptiness and not belonging would go away. It would finally be worth it.

But of course it wasn't.

We wonder why women don't stay in workplaces past a certain level. We talk about glass ceilings, quotas and flexible work, child care and job share. But we don't talk about the issues at the very heart of women's lives that eventually drive those who have found themselves on this heroine's journey (whether they know it or not), running as fast as they can from the structures that have kept them caged.

We don't talk about feminine betrayal. Of us, as women, betraying the feminine within ourselves. The fact that we've denied the core of who we are for so long, that it has taken away our very identity as women. That the betrayal shows up as stress, burnout, depression, isolation, divorce, anger—sometimes even as cancer in our breasts, our ovaries, our bones. That it's not our fault, as we didn't even know it was happening. Or that the betrayal wasn't really ours to own, but that of the patriarchy that existed all around us. And inside us.

As women, the balance we are really seeking is the balance between our masculine and our feminine. For both to reside peacefully, with equanimity, inside us. To be able to craft our own definition of success and not have to betray our feminine aspects, as we make our way in the external world.

AFFIRMATION
I reclaim my feminine soul.

DAUGHTERS OF THE PATRIARCHY

At every moment, a woman makes a choice: between the state
of the queen and the state of the slave girl.
In our natural state, we are glorious beings. In the
world of illusion, we are lost and imprisoned, slaves
to our appetites and our will to false power.

~ MARIANNE WILLIAMSON

Patriarchy. It's a word I have only really come to understand in the past decade. That may seem surprising for
someone who has researched women's studies, diversity, gender
and feminine power so intently. With a naivety that still makes me
curious, I worked inside the structures that define the very patriarchy itself—the all-encompassing, collective, cultural father—in
systems designed by men, for men, and which to this day are
primarily set up for men to prosper in. I was so ensconced inside
the patriarchy, I didn't even know it existed.

I strove to succeed by constantly, without fail, impressing my
boss—a role represented by a series of men parading through
my work life with the keys to unlock what I perceived to be my
very life success. As I did so, I followed the rules laid down by
hundreds, thousands, of years of oppression. And I didn't even
realise that was a massive part of the problem. Why I never felt
like I really fitted in; why I always felt on edge; and why no matter
the success, recognition or acclaim, I never felt like I had a secure
place in the world I was striving so desperately to belong in.

How is it possible that I and so many women that I speak to
aren't aware that this is our reality? Because this is the world
we have grown up in. We looked to our mothers for guidance

on how to be strong, independent women, only to find that they were daughters of the same patriarchy too, many asleep to the conditioning and conformity that ruled their lives. Different times, but the same culture and the same system.

The veil is finally being lifted. Many lifetimes of veils. And it is shifting. But we must open our eyes. We must question everything. Our individual and collective ideas about womanhood, who we are in the world, our very place in the world. We must ask questions. About the systems out there, and the systems within us that keep us enslaved.

AFFIRMATION
My eyes are open.

THE HEROINE'S JOURNEY

Women do have a quest at this time in our culture.
It is the quest to fully embrace their feminine
nature, learning how to value themselves as women
and to heal the deep wound of the feminine.
It is a very important inner journey toward being a
fully integrated, balanced and whole human being.

~ MAUREEN MURDOCK, *The Heroine's Journey*

A woman's journey is not linear. It's not a straight line and you can't plot it on a graph. It's cyclical, seasonal, emotional, relational. Women's lives take place in community, sitting in circle, gathering in tribe and in council. The path of the Heroine's Journey (as developed by Maureen Murdock) represents this, perhaps for the first time, articulating the stages of our path as women from separation to wholeness.

As Murdock states in her book: *Like most journeys, the path of the heroine is not easy, it has no well-defined guideposts nor recognizable tour guides. There is no map, no navigational chart, no chronological age when the journey begins. It follows no straight lines. It is a journey that seldom receives validation from the outside world, in fact the outer world often sabotages and interferes with it.*

The image of the heroine's journey is a circular path that moves clockwise, beginning with separation and ending with integration. Along the path are many stages: separation from the feminine, identifying with the masculine, the road of trials, finding the boon of success, awakening to feelings of spiritual death, initiation and descent into the Goddess, urgent yearning to reconnect with the feminine, healing the mother/daughter split, healing the wounded masculine and, finally, integration of the masculine and feminine.

In the work I do with women journeying into the feminine, when I outline the steps of the heroine's journey there is often a deep sense of knowing, of awakening, of a truth long buried coming back to them. The journey makes sense. They know it to be true.

Not all women walk this path or are aware that they are walking it. The journey is cyclical and one may be at various stages of the journey at the same time. I have found myself at the stage of finding the boon of success while simultaneously feeling the urgent yearning to reconnect with the feminine. It is a continual journey of self-development, awakening, understanding and expansion.

The journey starts when we hear the call, a sense that our old life no longer fits. If we choose to heed that call, which can come at any point in a woman's life—perhaps when she has a baby, when she goes through a divorce, as she reaches middle age, or perhaps when her children leave home—then the journey begins.

AFFIRMATION
I heed the call, the quest, of the heroine's journey.

IT STARTS WITH RESTLESSNESS

There is always, between ending and beginning,
the very briefest moments and in those moments,
change, deep volatile change, is possible.
To find that moment, to grasp it, embrace it, to
change within it, that is the thrust of evolution.

~ RHODA LERMAN, *The Book of the Night*

I wonder if it started this way for you, the path to waking up. To realising that there was something more waiting for you than what you had been told, or seen, or believed. To seeing a glimmer of light in a crack of your life, creating an opening into your womanhood.

Perhaps you started to get a little bit restless, like you no longer felt truly at home in your life, the way you once did. You started to itch a little. Not physically, but like an itch deep within your cells that you couldn't name or get a handle on.

Restlessness is the first sign. The sign of an awakening that is coming. It's often followed by seeking. Seeking out something to stop the restlessness that you feel. It may be a positive seeking: seeking out spiritual guidance, maybe a yoga or meditation teacher, a good coach, a therapist, the right book. You may find solace on your mat, in an art class, or in a women's circle. Or it can be less positive seeking. Distractions like shopping, drinking, sex, working too much, food or other indulgences, often reached for to dull the sharpness of the ache you have started to feel. To take the edge off the new-found awareness. To put you back to sleep, just a little, because you're not quite ready to wake up fully.

But still, you feel it. It is the start of your heroine's journey. There will be much journeying to do, and the path can seem arduously long as you traverse its heights, depths and winding rocky paths. It is not a journey for the faint-hearted, the meek or the incurious. But it is worth taking that first step past the restlessness. To even acknowledge the restlessness in the first place. And to sit in the discomfort of it until you are ready to move through to the next stage along the path.

AFFIRMATION

I sit in the restlessness of awakening into my womanhood.

MOVING AWAY FROM THE MOTHER

The mother wound is bigger than each of us.

~ DR. CHRISTIANE NORTHRUP, *Mother-Daughter Wisdom*

You look just like your mother. It's a sentence that used to make me cringe. As a teenager going through a decade-long rebellion, the very last thing I wanted to be told was that I looked like my mother. My mother was beautiful, feminine, gracious, polite and charming. She was the epitome of a lady. I was trying desperately to be anything but.

In my doc marten boots, ripped jeans, flanked by male friends swinging guitars from their hips, and often in a flannelette shirt with a packet of cigarettes in my top pocket (and the requisite thick black eyeliner), I was doing everything I could possibly do to not be my mother's daughter.

The first stage of the heroine's journey is where we separate from the feminine aspect of ourselves (represented by our mothers in many cases) and align with the masculine (often represented by aligning with our father). It's when we become the daughters of the patriarchy, where the masculine holds the power, the excitement, the sense of belonging we feel we are seeking. For many of us, it's where we encounter the first betrayal of our feminine self, where we first lose ourself—that self that may take us a lifetime to reclaim.

Moving away from our mothers may seem subtle, it may even be imperceptible. For those without a mother in their life, it may show up as disowning the feminine self. I didn't understand for a long time—for decades—why I would often look upon my father with longing, for the power he seemed to wield in the world;

and at my mother with a sense of dismissal, for the womanly and mothering duties that she performed with such grace. Even though she worked my entire childhood, I considered there was no power there.

Little did I know how much I had to learn, and am still learning, about the real power women wield in the world, and all that we hold inside of us.

AFFIRMATION
There is power in my feminine self.

DISOWNING THE FEMININE

The task for today's woman is to heal the wounding of the feminine that exists deep within herself and the culture.

~ MAUREEN MURDOCK, *The Heroine's Journey*

In order to make our way in the world, many of us women feel that we need to distance ourselves from aspects of the feminine, such as being too emotional or passive, as those traits have been labelled as negative and a barrier to success for women in the masculine-dominated workforce. Being a feminine woman could be seen as weak, inferior, less than—by men, as well as by women.

So as women, we learn to disown that sense of the feminine and anything that represents it. I remember coming back to work after having my son. I was thirty years old and had worked tirelessly for years to establish myself as a tough, fearless, inexhaustible worker, who would always get the job done with exceptional results. I had dispelled the myths about being female and what that meant in a mostly male workplace. I had found my place and been promoted as the youngest director ever, one of few women who had made it into the 'inner circle'.

And then I got pregnant. I was terrified that everything was about to change; that I would lose my footing and years of excruciating work would be undone. I turned thirty in the same week I was ready to announce that I was pregnant. At a birthday brunch with my girlfriends, this is the exchange that went down ...

Me: 'Guess what I got for my birthday?'

Friends: 'What?'

Me: 'A baby!!!!'

Friends: Blank stares. Gaping mouths. Utter shock. I was seen to be the most 'successful' and certainly the most ambitious of our group, and had never even uttered the possibility of having a baby, nor any desire to do so. It seemed about as plausible to them as an alien showing up for champagne brunch.

After the shock started to wear off, this came from a work friend, with a look of horror and concern on her face (she actually looked like she might cry): 'But what about your *career???*'

I was twelve weeks pregnant. Mild panic was quickly turning into a full-on anxiety attack. The truth was, I had no idea about my career. All bets were off.

I worked until the week before my son was born, even though I had a high-risk pregnancy, had to have daily blood-thinning injections, and was completely exhausted. I checked in with the office frequently while on maternity leave, which was meant to be six months but was really only three. Couldn't be away for too long, I thought, while secretly praying my maternity leave replacement was doing a terrible job.

The strategy to reclaim my power when I went back to work was simple: pretend I'd never had a baby, act like nothing had changed, get back to business as normal. Good plan, I thought. I recall walking around the office on my return, looking at the desks of more junior women with pictures of their kids and paintings done in kindy pasted to the walls and thinking to myself, 'Woah, bad idea lady, you shouldn't have all that stuff on your desk!'

To me, it was evidence of a life outside work; of family responsibilities that could be seen to detract from the ability to do your job; of motherhood, that thing that always negatively impacted on a woman's career but never on a man's. Evidence of being a woman. And none of that would help you to get ahead in that workplace, or any workplace for that matter. The feminine was something to be masked, covered up, stamped out, hidden at all costs.

For many of us, the workplace is when we first deeply disown and dishonour the most intrinsic parts of ourselves, for fear of not fitting in, of standing out for the wrong reasons, of disobeying the patriarchal laws of the land.

And many of us don't even know the value of what we have lost.

AFFIRMATION
I honour my feminine self.

FATHERS' DAUGHTERS

*Many of us are unaware of our devotion to the values
and standards which our 'fathers' represent.
We have unconsciously accepted ourselves as daughters, and
unconsciously act out little girl roles in relation to men.*

~ MARION WOODMAN, 'THE EMERGENCE OF
THE FEMININE' IN *Betwixt and Between*

Disowning the feminine and aligning with the masculine
shows up in our lives in many ways. Cloaking ourselves
in the armour of masculinity. Seeking validation, approval and
recognition from the masculine, represented as the individual
and collective father.

Striving for external success. Using external success as our
barometer of self-worth. Bypassing what we deem to be acceptable
and competent, as we hike our way to the extraordinary. A rigid
orientation to results. Following linear and structured processes.
Staying within the lines of the patriarchy. Confirming to the
norms of the structures we live and work in. Being a good girl.

Shielding ourselves from our perceived feminine weaknesses—
our feelings and softer sides. Squashing our vulnerability, our
creativity, and what we have come to know as our untrustworthy
femininity. Burning ourselves out to do more, go faster, be better.
Spinning our wheels in an endless pursuit of the power we seek,
even though—in perhaps the greatest irony of our lives—we
don't realise that it doesn't and never will belong to us, because
it's not ours to own.

We ignore our tiredness and exhaustion; deny ourselves the
need for rest, support, to be nourished and nurtured, to listen to

and honour our bodies, all for fear of falling behind. Our lives are dictated by a long list of 'shoulds'. Nothing we do is ever satisfactory, good enough, or worth enough. The way we align ourselves to the masculine and to the patriarchy is endless. And it's endlessly exhausting.

To undertake our own heroine's journey, we need to step out of the identity of being our father's daughter and claim our own identity. At the core of it all is the longing to be loved. To be validated. To be safe. To be seen. I've been there. You may have been there. We are a generation, generations, of 'fathers' daughters'.

As was my client Lisa. She drove and pushed herself so hard for so long, that one day she just collapsed. Calling me in floods of tears, she was clearly distraught and beyond exhausted. 'I'm so over it,' she sobbed, 'I just can't push anymore. What am I driving myself so hard for?' she asked, desperate for the self-torture to stop. 'I feel like I'm constantly fighting for approval from everyone! My boss, my husband, my father, even my boys for God's sake. Why do I feel like this all of the time? I just want it to stop.'

I waited as Lisa's breath calmed and her tears subsided. It was like she'd had a full body release with her admission, like an energy clearing through her realisation.

'Lisa, you hold the keys to release these patterns of behaviour,' I said gently. 'The first step is what you have just done, which is to become conscious of the fact that you are not living the life that you want. That it's based on other people, mostly men's, opinions of you and demands on you. You're striving for their validation and you've forgotten or completely ignored your own approval and what you want for your life. It's time to take back your power, over your decisions and your life.'

There was a path ahead for Lisa, as there is for all of us, as we come into the knowing of what truly drives us and why we act the way we do. But stepping into the light of the truth is the first critical step in coming home to ourselves.

AFFIRMATION

I step out of the shadows of the masculine.
I reclaim agency over my own life.

THE DESCENT

A woman who has made the descent has experienced
the devouring, destroyer aspect of the feminine, which
is in the service of the death renewal of herself.

~ MAUREEN MURDOCK

When a woman starts to awaken to the realisation that she is not whole within herself, that the internalised patriarchal father is calling the shots in her life, she starts her initiation into the quest. When she decides to stand in her fear, instead of letting it stop her, and to step out of the systems and norms that have kept her caged, she starts her descent.

This may involve great periods of feeling lost, abandoned, sad, angry, resentful, and full of questions for what was and what will be. There may be a longing to reconnect to Mother Earth, to ground in the sacredness of nature. Moon and hormonal cycles become more important, as she wants to find her natural rhythm, rather than the masculine beat she has been marching to. It can be a challenging and yet illuminating time for women, and it's a journey that can't be rushed. For some, it may last weeks, yet for others it may take years to fully descend. While the external world, friends, family or loved ones, will ask her to hurry up and 'get back to normal', she knows that she must sit, wade, be patient with herself, and let the unknowing unfold into knowingness.

It's a path of reclaiming the lost parts of our womanhood, individually and collectively. It's not just each woman who must descend on her own, but entire cultures and societies, as we learn once again to value all that is woman and feminine and sacred. As we come out the other side of our descent, we are finally ready to get back in touch with the feminine within ourselves, and to seek out that which will make us whole. The journey is about seeking the sacred feminine. The journey is about reclaiming the Goddess.

AFFIRMATION
I allow myself to descend.

SEEKING THE FEMININE

We are becoming the men we wanted to marry.

~ GLORIA STEINEM

For a long time in my life, I was deeply out of touch with the feminine. You could see it as soon as you looked at me. While I may have seemed feminine at first glance, judging by my hair and how I dressed, a closer look would reveal my hard edges, sharp corners and icy demeanour. Those edges were my armour, my cloak, my mask. They were my very survival mechanisms.

Not that different from you I would imagine, in smaller or larger ways. Most of us have been there, deeply ensconced in the masculine. The way we work, live, play even. We show up like that in our place of work, then wonder why our relationships struggle when we can't switch it off when we get home.

It wasn't until recently that I started to realise something was missing. That there was meant to be another side to me. Not just the softness of the feminine, which I was desperately in need of, but also the fierceness that comes from a place other than masculine power.

So I went seeking. It was a slow process at first, and it would take years to find my way back to her. I stumbled and fought her, as I grappled with retaining what I perceived as the power in the masculine that I wasn't ready to let go. I didn't fully understand that it was a false power, and would continue to slip through my fingers like grains of sand on the beach.

As I finally gave up the fight and declared I was ready, I intuitively knew where I would find her. On my yoga mat. Deep in meditation. In Mother Nature. Inside my creative practices, like writing and painting. In the softer side of my mothering. In the nurturing side of my close relationships. In the open and womanly side of intimate ones. In spiritual texts of wise women who had come before me. In my rose essential oil and the bloom of flowers. In stillness and silence.

She was in my heart. Before her, I had only walked life in my head. My soul had the work of reaching her and connecting the two.

It can be a hard path to walk, holding onto that feminine essence in such a tough world. We have to be dedicated to the path. To retain our soft centre, when the world tells us to harden our edges. To sit in our vulnerability, when we are expected to have everything under control. To fill our longing to create, rather than just our need to get things done.

We must seek out the feminine side of ourselves, even though it is so inherently and divinely ours. Those of us who were born with it, and those who weren't but align with it naturally. We must welcome her in, open our arms and our hearts, create a place for her, and make it safe for her to stay.

AFFIRMATION
I seek out the feminine and hold her close and sacred.

LONGING FOR HOME

I find that many women who have embraced the
masculine hero's journey have forgotten how to foster
themselves. They have assumed that to be successful
they have to keep their edges sharp, and in that process
may have ended up with a hole in their hearts.

~ MAUREEN MURDOCK, *The Heroine's Journey*

As we come to the other side of our heroine's journey, and begin to heal the mother/daughter split and integrate our feminine and masculine aspects, what we are really longing for is home. A sense of home within our bodies and communities. A sense of home within ourselves.

When we started our journey, we knew that we had lost ourselves, feeling out of sync with the woman we used to be. As we stopped long enough to breathe into that loss, we realised we were desperate to reclaim it. All of it.

As we come home to ourselves, we begin to reclaim those lost feminine aspects like intuition, creativity, our sexuality and our joy and lightness for life. We may feel the need to nest, recreating our home environments and nurturing our spaces and those within them. We might take up new creative projects, or rekindle an old creative love we used to have. We may indeed slow down in our career, take a lesser role, or leave a job we now see as constricting. We may choose to walk a different path, take a different career, or stop working altogether.

Many people won't understand these choices. They will think you have settled, opted out or abandoned the feminist cause. But this journey is less about approval and recognition from the outer world, and all about finding your own voice, and making your own choices, on your own terms.

As you walk this path, there may be less external rewards, certainly from those who retain a patriarchal mindset. But as you find the courage to continue, you will find other women on the path, perhaps gather in sacred spaces together, and find comfort and joy in co-creating a new paradigm for yourself and for other women that we can all find a place called home within.

AFFIRMATION
I come home to myself.

LEAD LIKE A WOMAN

*It's not enough to simply say that women are leading
the way; we must now become the women who do it.*

~ MARIANNE WILLIAMSON

Maureen Murdock writes: *The path of women's leadership has
no well-defined guideposts, no map and no straight lines. It is a
journey that seldom receives validation from the outside world, but instead
faces sabotage and interference.*

Over the years, I've seen these words play out in the lives of
women I've worked with, as well as for many of my girlfriends.
I've coached hundreds of women and listened to thousands more
talk about the barriers that rise up like prison gates, as they do
everything in their power to ascend. Yet no matter what they
try, they remain stuck behind a sea of men who seem to have a
never-ending claim on the power seats of leadership.

These women continue to morph and twist themselves like
pretzels into what they think their boss or those in power want
them to be, modelling the behaviours of successful men, in order
to be accepted into the club. And yet success can harden those
who do break through, turning them into bad clones of the men
they have been emulating on their rise to the top.

This is the very epitome of the 'leading like men' model;
women unknowingly becoming part of the fabric that keeps
the patriarchy entrenched. And as we have already discovered
through the heroine's journey, it's unsustainable for a woman
to disown and betray her feminine self in order to conform. At
some time, in some form, she will come undone.

I co-wrote a book and co-founded a company called *Lead Like A Woman* to bring a new model to light that would create a path for women to follow, to do things differently. More authentically. With a balance of the feminine and masculine traits we have already discussed. It's not only essential for women to step into their feminine traits like empathy, vulnerability, intuition, collaboration and creativity—it's essential for men and for the sustainability of the world today. We know this to be true. Research confirms it. And women's stories, and those of men who are sick and tired of the status quo—literally and figuratively—validate it.

The world needs us to be women in our power. In our feminine power. The world, and our very soul, needs us to finally step into leading like women. It takes vision and foresight. It takes courage and conviction. It takes every aspect of the strength and softness of our womanhood.

You are absolutely up to the task. And the women behind you are watching and waiting for you to lead.

AFFIRMATION
I am ready to lead like the woman I am.

YOU ARE SAFE TO SOFTEN

Stay soft. It looks beautiful on you.

~ NAYYIRAH WAHEED

It's time. To remove your mask. To take off your armour. To lay down your arms. The cloak of masculinity that you wear as protection from the patriarchy is too heavy to carry now. Lay it down. Please lay it down.

We have been fighting for so very long. For equality. For freedom. To be heard. To be seen. For agency over our very lives. It has taken all of our energy. We have had to be so strong. There weren't enough of us to carry the burden of that fight. There weren't enough of us ready to rise.

But we are rising now. In the millions. And in that strength, we can soften. It's time.

To step into our feminine essence. That part of us that has been denied and locked and hidden away.

To own our feminine power. That which has frightened the masses, even frightened ourselves at times, as it scared us of the power we are capable of.

To stand with all women. In sovereignty. In solidarity. In true sisterhood. It's time.

Embrace your femininity. Your vulnerability. Your beautiful inner world of creativity and light and deep ancient wisdom. Your softness is where your true strength lies.

AFFIRMATION
I embrace the softest parts of myself.

WELCOME TO THE CLUB

*Sometimes we are just the collateral damage in
someone else's war against themselves.*

~ LAUREN EDEN

Welcome to the club. The motherhood club. We come into
it from different places, walks of life, different ages, with
varying expectations. Full of hope, excitement, perhaps anxiety
for what is to come. And many of us eagerly look forward to
becoming part of a community of mothers, all going along on
the same journey.

And being part of the club can feel amazing. Open. Warm.
Welcoming. Supportive.

Sometimes it feels like that. But the motherhood club can also
feel remarkably different. And it can bring forward shadows and
projections that are the very worst of us and society. Exclusion.
Imperfection. Inspection. Guilt. Judgement.

I remember it all too well from when my son was young. I hear
it from my clients who are mothers and from women who sit
together in circle at my events. Exclusion. Cliques. Did I mention
judgement? And the comments: 'Oh are you *still* feeding your
baby that processed baby food?' from a woman in my mothers'
group, as I struggled to juggle a failing marriage, my job, study
and a fussy baby. Said with a laugh, but what she was really
saying was, 'You're such a bad mother, why can't you cook and
blend organic pumpkin and peas like the rest of us?'

In primary school, it was the side glances from the stay-at-
home mums to the working mums, full of judgement for not being
there for school pick-ups and play dates. The result was not just

exclusion of the mother from the cliques, but of the children as well. Little did they know that for many of those women, work was not optional but a necessity, for paying the rent or the mortgage, and their judgements just made it that much harder.

And on it goes.

Of course, the responses are often just an outward projection of the inward battle that many mothers face when looking at their own inadequacies. An outward reflection of their own inner war. Of course. But we can know that and still not have it any easier. We make it so very hard for ourselves. And for others.

The 'club' used to be so different. Thousands of years ago, perhaps even hundreds of years ago, women would share the caring of children, raising them together. It really did take a village and the village was there. Today, it still takes a village but the doors are closed and the village is empty. We struggle alone, getting through it instead of supporting each other.

We can do so much better. We can be a little kinder. We can ask, 'How is the baby?' and really listen for the response. We can offer help. Be more inclusive. Offer support. Welcome new people in. Welcome in all genders, parents and carers. We can open up the club to everyone. And let everyone belong there.

AFFIRMATION
I am non-judgemental and inclusive in my
mothering and create community for all.

WE ARE ALL MOTHERS

Biology is the least of what makes someone a mother.

~ OPRAH WINFREY

'Do you have kids?' It's a question that can invoke pride, love and identity for those women who have children. And it's a question that can invoke pain, longing, suffering—anger even— for those women, and those who identify as women, who have chosen not to, or not been able to, have children of their own.

We were not all destined to be mothers of our own children. I have single girlfriends who longed for their own families, but it wasn't in the plan for them. I know women who have chosen not to have children, own that choice and are happy with it. I know women who terminated pregnancies when they were much younger and then deeply regretted the children that they had lost—haunted and tortured by choices they were too young to make. And I know married people, gay and straight, who were unable to realise their dream of becoming parents, despite expensive and painful IVF treatments.

But whether we have had biological children or not, as women in the world we are all mothers. In unseen ways, every moment of every day, we hold the mothering energy of the planet and all its people. We are the collective mother.

I feel like the mother to all children. I feel it in my body. The little boy who just skinned his knee on the footpath. The baby smiling at me from the pram, as she drools over her half-eaten biscuit. The emaciated child on the television ad for a world hunger charity. The boy standing alone at his locker on the first day of high school, crying as he can't get the lock open.

The refugee children separated from their parents at the border, screaming and traumatised. The joy and tears of a sixteen-year-old, after a great performance on a talent show. The boy who died by suicide in the school bathroom, wracked with pain that we will never know about. The teenage girl shivering with far too few clothes on, trying to find her self-worth in external validation. The children who die in school shootings and the kids who are traumatised by them, because we adults have failed to protect them.

I feel like a mother to all of them. The pain in my heart, the wrenching in my gut, as I look at sufferings large and small, is palpable. The joy I feel when I see a child or teenager learn something new about themselves and what they are capable of. And I know I am not alone in these feelings.

Mothers come in an innumerable variety. Old, young, single, married, gay, straight, biological, chosen. It's for all of us to undertake, mothering the children of the world. Mothering the world itself. We have the power to nurture, inspire, give, heal. To create a sense of worth and belonging. To connect and nourish and empower. All women. All children. It is our work. This is women's work.

We are all mothers.

AFFIRMATION
I am a mother on this earth, to all of God's children.

YOU CAN DO ANYTHING
(BUT NOT EVERYTHING)

That isn't armour you've wrapped yourself in. That's a cage.

~ L.E. BOWMAN

We still talk endlessly about balance or our lack thereof. We struggle with the juggle. We are exhausted. In many cases we have thrown our hands up in the air, dropped our heads in despair, and figured that we would just have to settle for this life, unsatisfactory as it feels, because this is just the way it is.

But one simple realisation can lift you out of that feeling: *You can do anything, but you can't do everything.*

You can do anything, but not everything. You are wildly capable and you have the world available to you. But you are still going to have to choose.

Choose what the priorities are. What is on your 'yes' list, your 'not now' list, and your 'no' list. What is for today, what will have to wait. Which direction you go in. What roles you take. The clients you choose. Which business you start. When it's the right time to push ahead with your career and when it's time to take your foot off the pedal.

Sit in the liberation of knowing that you get to choose what's in, what's out, and what it all looks like as it comes together. And yes, how you balance the choices that you make. You are a liberated woman. How empowered you are is up to you and the choices you make.

AFFIRMATION
I am empowered to choose.

TAKE UP MORE SPACE

We cannot live what we are here to do without fire.

~ JULIE DALEY

As little girls we are taught how to play small: be quiet, be nice to your brother, don't speak too loudly, do as you are told. As we grow and develop, some of us rebel, but most of us have the need to conform, to comply, to fit in wherever possible deeply buried in our subconscious. That stops us from taking up too much space in the world. From speaking too much or too firmly. From shining too brightly.

And the fear is deeply ingrained and very real, long before we came into this life. Deep within our bones and heritage we have the knowing of the stories, even if we have never heard them before. Stories of women being shunned, cast out, killed, and burnt at the stake for speaking the truth, for being healers, teachers, for being deemed witches. For being seen. For being heard. For taking up space in a world where we were not meant to take up space.

In her brilliant book *Burning Woman*, Lucy Pearce writes: *Free-thinking, powerful, passionate women are dangerous to a conservative male-dominated culture.*

We see it every day, especially when we witness women in public life being torn down or ridiculed, with the attention largely placed on how they look, sound, what they are wearing, and their dress size. Think about Hillary Clinton in the US presidential election. Or a movie star who has the audacity to speak out on issues. A business leader who publicly goes against the grain. Any famous woman who dares gain weight, so is instantly shamed on the cover of trashy magazines.

We've been told loudly and clearly and we have listened: We speak, we burn. We take up space, we burn. We stand out too much, get ready to burn.

However, the new womanhood is filled with women who are ready to be seen. Ready to be heard. Ready for it all. It's time to burn, to lights things up, to set the world on fire with our power and passion and presence.

So stand up, speak out, put yourself forth, and take up your space in the world. We are so very ready for you.

AFFIRMATION

I claim my space and stand in my power.

PART 10

Sovereignty

UNTO HERSELF

Be really whole and all things will come to you.

~ LAO-TZU

This book took on a life of its own. It started as a small book, my intention simply to provide some encouragement and inspiration for women, so they could live their lives in a better, happier, more fulfilled way. That's still my intention. But the book, and my muse, had other ideas for how to bring that to the world. As I worked on what felt like the fifteenth revision of the outline, the chapter formation finally became clear.

There were many things that were a given, like writings on clarity, purpose, wellbeing, sacredness. But I knew deep down in my soul that all of my work and writings, along with my life's journey, had brought me to a point where I could finally talk about one of the most meaningful topics there is: womanhood. What it's like to be a woman today, what it means, how we step into our power. How we care for ourselves, our loved ones, the world and the planet. How we rise and help others rise. And as I continued feeling into it, one word kept appearing in front of me, swirling into my consciousness like a promise on a breeze: sovereignty.

Sovereignty. It's not a word we hear very much these days, certainly not in relation to women. What did it mean? Why was this word showing up for me, following me around, permeating my thoughts, calling my name? It started years before writing this book, but I kept flicking it away like an annoying bug. But the bug turned into a butterfly and I realised that the muse, the

Goddess, was leading me here to talk about this most important facet of our lives.

After all of my research into sovereignty, it comes down to this for me: *being a sovereign woman means being a woman unto herself.* What does that mean, you may be thinking, just as I was? It's something that becomes unveiled little by little. As we discover how we really claim our power and become the women we want to be—the women we were born to be.

This is about how we finally come to ourselves. This entire book has been leading to this point. We can journey for a lifetime to arrive here, although some women (and I see more of them every day) seem to have an innate sense of their own sovereignty. I'm not sure where that comes from, but my sense is that the younger generations, particularly women I see in their late twenties and early thirties, seem to have a grasp of this. They have a clear sense of themselves, who they are, how they stand in their power. For many of us raised in different times, with different cultural and internal narratives, it has taken longer for this sense to take hold.

It doesn't matter how we come to it or how long it takes. Only that we are on the path to claiming ourselves as sovereign women. That we become women unto ourselves. And that we find safe passage there.

AFFIRMATION
I embrace the journey home to my sovereign self.

LIBERATION

Above all, be the heroine of your life, not the victim.
~ NORA EPHRON

I was looking for a new Sanskrit mantra to work with in my morning meditation practice. As I studied the teachings from sacred texts, one particular chant landed with me. In all the years of my practice I had never seen this one before.

Om Namo Bhagavate Vasudevaya.

Liberation. It stunned me. I couldn't move past it.

What did I need to be liberated from? I thought to myself.

After no more than a beat, the answer came. *Everything.*

Limiting thoughts and beliefs that were holding me back or keeping me stuck.

Old relationship wounds still buried deep in my heart, not allowing me to move forwards and find real love.

Decades of torment around food, my body, how I looked, what others thought of me.

Negative blocks around money I didn't even know I had.

Anxiety and fear buried deep within my root and sacral chakras, keeping me from feeling safe in the world.

A steady state of panic that would cause me to hold my breath then catch it, gasping for air to revive my soul.

Everything that I didn't even know I needed to be liberated from, until I removed the layers.

But first I had to descend, by painfully removing distractions and addictions. Through yoga and meditation practice. Through chanting and prayer. Through stillness.

Beyond liberation comes the thing I believe we are all seeking most in this world, even if we don't fully realise it. Peace. Just peace. And love. The longing is palpable.

AFFIRMATION
I am liberated from anything that is holding me back.

QUESTIONS ABOUT POWER

Women are very confused about power, and actually so are
men. Feminine power isn't something we go out and acquire;
it's already within us. It's something we become willing to
experience. Something to admit we have. Until we do, our
positive power lies unexpressed. It's there, but it's not working.
We're wired for something we don't know how to access.

~ MARIANNE WILLIAMSON, *A Woman's Worth*

I've long been fascinated with power. Who has it, why they
want it, what they do with it. So much so that I started a PhD
on the topic. What I really wanted to investigate was women and
power. How was the power that women hold when they are most
aligned different from that of men in the same domain?

I had seen nearly every woman I came into contact with in
my working life deeply entrenched in the dominant power structures and behaviours yielded by successful men in the workplace;
they were ambitious, political, hungry, self-serving—all decidedly
masculine power traits. In some cases, the women were more
masculine than the men (for a long time I was one of them).
I thought this was just the way it was in the world of work.

But as I left that world to embark on my entrepreneurial
journey, including writing more books, doing more research and
developing my own identity in the world, independent of the
corporate hierarchy I had grown up in, I started to ask different
questions about what success models and power structures could
really look like. Could women hold power differently from men?
Should they? Was there a difference in gender, deeper than what
we see on the surface, that influences our authentic power models?

Was this misalignment with power one of the reasons why so many women leave workplaces when they hit upper management, because they no longer feel like themselves and no longer want to play the game (even if they can't name that as the reason)?

The answers seem so obvious to me now. After many years seeking those answers, researching them, watching the stories unfold with my clients, and co-founding *Lead Like A Woman*, a company solely focused on helping women step into authentic feminine leadership, it all seems so clear.

The answer is, of course. Of course women, when in alignment, hold their power differently from the way men do. Of course women, when most authentic, sit deeply into their feminine traits, rather than solely in their masculine traits that are so dominant at work. Of course, women want to show up as themselves in the truest sense, and have that be accepted.

There is another side to power. A softer, more intuitive, collaborative and more holistic side. Call it feminine power, authentic power, personal power or aligned power—the words don't matter as much as the intent. To be true, caring more about the whole than the self, using power for the greater good and not just as power over others. Caring, period.

Feminine power can still be fierce, and indeed it is. But it's fierce with purpose, rather than because power makes it so. It's a power that we could all use more of. It's a power that can create revolutions and change the world for the better. And the truth is, it's the only power that can.

AFFIRMATION

I align my power to my most authentic self.

YOUR POWER IS REAL

Power's not given to you. You have to take it.

~ BEYONCÉ

You are much more powerful than you know. And you give your power away in many ways that you don't even realise. When you say 'sorry' without needing to. When you say 'yes' when you desperately want to say 'no'. When you take on extra work when you already have a full load. When you excuse bad behaviour by letting people off too easily. Or when you make compromises that minimise or diminish yourself in ways that chip away at your soul.

There are big ways you leak your power. Staying in the wrong job or in a relationship you have outgrown. Squashing your dreams to keep other people comfortable. Staying silent when you want to scream. Denying who you truly are because you've become comfortable in a different, lesser version of who you know you could be.

One of the ways we deny ourselves our power is by telling ourselves that we don't have any. But you do. In a million small and profound ways, you are powerful beyond measure. Your voice is powerful. Your spirit is powerful. Your will, presence and intent are powerful.

How do you wield all of this beautiful power that you have? Do you hide it, diminish it, apologise for it? Do you give it away to people who misuse it, who can't be trusted with it? Do you run away from it? What would it feel like to truly own your power? To name it, claim it, step into it. To acknowledge it for what it is, for how it makes you who you are, and who you can become.

To stand powerfully in the world, trusting that your true power is your very essence. It's who you are, not what you do. You take it with you wherever you go, in every circumstance.

When you feel it evades you, or has been taken away from you, you can call it back to you in an instant. Say this with me: *I call all parts of myself back to me now. I call my power back to me now. My power is real. I claim it. And I own it.*

AFFIRMATION

I own my power.

EMBRACING THE GODDESS

The practice of tuning into the energies of the
Goddesses is a form of sacred feminism—not
political feminism, but feminism of the soul.

~ SALLY KEMPTON

The emergence of the Goddess in popular culture has been expanding into the broader cultural narrative in recent years. I've been watching this with interest over the past decade, as my own journey and research into womanhood, feminine power and spirituality has unfolded. The first time I recall learning about the Goddess was when reading *A Woman's Worth* by Marianne Williamson when I was 23. I was transfixed. She wrote about glorious queens and slave girls and how we all needed to 'embrace the Goddess', a phrase I wouldn't come to understand until decades later.

But what exactly is a Goddess, and how do we embrace her? These are valid questions, especially if you have come to this conversation for the first time. Goddesses are deities that are female representations of the Divine. They are found in traditions from all over the world, dating back centuries, and in religions such as Hinduism, Buddhism, paganism and ancient cultures of Egypt, Greece, the Celts, Africa, Japan, the Americas and many more. From ancient myths and stories we learn that Goddesses embody a vast array of archetypes, including warriors, lovers, magicians and mothers, and represent both the light and the dark. Each Goddess has specific traits, talents and rituals that are associated with her, and we can conduct sacred rituals to a specific Goddess when we want to work with her.

We may have different images come to mind when we think of the term 'Goddess': a modern-day gorgeous woman with flowing golden locks and an ethereal dress; a nurturing women, perhaps a picture of Mary, kind, strong and welcoming; or perhaps we see a dark Goddess wielding power, like Kali Ma or Durga, ready to fight and protect at any moment. The Goddess is complex, multifaceted and all representations form part of what we know to be the Divine Feminine.

The writings of Rafael Espitia Perea deeply resonate with me. She describes a Goddess as a woman who has explored both her darkness and light, can fall in love with the possibilities within herself, and as a woman who emerges deep from within her very self. She describes her as a woman who knows of her own magic. As Perea writes: *She is a woman who radiates light. She is magnetic. She walks into a room and male and females alike feel her presence. She has power and softness at the same time.*

A Goddess is sovereign, a woman unto herself. The journey and practices in this book all lead us back to our inner Goddess, our Divine centre of being, our most sovereign self. To becoming firmly grounded in our feminine essence. To not just understand our true worth, but to know it.

Embracing the Goddess within takes us on a path to further connect to our sacredness. We return to her again and again, as we come further home to ourselves.

AFFIRMATION
I embrace all parts of my Goddess being.
I celebrate the Goddess that I am.

FACING YOUR SHADOW SELF

There are parts of me that always remain unnameable,
messy and reckless; but I refuse to apologize for it anymore.

~ KAITLIN FOSTER

Psychiatrist Carl Jung defined the term 'shadow' as the unknown dark side of our personality. He called it dark, because it consists of the negative aspects of human emotion and impulses such as anger, rage, lust, striving for power, greed, selfishness and envy. Our dark emotions can lead us to unhealthy actions and behaviours like addiction, lying, depression, toxic relationships and shame. Anything we look upon as negative or unacceptable, or that which we deny, becomes part of our shadow self. These parts are often disowned, leading to what we know as projection onto others, so that we don't have to identify it or confront it within ourselves.

It serves us well to get to know and understand our shadow and learn what it has to teach us, rather than deny it or hide from its truth. While it may seem scary to do so, honouring our imperfections and acknowledging where we play in the shadows in our lives is part of our path to sovereignty.

In getting to know your shadow, look out for ways you hide parts of yourself that you deem to be unacceptable, unlovable or shameful. Your shadow lurks in the parts of you that you feel no-one would love if they saw the 'real you', which is often your shadow in hiding. It can show up in thoughts like these:

- *My kids are driving me crazy. I'm so frustrated with them I just want to scream in their faces.*

- *I'm so hopeless at everything. Why can't I do anything right?*

- *I hate how I look, I'm so fat and ugly. No wonder I'm eternally single. Who would want me?*

- *All I can think of is the big glass of vodka I am going to drink when I get home. I drink every night, is that bad?*

- *I feel so ashamed about my childhood. No-one would love me if they knew.*

- *My mother is so awful, I can't stand her! She is always trying to control everything I do.*

- *I'm sure my husband is cheating on me. I keep checking his email and phone, so I can catch him.*

- *I wish I wasn't so insecure. But I just hate myself. I'm so sad all the time. I don't know what to do.*

- *Those mothers at school are such complete cows. All they do is judge me. I feel like such an outcast.*

It can be pretty confronting to face our shadow selves. But if you made a list of where your shadow shows up in thoughts and actions, what would you find? Probably nothing vastly different from these feelings and stories that we all share in some way, in our most private thoughts.

Go gently here. As you start to get to know your shadow, step in with grace and compassion. Acknowledge where you see darkness, and accept those parts with love rather than shame. The more you can reclaim all parts of yourself, even those parts that you don't like or want to see, the more you will be able to reclaim and own your power.

AFFIRMATION

*I witness and embrace my shadow self
for all it has to teach me.*

THE DARK GODDESS

The dark side of the feminine is vicious; it's a killer.

~ MARION WOODMAN, *Conscious Femininity*

As much as we might like to, we don't live our lives solely in the light. No matter how conscious or awakened we are, we can't live in the light without the darkness. Growth happens in the dark. Renewal, rebirth and possibilities happen in the dark. They wait for us in the form of the Dark Goddess. When other avenues have failed us, when we're feeling vulnerable, scared, lost, or when we're ready to let go of our perfectionism and transform, she waits for us, a beacon of light amid the shadows of our life.

The Dark Goddess (She who is Lilith, Inanna, Pele, Medusa, Kali Ma, Durga, Hecate and more) helps us to get in touch with hidden and often repressed parts of our womanhood. The Dark Goddess can play a deep and transformative part in our heroine's journey. If we invite her in. If we are willing.

She often represents the scary part of the darkness. When we quickly reach to turn on a light, she asks us to sit with her in the blackness. Rather than stay on the surface of our feelings, emotions and life challenges, she wants us to descend, to go deeper and get dirtier than we have ever done before. She knows that our unveiling happens there, deep in places that are sacred but perhaps also feared.

Embracing the Goddess is a beautiful part of our journey of coming home to ourselves. But to return home as sovereign women, we need to claim all parts of ourselves, our whole selves, not just the parts that we love in the light of day. For the Goddess is both light and dark, calm and fierce, gentle and wild, compassionate and ruthless. Like two sides of a coin, she is not one without the other. And neither are we.

For us to be fully in our feminine power, we must embrace the darker aspects of the feminine that have been long suppressed, through thousands of years of patriarchal reign. Those aspects of our feminine self that we have been told have no place in a paternalistic society—our most sensitive selves, our rage, our sexuality, our fierce feminine power—are ready to come to light, and the Dark Goddess wants to help us unveil them. Indeed, she insists that we do.

In these times of women rising, we see the Dark Goddess everywhere. We see her in women marching through the streets, protesting for women's rights and human rights. We see her whenever a woman stands up to the powers that be and says, 'no, I won't stand for this'. We see her in women's movements, when women come out from the shadows to cast light on how they have had their power taken away, and are now reclaiming it by using their voices. We see her in women and mothers fighting in all their rage for social justice. We see her everywhere. And she is a sight to behold.

We experience her when we sit in our pain, fear, anger and rage for the state of the world and humanity. When we feel into our depths and truly experience our shame, sadness, grief, despair and longing to wake up, transform and be who we truly are in a world that never sees us. We feel her when we are ready to embody our wisdom and step into and own all of our feminine power, not just the parts that we think are socially acceptable.

The Dark Goddess asks us to finally take off our masks and with all of our strength, humility and realness, heal the wounded feminine that resides deep within us. To embrace not just our prettiness, our purity and our positivity, but the depths of our darkest, grittiest, rawest selves. To fully allow her to come to us, work through us, and unite the polarity that enables our wholeness.

Maiden of the Shadows, Great Mother of the Darkness, Wise Crone of the Underworld, I call to you. Enter this sacred circle and grant me the vision to peer into the Dark. Guide me into the Mysteries and give me the wisdom of my own abyss. Be here now.

Amber Zeta

AFFIRMATION
I am no longer afraid of the dark. I embrace all parts of myself, and reclaim those parts I have long kept hidden. I love myself into wholeness.

BECAUSE I CAN

Life shrinks or expands in proportion to one's courage.

~ ANAÏS NIN

I was at a Stevie Nicks concert, on the *24 Karat Gold* tour. Stevie told her team and the concert producers that she was going to do things differently this time. She was going to tell lots of stories in between the songs. They told her she couldn't do that, that no-one would be interested. 'Yes, I can and I am,' she told them.

It was a pattern of agency that played throughout her life.

On stage, Stevie told the story of being on her honeymoon and driving in the car with her new husband, when Prince's song *Little Red Corvette* came on the radio. Stevie immediately grabbed a piece of paper and a pen and started writing down a poem. Her husband looked at her and asked, 'What are you doing?'

'I'm writing a poem to this song,' she replied.

'You can't do that,' said her husband, 'It's Prince's song.'

'Yes I can,' said Stevie, as she continued, 'I'm doing it now.'

She did write that poem. She later went on to record the poem as lyrics over Prince's song. Not only that, but when they were recording the song in LA, Stevie called Prince, who she had only met once, told him what she was doing, and invited him into the studio to play on the song. He came, they recorded, and she split the proceeds with him 50/50. 'I can,' she said. 'I'm doing it.' It was a consistent theme in her life.

You have agency over your own life. Sovereignty. You can do the things you want to do. You can simply choose to, just like Stevie Nicks. Your life. Your choice. Think of Stevie sitting in that car, writing a poem to a song on the radio, written and recorded by one of the most famous artists in the world.

'I can,' she said, writing away inspired. 'I'm doing it now.' She didn't ask for permission. She didn't seek approval. She followed her inspiration. Trusted her muse. Trusted herself. And did exactly as she chose to.

And you can too.

AFFIRMATION
I can do exactly what I choose to do.

TRUST YOUR OWN WISDOM

One is not born, but rather becomes, a woman.

~ SIMONE DE BEAUVOIR

I grew up asking questions. Mostly, I grew up seeking opinions. I remember in my teens never making a decision unless I had canvassed the opinion of all my friends, male and female, to see which action I should take next. Should I go to this drama school? Should I smoke the weed? Is this skirt too short?

As I got older, you would think that the questions would lessen, as I learned to tune in to my own inner answers. But I must have missed the memo on that, because I was well into my thirties before I really started listening to the only voice that mattered. My own.

How often do you ask others about what you should do? Who do you ask: your partner, best friend, sister? Your mother, father, kids even? In many ways, it's much easier to ask others rather than trust ourselves. We can then place the blame on someone else if things go wrong (subconsciously, if not literally). We get to take less responsibility for our actions. And it takes less work, less inner work anyway. Getting to the heart of our own truth requires processes that can be uncomfortable, tiring and full of complexities, especially if we haven't traversed those waters before.

When we stop looking outside ourselves for answers and turn inward, to our own inner wisdom and guidance system, we stop churning and burning our energy. We stop questioning what we think we believe. We learn to find the calm in our self-created chaos, to understand grace and ease. And we learn that whatever decisions we make, when they come from our core, our own inner knowing, we will be just fine.

To have sovereignty as women, we need to be unto ourselves in all ways. We need to learn to get quiet. To ask ourselves the right questions. We need to be able to hear the answers. And then trust our own guidance.

The first step is to stop yourself when you are seeking opinions. Catch yourself mid-sentence, after the fact, or while the question is still forming in your brain. Then pause. What is it you are really seeking the answer to? If you sat with it for just a few moments, what answer would you come up with, given the opportunity?

Sit with that. Feel into that. Over time, you will learn that you really can trust yourself. And you can trust that your life is unfolding, just as it should be. Relax into that knowing, and take rest there.

AFFIRMATION

I listen for my own inner wisdom and trust it.

WHO WERE YOU BEFORE?

*To be nobody but yourself in a world which is doing
its best day and night to make you like everybody
else, means to fight the hardest battle which any
human being can fight and never stop fighting.*

~ E.E. CUMMINGS

Who were you before the world told you who to be? Before
you were labelled, shamed and crafted into who the world,
society and your parents wanted you to be? Can you remember?

I was a bright, talkative, creative child. From an early age,
I never wanted to do anything other than perform. Dance classes,
elocution lessons, drama school, music productions. It was my
life and I loved it.

I turned into a rebellious teenager, always pushing the edges
of what was acceptable. It got me into a world of trouble, but
also primed my spirit and developed my grit. I knew I didn't
want to have a 'normal' life. As a wild teen, I never dreamt of
getting married and having babies, just of living a big life that
meant something.

When I was an eighteen-year-old student at an inner-city
performing arts school, we'd climb out on the concrete window
ledge of the dance studio at lunchtime. We'd sit there five stories
up and watch people we called 'clones in suits' rushing about,
getting lunch and trying not to be late back to their desks.

We would laugh at them, scoffing at their compliance. At
how normal they were. At the boring lives we thought they must
live. We were wild, free, creative and fabulous. We were bold
and thought we were so badass. We were so young and naïve,

but had a very clear sense of ourselves, our place in the world, and who we wanted to be. We hadn't yet hit that age when it was our turn to grow up, to be told to get real jobs and conform. We said we never would. Some of us did, thinking it was the only option in a world that was built on that very compliance.

I look at my son who is now the same age I was back then. I've always told him to question everything. To reject the notion that he has to be anything other than who he is. I have watched with curiosity as he has grown about who that person is, and let him develop as much as I was able without interfering or directing him to be anything other than himself. Hopefully, he will not a have a 'before', just a 'now', of being who he is destined to be. Of who he wants to be.

Who are you really? Who were you before? Who do you want to be?

AFFIRMATION

I am fully myself. I am who I want to be. I live life to my own beat.

CHOOSE YOURSELF

You can never leave footprints that last if
you are always walking on tiptoe.

~ LEYMAH GBOWEE

We grow up waiting to be picked. Think about it for a minute. As children, we wait in the schoolyard to be chosen for games, to be invited to sit at the lunch table, to get chosen for the party invite list or to be picked for the sports team. We desperately hope we aren't that kid who gets picked last, for what that would mean for our perceived popularity. As we get older, it's about getting picked for jobs, for projects, and for those university placements we were always told were crucial to our future. When you really think about it, we spend our whole lives waiting to get picked.

When do we choose ourselves? I first considered this concept when reading Seth Godin. He's one of those authors who makes me actually stop reading to think. To consider what I have just read. To let it sink in. To let it settle and marinate.

I recall the first time I read about his seemingly bold concept. *What do you mean you can choose yourself?* I thought. I had spent my entire life waiting to be picked. As a performer growing up, I was always waiting to get picked for a role: for the dance concert, as the singer in the band, the actress in the play, the model for the photo shoot. I was groomed and moulded to be as pretty, likeable and flexible as possible, to ensure that I would be the chosen one. And on it went as I started dating in high school, and then entered the workforce. It happened everywhere, in every situation. Waiting to be chosen.

So what on earth was Seth Godin talking about? As if it could be that simple. We have bosses and clients and things to comply with and conform to. We have prospective partners we want to be picked by. Millions of authors or entrepreneurs waited decades to be picked by Oprah, as getting on her book club list or in her annual favourite things collection guaranteed massive success. As writers, we wait for the publisher to say our book is worth enough to publish. Musicians have always waited for that elusive record company to agree to make them a star. The list goes on and on.

We are always waiting for the next authority to tell us that we are the chosen one. Our lives depend on it. Or do they? Godin tells it like it is: *You want the authority to create? Sorry. There's no authority left. Oprah has left the building. Once you understand that there are problems just waiting to be solved, once you realise that you have all the tools and all the permission you need, then opportunities to contribute abound. Not the opportunity to have your resume picked from the pile, but the opportunity to lead.*

Being a sovereign woman means taking charge of your life. Of no longer waiting for another to recognise you, validate you or choose you. As women, we have important work to do in the world. We are here to make a contribution, to teach, lead, serve, nurture and create.

The time to be chosen is over. Take your power by the reins. Choose yourself.

AFFIRMATION
I take my future into my own hands, and I choose myself.

KNOW YOUR TRUTH

*We may act sophisticated and worldly but I believe we feel
safest when we go inside ourselves and find home, a place
where we belong and maybe the only place we really do.*

~ MAYA ANGELOU

To truly come home to ourselves, we need to have a safe
place to come home to. We do that by getting to know
ourselves, listening for and learning the truth of who we are,
what we believe, what we need, and then trusting that truth.
This can be the most challenging journey for us as women. Our
stories have been narrated for us by others, who have had their
own view of who we are and how we should be in the world. It
can take a lifetime to unravel those voices that play inside our
minds, to turn off their tracks and start to play our own.

For many of us women the voice is that of our mother, but it
could also be a father, grandparent, sibling or another dominant
person from our childhood or formative years. Learning to discern
between that voice and our own is part of the work of finally
being able to claim our sovereignty.

Tune in to your true voice. When you are in your most quiet
spaces, perhaps during meditation or after prayer, know what
your own voice sounds like. Listen for your truths, the ones that
linger on the surface of who you are, and the ones that rest deep
down within your soul. What do you believe? Write it down.
What do you feel about situations, people, your work, relationships, your place in the world? Sit with this truth.

Before you ask what someone else thinks, practise asking yourself this question first: *What do I think and feel about this?* Ground

yourself into your knowing. It doesn't mean you never care what others think, only that your truth matters first and foremost.

You are your home and your place of belonging. You are your safe place. Get to know who you are there. Know your truths. All of them. Feel the sense of being and belonging that comes when you can trust yourself fully, and know that you will always be safe within yourself.

AFFIRMATION

I am safe and at home in my truth.

HONOUR YOUR STORIES

I hope you will go out and let stories, that is life, happen
to you, and that you will work with these stories ...
water them with your blood and tears and your laughter
till they bloom, till you yourself burst into bloom.

~ CLARISSA PINKOLA ESTÉS, *Women Who Run with the Wolves*

How many of the stories in your life would you like to change? The things that have happened to you, choices you have made, decisions that shaped your life for the better, or for worse. We all have them. I could write a book on mine. They aren't necessarily regrets as such, more things that we wouldn't have chosen for ourselves if we were writing the script of our life.

I often look at my son's female friends, young women from seventeen to nineteen with their lives ahead of them. I think about the events that happened in my life around their age, the choices I made, the lessons I had to learn the hard way. The relationships that didn't serve me, the men who didn't respect me, the drinking, partying, drugs, lack of self-care, lack of self-respect. I know it was all part of my journey, part of growing into myself and the woman I would become. Of what I was here to teach that I first needed to learn. But for the longest time I shamed myself for who I was, how I was in the world, and the darkness with which I looked upon those stories.

When I look at these young women, I am overcome with waves of compassion for myself. They look like fully-grown women, but they are just babies—buds waiting for enough sunlight and rain to blossom into their full beauty and potential. My self-compassion carries over to my twenties and my workaholic, borderline alcoholic self, that led me to work too hard, play too hard and neglect the marriage that, if I had been honest, I had never wanted. And then through my thirties, with divorce, single motherhood and all the other lessons that would further develop me into my womanhood.

Our stories are our path. And while they will never define us, they do shape us. We may not have chosen them. We may hold deep shame because of them. But if we can step out of that shame for just a moment, if we can bear witness to who we are in our soul, then we can also bear witness to the glory of the woman growing into her sovereignty.

We can honour our stories for who they have helped us become. And recognise that our journey has been made more beautiful and precious by every flawed step along the way.

AFFIRMATION

*My stories have been my becoming. I honour
them as a sovereign woman.*

SOFTENING INTO FEMININE POWER

Feminism isn't about making women stronger.
Women are already strong. It's about changing
the way the world perceives that strength.

~ G.D. ANDERSON

Sarah is in her mid-thirties and works in a manufacturing business. She came to me two years ago because she wanted to step more into her feminine traits. These weren't the words she used to describe her struggles, as they rarely are. She said she was feeling exhausted, having marriage issues, and struggling to feel like a good mum to her baby.

After working together for six months, she had come to terms with how far out of balance she was in the area that mattered most—with her feminine and masculine energies. After showing up for work each day in a deeply masculine environment, she couldn't switch off when she went home. So she was showing up at home with the same hard edges that she thought she needed for survival at work. And nothing she was doing was working.

Slowly, as we unpacked the beliefs, stories and expectations she placed on herself, those hard edges started to soften. Tiny piece by tiny piece, curved lines started to appear where sharp corners had once been. As she embedded new practices into her life (breath work, short meditations, getting back to nature through walking, using deeply feminine essential oils like rose to open her heart, and mindfully and physically changing her state when she finished work), she came home to herself a little more. And in turn, she reconnected in her marriage and even started to thrive more authentically at work.

It's the softening that happens when we start to reclaim our womanhood. It's scary at first, because we think the world will eat us alive without our steel cages to keep it at bay. But we come to realise, moment by moment, that we can be safe in the feminine glory of our womanhood. That we don't need to play the game the way it has been laid out for us. And that the only way the game will change is by all of us learning to soften into our feminine power and living and leading from that place.

AFFIRMATION

I soften into the strength of my feminine power.

SPEAK TRUTH TO POWER

When we speak we are afraid our words will not
be heard or welcomed. But when we are silent,
we are still afraid. So it is better to speak.

~ AUDRE LORDE

Rachel was sitting in her boss' office. A mid-level manager doing great things in her company, and with an impeccable reputation, an issue had arisen. One of her team had made a complaint against her. It was a pretty serious complaint, detailing how this person thought she misbehaved as a manager and listing page upon page of examples.

The facts were that this woman had just been let go from her role and she wasn't happy about it. The facts were that Rachel had a flawless record as a manager, was a star performer with a bright future, had been mentored by the divisional CEO as a future leader, and was well-respected by her team and peer group.

But the facts weren't at play here. Rachel's manager had told her to come to a meeting with human resources and just listen. Not talk, just listen. She was told not to 'be defensive'. She hadn't been shown the letter of complaint. No details had been shared. Her manager had gone so far as to say that the woman was 'completely mad'. But still, 'process had to be followed', which meant an investigation had to ensue.

In our discussion before this meeting, Rachel told me, 'I guess I just go into the meeting and take whatever they dish out. I don't want to be seen as being defensive, so he has pretty much told me not to say anything.'

'How do you feel about that?' I asked her.

'Well, not great. I know I haven't done anything wrong. I know she is barking mad and everyone else knows it too. So why do I have to just sit there and take it? Why can't I speak up, ask questions and defend myself, without being defensive about it all?' she asked, upset that she felt she now had a black mark on her untarnished management record that could impact on her future.

I paused as I contemplated her questions and situation. I understood how it felt to hold your tongue and deny your own sense of self and power, in an effort to comply and not rock the boat further.

I looked at Rachel, at this strong, powerful, successful woman sitting in front of me.

'You can,' I told her. 'You can speak up. You can use your voice. You can defend yourself and ask questions and challenge the status quo in your own way without being defensive. You can stay grounded in your power and back yourself. You can do all of those things, even though they have told you that you need to comply and behave according to their codes and rules around what is appropriate. And you can do it all with respect— for yourself and for them.'

You can speak truth to power. It's your choice. You have your own power, even when it doesn't look or feel like you have any. Choose it. And when you feel called to, always use your voice.

AFFIRMATION

I stay in my personal power, regardless of the situation.

CREATE AGENCY OVER YOUR LIFE

You are the one that possesses the keys to your being.
You carry the passport to your own happiness.

~ DIANE VON FURSTENBERG

I was at the beach yesterday. I'd been for a walk in the morning winter sun, and had gone to sit among the trees at the far end of the beach for some solitude and meditation. I was lingering among the century-old trees before finding my seat, when an older woman and man walked slowly past. I caught a snippet of their conversation for a few minutes, as they ambled past me.

'You know, in the entire time they've been married, she hasn't had any control over her own life!' I heard the woman say to the man, seemingly exasperated.

'What do you mean?' he asked her. I didn't know who they were taking about, or the relationship of the woman in question, but it was clearly someone the older woman knew quite well. Perhaps a daughter, or a close friend.

'I'm worried about how isolated she has become. She has never driven, as she doesn't have a licence. She doesn't work outside the home and is completely absorbed in the children, at the expense of everything else. I'm not sure if she has many friends. I mean, she has never even paid a bill during their entire marriage! He's in charge of everything, in charge of her. It's hopeless. She doesn't even have access to their finances, no control whatsoever over her life,' the woman sighed, clearly concerned at the situation.

As they walked away past me, I caught the last of the woman's words. They lingered in the cold morning air, like a question calling for the Universe to provide an answer. I didn't know anything about the woman they were speaking of, but I knew one thing: it sounded like this woman had little agency over her life.

Having agency essentially means having a sense of control over one's actions in the world. As a woman, this is exceptionally important. Not all women have this opportunity, but as a woman reading this book, I am hoping that you are in a position to be able to.

I am often witness to situations where a woman has little or no agency over her life. She may not have the choice to work, as her spouse wants her to stay home with the children. She may not have access to the family finances, everything being controlled by the main breadwinner. She may still be under the domain of her father, which is patriarchal control in the truest sense. Or perhaps her stories and beliefs have kept her in a pattern of submission, or with only a minor sense of control over her life and work choices.

A woman can appear to have total agency over her life and choices, but then a situation like having her first child and giving up her work changes that dramatically; over time, she may lose her self-confidence and financial independence, and her sense of agency along with it.

Creating agency over your own life is an essential part of reclaiming your sovereignty and being in your power. Take small steps if you need to, or maybe a giant leap is required. Define for yourself what agency in your life looks like: getting a part-time job, taking the next career step, setting up a small business while raising the kids, leaving an abusive relationship, managing your own finances, taking charge of your superannuation, paying the bills, being independent, understanding the entirety of your family money situation. The list goes on.

Define this for yourself, then create that agency over your life, so you have the power and autonomy that you need to truly take care of yourself.

AFFIRMATION

I have autonomy and agency in my life.

LET KALI BURN IT DOWN

Finding your Kali is always about liberation.

~ SALLY KEMPTON

Goddess Kali is the dynamic force of liberation. She is known for bringing about endings and transformations, and reminds us that the death of the old allows the way for new creation. Kali can help free us from beliefs and concepts of self that keep us stuck, hidden from our true selves and who we are destined to become.

We can do sacred work with Kali when we are finally ready to step out from behind the shadow of our ego, our small self, and remove the social masks that we think make us acceptable. When we are ready to find freedom from that which keeps us stuck, when we are no longer prepared to hide, when we are so sick and tired of our own lies and betrayals of self, then maybe, just maybe, we are ready for Kali. She will smash our self-limiting beliefs, shine searing light on our false personal identities, and remove anything that stops us from seeing who we truly are.

Meggan Watterson, author of *Reveal: A Sacred Manual for Getting Spiritually Naked,* shares her teachings:

> *Kali is called the Mother of the Universe. Her intentions are 'I release all that doesn't serve me. It's time to be the truth of who I am.' Kali first appears in the 6th century in the Devi Mahatmya, a Hindu text that describes her as having been called forth from the forehead of the warrior Goddess Durga, when the Gods had thrown the world so out of balance that what they needed was the fiercest form of the Divine Feminine in order to bring the world back into balance. Of course*

the world can also mean our own mind and our own thinking, but
the world within the Devi Mahatmya was surrounded with demons
that represent the tiny mad ideas of the ego, the false beliefs, that
keep us from being the truth of who we really are.

Calling on Kali and connecting with her is a deeply sacred act. You can invoke Kali by chanting her mantra, *Om Kali Om*; visualising her in meditation; journalling with her, asking her what she wants you to know or what needs to be destroyed in your life; getting a Kali statue or picture, praying to it and making offerings as a sign of your respect and gratitude; setting up an altar to Kali, with a black cloth, red candles and crystals, spicy incense and her image, along with a skull image or symbol. Make sure you are clear on your intention before calling her in and don't do it lightly. Be grounded in your energy and ready to have the veils lifted from your life.

Kali is the destroyer—destroyer of ego, lies, sabotage, self-betrayal, false identity, stories, beliefs and anything that keeps you from your soul's truth. When you are ready to fully step into your wild feminine power, to be a sovereign woman, then call on Kali to burn down all that no longer serves you. It will be worth the journey, even though it will rarely be gentle. Because in the smouldering embers that remain at the end of the fire, you will find your truth. Unencumbered, unfiltered, unashamedly you. In all of your fierce, feminine, powerful, sovereign glory.

AFFIRMATION
I call on Kali to destroy all that is not
true and liberate me into the light.

READ ALL ABOUT IT

If no-one ever hears it, how we gonna learn your song?

~ EMELI SANDÉ

I've been meditating on the song *Read All About It* by Emeli Sandé. We live in a world where women's voices are rising, but in no way are they rising fast enough, loudly enough or in large enough numbers. We still silence ourselves, and one another, in a million ways, both conscious and unconscious. And it hurts us in ways large and small, like a million tiny paper cuts that we may not be able to see easily but that pain us to our core.

As women, it really all comes to down to us claiming our power. Not the masculine model of power that we've been raised with as the idealistic version of success. But the softening and opening that comes when we come home to ourselves, to our true essence. It can be 'quiet power', as Susan Cain refers to it. Or it can be loud, fierce, roaring power that shakes the ground we walk on. We need both. We need it for ourselves as women, and we need it for the world.

The world is in crisis. And while we may look away because it's too painful to see the dreadful atrocities that happen every day, we are the ones who can help change it. With our voices, our hearts, our strength and the unique feminine power that only we have access to. This power that nurtures, that listens, that brings people together and unites, that looks for peace, that creates harmony and that can heal the wounds that seem impossible to heal.

In her beautiful song, which I encourage you to listen to, Emeli sings of the pain of knowing you have the voice to create change, and yet remaining silent. Of sitting in that silence for fear of being judged, for saying the wrong thing, or for being different. Of hiding in the shadows rather than stepping into the light.

My heart aches as I listen to this song. It aches for the pain in the world that I can't change. For the people who suffer so needlessly and for the injustice that is seemingly everywhere. For the women who still don't have a voice, and for the women who do but feel like they are never heard.

But my heart also leaps and expands as I think of the positive change in the world that is possible when we women continue to find our voices, step into our power, and rise up collectively to create a new world. A world where every woman and child has a voice. And where we are not afraid, we stop biting our tongues, and we remove ourselves from the shadow of silence as we step into the light.

What light is waiting for you to step into? What power are you hiding from? Where are you staying silent?

It's time to use your voice. It's time to speak. It's time to rise.

AFFIRMATION
My voice is rising.

THE MILLIONTH CIRCLE

Love in action is the answer to every problem in our lives
and in this world. Love in action is the force that helped us
make it to this place, and it's the truth that will set us free.

~ SUSAN L. TAYLOR

Jean Shinoda Bolen is a sacred activist for the global women's
movement. A Jungian analyst, psychiatrist, writer and speaker,
she is the author of twelve influential books including *Goddesses
in Everywoman*, one of the books that introduced the theme of
Goddess culture to women the world over.

Perhaps though, her most pivotal work for me is captured in
her books *The Millionth Circle: How to change ourselves and the world*,
published in 2003, and the follow-up published a decade later,
*Moving Towards the Millionth Circle: Energising the global women's
movement.*

In the following excerpt from *The Millionth Circle*, Bolen
describes how every woman can be supported by a circle of
women with a sacred heart, and how women coming together in
circle will be the activism that changes the world—finally leading
us out of a cycle of patriarchy and into more balanced times:

> *In more ways than one, women talk in circles: listening, witnessing,
> role modeling, reacting, deepening, mirroring, laughing, crying,
> grieving, drawing upon experience, and sharing the wisdom of exper-
> ience, women in circles support each other and discover themselves,
> through talk.*

The metaphoric millionth circle represents the tipping point
into a post-patriarchal era, based on the premise that when a

critical number of people change their perceptions and behaviour, a new era can be born.

Whether your circle is three girlfriends sharing a soul's truth over a glass of wine, a mentoring circle, a business mastermind or a circle for social activism, the time to gather is here. Form your circles in whatever way you are called to. For together, and only together, we will rise.

AFFIRMATION

Sacred circles activate change.

GO OUT LIKE A COMET

You are not a powerless speck of dust drifting around in
the wind. We are, each of us, like beautiful snowflakes—
unique and born for a specific reason and purpose.

~ ELISABETH KÜBLER-ROSS

One of my favourite episodes of *Super Soul Sunday* is the interview between Oprah Winfrey and Jean Houston. I must have listened to it at least half a dozen times. They discuss many things, most notably consciousness, being a woman, the state of the world, purpose, the hero and heroine's journey, ageing and fulfilling their purpose.

Towards the end of the conversation, they are discussing what it's like for Jean to have reached the age of 75. Jean then turns the question on Oprah, asking her where she wants to be at 75. This is what Oprah said.

I want to fully embody the calling. I think I'm sort of touching around the edges of it. And I knew that for me to release the Oprah show, which was very comfortable for me to do, and to step into this next generation of being able to reach people at a different level, I knew that that would be challenging. But I want to go out like a comet, knowing that I really fulfilled the mission. That's what I want. And at 75, I want to be able to sit here on a Sunday morning, saying I am doing exactly what I want to be doing. I want this platform that we are speaking on right now to be an international worldwide service for people, and I want millions of people to join us all over the planet in the gathering of our community here to talk about these ideas that become idealized and actualized within the human spirit. That's what I want.

A woman of substance and sovereignty, and with the utmost clarity, she has a greater vision that she is showing up for every single day. Her legacy is still beyond her, there is more to do, even after all she has created and all that she is. There are more people to serve. More consciousness to raise. More light to bring. What a beautiful and inspiring example of a woman standing in her purpose, in her power, in her mission, and in partnership with those who walk alongside her.

I want to go out like a comet, knowing that I really fulfilled the mission.

May we all know this sense of purpose. And we may we all rise up to meet it.

AFFIRMATION
I fully embody my purpose and mission.

ACKNOWLEDGEMENTS

Writing this book taught me about so many things: creation, surrender, courage, friendship and womanhood. Sometimes you really do just have to trust those soul whispers, take a deep breath, let go and see what happens. I'm not the same woman coming out as I was going in, and for that I am so deeply humbled and grateful.

Thank you to Hay House, and especially Rosie Barry, for giving this book the time it needed to unfold, and for trusting that she would be delivered at exactly the right time. She was. Thank you to Laura Yorke for believing in the resonance of this work, for women and for the world, especially right now.

To my family, thank you for the endless love and support that sustains me always. Thank you to my sacred soul sisters who have held space for me, while I was unfolding into the woman I needed to be to write this book. You know who you are. Thank you for seeing me, allowing me to see you, and for sharing the journey. And to my teachers and all of the women who have come before, I am forever thankful for your contributions and teachings. Neither my work, nor my womanhood, would be possible without you and all I have so humbly learnt from you.

Special thanks to Louise Robinson, for reading early pages and giving me such beautiful encouragement; to Bec Van Leeuwen for your sisterhood, your cherished long voice messages that fuelled my fire and for your deep belief in me and this work; to Justine Peacock, for holding space for me, even in the hardest moments, and shining the light when I really needed it (and for those roses which were magical in the final push).

To all of the awakening women of the world, this book was always for you. You are the light that the world needs. I see you. And I believe in you. May you embrace your path to womanhood, find your path to rising, and may we always raise each other higher.

ABOUT THE AUTHOR

Megan Dalla-Camina is a bestselling author, women's mentor, founder and speaker passionate about helping women rise. She works with female entrepreneurs on all aspects of their businesses; speaks to audiences around the world on topics of women's empowerment, entrepreneurship, leadership and wellbeing; runs women's leadership development programs for some of the worlds largest and most innovative companies; and writes about things that matter to modern women.

She is the Founder of Sacred Living Co, a website for women who are seeking more simple, soulful ways to be in the world; Co-Founder of Lead Like A Woman, an award winning leadership development company with a journey for women wanting to live and lead with authenticity and confidence; and Founder of Sacred Essentials Co, a collaborative wellbeing and essential oils business.

Her work has been featured in hundreds of media outlets around the world, from CNN, NBC and Fast Company, to Elle, Marie Claire and Forbes. She is the author of two best selling books *Getting Real About Having It All* and *Lead Like A Woman*. Megan writes weekly at megandallacamina.com with collections, inspiration and empowerment on love, wisdom and tools for rising.

You can connect with Megan on:
Instagram @megandallacamina
Facebook @megandallacamina
Twitter @mdallacamina

RESOURCES

To further support your journey, please download the free
Simple Soulful Sacred Journal at megandallacamina.com/
sssjournal.

Also by Megan Dalla-Camina

Getting Real About Having It All:
Be Your Best, Love Your Career and Bring Back Your Sparkle

Lead Like a Woman:
Your Essential Guide for True Confidence, Career Clarity,
Vibrant Wellbeing and Leadership Success

Printed in the United States
by Baker & Taylor Publisher Services